Editing by Ma Dhyan Sagar, B.A.
Sutra translation by Swami Anand Vandano
Typesetting by Ma Anand Disha
Design by Swami Deva Anugito, B. Arch.

Photography by Ma Himani, Swami Veet Shastro,
Swami Samarpan Avikal
Outside cover and inside cover painting by Osho
Inside paintings by Swami Deva Prashant

Production by Swami Prem Visarjan, Ma Punyo, Ma Anand Ritu
Printing by Mohndruck, Gütersloh, West Germany
Published by The Rebel Publishing House GmbH,
Venloerstraße 5-7, 5000 Cologne 1, West Germany
1075 N.W. Murray Road, Suite 258, Portland, OR 97229, USA

Copyright © Neo-Sannyas International
First Edition
All rights reserved

No part of this book may be reproduced
or transmitted in any form or by any means
electronic or mechanical including
photocopying or recording or by any information storage
and retrieval system without permission
in writing from the publisher.

ISBN 3-89338-079-5

I Celebrate Myself

I Celebrate Myself

GOD IS NO WHERE:
LIFE IS NOW HERE

OSHO

Table of Contents

CHAPTER 1
The Grand Rebellion
1

CHAPTER 2
Ringing Bells In Your Heart
47

CHAPTER 3
The Paradise of Yourself
83

CHAPTER 4
Showering Invisible Flowers
121

CHAPTER 5
Don't Knock – Wait!
151

CHAPTER 6
Come to Your Own Festival
193

CHAPTER 7
Existence is Celebration
241

Introduction

BY
SWAMI DHYAN YOGI

In this book Osho says:

"Meditation is a rebellion, perhaps the most fundamental rebellion against all fictions, against all lies and against all those who are living on those fictions and lies... I teach you rebellion. I teach you revolt."

Doesn't sound much like a standard religious text, does it? It isn't.

It is *the* religious text, the Zen manifesto, a prescription for freedom from the doctors of the soul; a discovery of the world *as it is*. Not as the priests and pundits would have us believe.

It is not a rebellion of war and destruction, but a revolt for creativeness, for individual human dignity and for... there is almost no word for it...religiousness. Not an organization, but an understanding.

This is Zen: gritty, real, stark, funny, touching, and astoundingly simple. Osho has said that Zen is the only living stream of religion on the earth, everything else is just "dead." It is no wonder that some have predicted that Zen is the coming religion of the 1990's and beyond.

Just the absurd beauty of life and humanity lifted with Osho's insight into prayer and limitless gratitude.

It contains some of the most famous and timeless Zen anecdotes, each marking a disciple's jump from the animal to the divine.

A split second that separates what we are from what we *could be*.

This split second *is* Zen. In this tiniest of all gaps is the first real glimpse of the universe as it is. Sounds absurd?

It is. And it isn't. But one clue can be given. Most everybody is in a joke, and calls it life. The man of Zen discovers life, and calls it a joke.

Swami Dhyan Yogi

Note to the reader

The end of each discourse in this series follows a certain format which might be puzzling to the reader who has not been present at the event itself.

First is the time of Sardar Gurudayal Singh. "Sardarji" is a longtime disciple whose hearty and infectious laughter has resulted in the joke-telling time being named in his honor.

The jokes are followed by a meditation consisting of four parts. Each stage of the meditation is preceded by a signal from Osho to the drummer, Nivedano. This drumbeat is represented in the text as follows:

The first stage of the meditation is gibberish, which Osho has described as "cleansing your mind of all kinds of dust...speaking any language that you don't know...throwing all your craziness out." For several moments the hall goes completely mad, as thousands of people shout, scream, babble nonsense and wave their arms about.

The gibberish is represented in the text as follows:

The second stage is a period of silent sitting, of focusing the consciousness on the center, the point of witnessing.

The third stage is "let-go" – each person falls effortlessly to the ground, allowing the boundaries that keep them separate to dissolve.

A final drumbeat signals the assembly to return to a sitting position, as they are guided in making their experience of meditation more and more a part of everyday life. The participants are guided through each stage of the meditation by the words of the Master, and the entire text of each evening meditation is reproduced here.

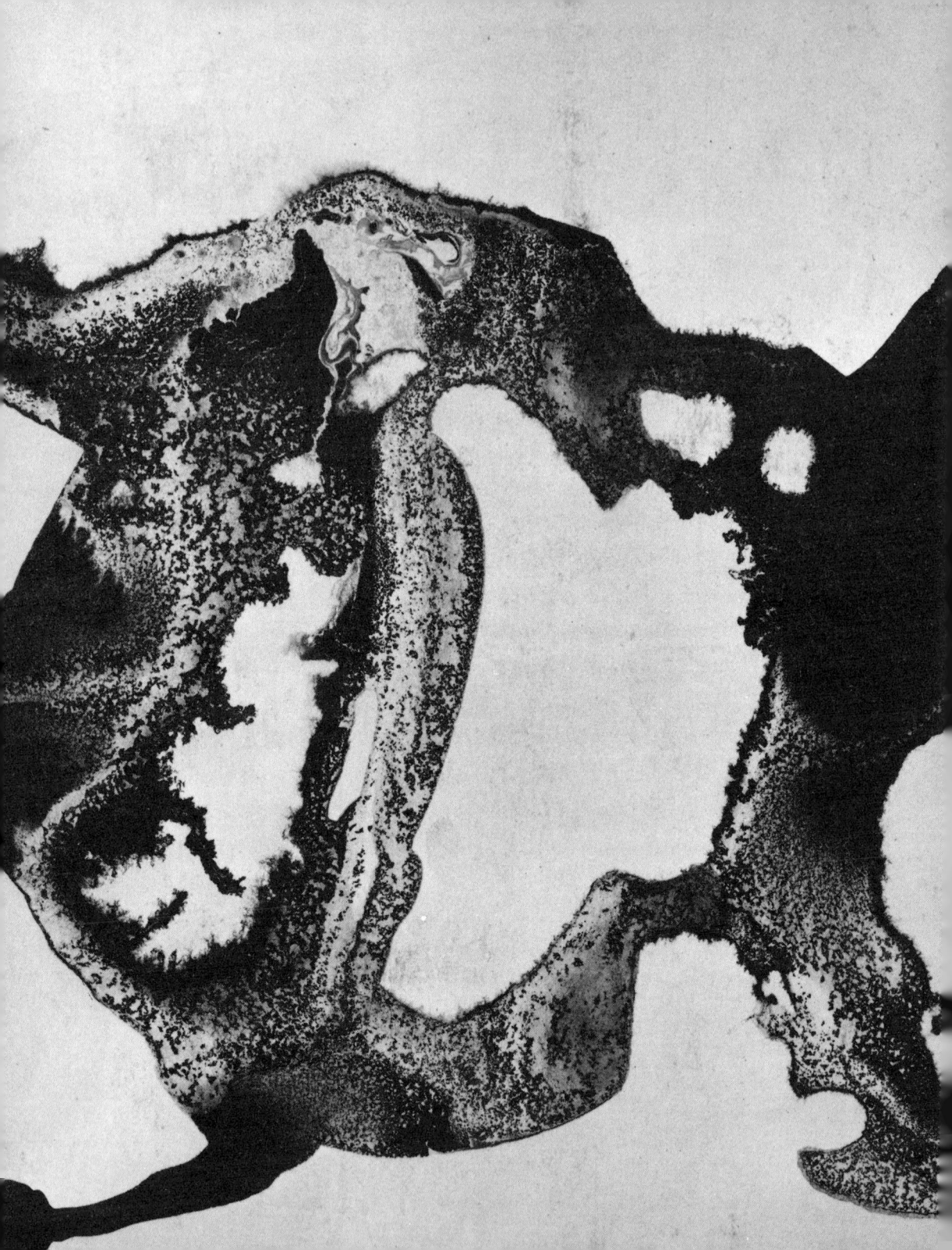

CHAPTER 1
The Grand Rebellion
FEBRUARY 13, 1989

THE SUTRA

Our Beloved Master,

Sekitō said:
"My teaching, which has come down from the ancient buddhas, is not dependent on meditation or on diligent application of any kind.
"When you attain the insight as attained by the Buddha, you realize that no-mind is buddha, and buddha is no-mind; that no-mind, buddha, sentient beings, bodhi, and klesa, are of one and the same substance while they vary in names.
"You should know that your own no-mind essence is neither subject to annihilation nor eternally subsisting, is neither pure nor defiled. It remains perfectly undisturbed and self-sufficient. The same is so with the wise and the ignorant. Your no-mind essence is not limited in its working, and is not included in the category of mind, consciousness, or thought.
"The three worlds of desire, form, and no-form, and the six paths of existence are no more than manifestations of your mind itself. They are all like the moon reflected in water or images in the mirror. How can we speak of them as being born or as passing away?
"When you come to this understanding, you will be furnished with all the things you are in need of."

Friends,

ood evening. And good news…!
This evening we are starting a new series of talks:
I Celebrate Myself: God Is No Where, Life Is Now Here.

The statement of Friedrich Nietzsche that God is dead is only symbolic, because God has never been in the first place – not even born. How can he be dead? But it was a tremendously powerful symbol to declare that God is dead.

It was a recognition that we have been worshipping a lie. And it was not only worshipping, we were being destroyed by a lie. We had been exploited by the priesthood of all the organized religions. Our dignity has been destroyed. We have been turned into puppets in the hands of a fiction.

His declaration that *God* is dead simply means that *man* is born. That is the other side of the coin. And because man is born, he brings freedom to the earth, he brings joy to the earth, he brings dignity to the earth. And he destroys all that was clinging to the ultimate lie, God – all the superstitions, heaven and hell, all theologies, all religions…all kinds of false programming of man's being. They have also died with God.

Hence, I celebrate myself and I celebrate you.

Friedrich Nietzsche's statement also includes another part: "God is dead, therefore man is free." God was the slavery of man, he was the bondage. He was the prison that did not allow humanity to rise to its ultimate heights. He was keeping the whole of humanity reduced to subhuman beings, sinners. His death is a great moment to celebrate.

His death means man has come of age. He is no longer a child and he does not need a father figure. He can stand on his own feet. He is not a sheep, as all the religions have been telling him, and he does not need any shepherds. Jesus, Krishna, Mahavira, Mohammed, Moses...no prophets are needed, no saviors are needed, no messengers of God are needed. They were all megalomaniacs, and in the name of God they have been pushing human consciousness to the lowest levels of existence.

The death of God cleans the whole sky outside and cleans the inner world also, completely – cleans you of all the belief systems, cleans you of all prejudices, cleans you of all guilt. That is what he meant by freedom. Freedom from guilt was possible only if God was dead. And once you are free from God you have the whole sky to yourself, inner and outer both – you can open your wings in utter freedom. Without any inhibition, and without any suppression, you can live your life with joy, with song, with dance.

God not being there is a great event, the greatest event that has happened in the whole history of mankind. The absence of God gives you a certain solid presence. For the first time you are individuals, independent souls – not creatures who have been created, but individual consciousnesses which have been in existence from eternity to eternity.

This is a glorious moment for those who can understand all the implications of God's death. They will immediately celebrate it, because it gives you a new sense of direction, a new uniqueness, a new destiny. It makes you a master of your own destiny. Nobody is there to guide you, and nobody is there to dominate you, and nobody is there to give commandments to you.

For the first time, in Nietzsche's statement, man comes of age. But very few people have heard that God is dead and they are still worshipping him. They are still praying in the churches, in the temples, in the mosques. They are still holding the lie as if it is the truth. And because of that lie their whole life becomes phony. They cannot laugh, they cannot enjoy. Their only duty, propounded by all the religions, is to be masochists – torture yourself as much as you can. The more you torture yourself, the greater saint you are.

All the religions have been preaching nothing but masochism. That gives me a deep insight into God.

Mankind has to be masochist, guilty – torturing himself, torturing and destroying his own roots in nature, going against nature...suffering all kinds of stupidities because God was a sadist. All the religions, unknowingly, are propounding a God that is a sadist. He loves humanity to suffer. He loves people to torture themselves. He does not like your laughter, he does not like your joy. He does not like your pleasure, your blissfulness, your cheerfulness. He does not like your songs, and he does not like your dances and your celebrations. He has taken away all that was beautiful on this earth. He *hates* the earth! He is against the earth. He is against life itself.

So what, in the name of God, your saints have been doing all these thousands of years is nothing but committing a gradual suicide. The more dead you are, the more you will find followers. The more alive you are, the more religions will condemn you, the masses will condemn you, all the idiots of the world will be together to destroy you.

Joy is not acceptable. Laughter is not acceptable. A sense of humor is not part of any religion. Life has become sad...misery, anguish, anxiety. Who is responsible for all this? The first responsibility is a fictitious God who is represented by the priesthood around the world. Millions of people in this priesthood are living on your blood. They are parasites, not priests. And their whole function is to keep you miserable, because only a miserable person can bow down to a fictitious God. And they have been respecting those – giving them prestige and honor – who were nothing but insane people.

Anybody who goes against life is insane.

Life is all that we have.

If you go against it, you are committing suicide. Maybe it is very slow suicide – it may take a few years for you to die. One religion, Jainism – unfortunately I have been born into that religion – even supports the idea of suicide. Other religions unconsciously support it, but Jainism is clear about it.

It preaches that if you want to commit suicide, commit it because this life is not worth living. This earth is not your home, your home is beyond the clouds. They call it *santhara,* but it actually means slow suicide. Whenever a man goes on santhara, he becomes immediately a great saint. Santhara is a fast unto death – no food, and in the end no water. For a healthy man to die it takes almost ninety days, and those ninety days are of immense self-torture. Jainism is simply making conscious that which every religion has as an implication.

What have all the saints of the world been doing? And what is saintly in their actions, in their behavior, in their style of life?

A man who was worshipped very much by the Christians in Egypt, remained sitting on a high pole for twelve years! It was a ruin of an old palace, and only one pillar was standing high. It was very difficult; it was a small place to remain on for twelve years. He could not sleep – he had to tie himself to the pillar. He could not come down even to go to the toilet, so he was defecating from the pillar, pissing from the pillar...and people were worshipping him...!

He must have suffered immensely just to get this honor, honor from the ignorant masses. Just to get this prestige of being a great saint, he was living in utter dirtiness, ugliness. And he dropped from the pillar only when he died. A great memorial exists in his name because he has done the greatest penance against the original sin of Adam and Eve.

Strange ways have been found how to take your pride. Now, Adam and Eve have committed a sin? I don't think they have committed any sin. They were simply provoked by God to eat from the Tree of Knowledge and from the Tree of Eternal Life. To prohibit anything is to provoke – it is a simple psychology. God could have learned much from Sigmund Freud.

In the Garden of Eden where God lived, there were millions of trees. If he had not prohibited those two trees, I don't think that even by now we would have found them...millions of trees with beautiful fruits. We would have still been chewing grass in the Garden of Eden just like the buffaloes. If anybody committed the sin it was God himself.

And why did he prohibit his own children from eating from the Tree of Knowledge? No father would do it. Every father wants his children to be as wise as possible. And why should a father prevent his own children from eating the fruit which will make them eternal, immortal. Every father would love – even ordinary fathers on the earth would love their children to be immortals.

What kind of God was this? And if this is God – who prevents his children from becoming wise, from becoming Socrates, and Gautam Buddha, and Lao Tzu – this is not a god worth having. If he has not died by himself, then somebody has to murder him. He has tortured humanity enough.

And strange is the fact that it was the Devil who persuaded Eve to eat from the Tree of Knowledge. He showed her why God was preventing them. He does not want anybody to be equal to him – and you call this God compassionate? And you call this God love? The Devil was far more loving, far more compassionate! In fact, he showed man the way of wisdom, the way of immortality.

God is preventing his own children because he does not want them to be wise, he does not want them to be immortal. If they are immortal and wise then they will be equal to God, and he is afraid of their equality – a very jealous God. In fact, the Old Testament declares it through God himself. God says, "I am a very jealous God." He certainly is. He was jealous of his own children. He is not even worthy to be called a father. If the Devil had not told Eve, "You have to eat these fruits, only then will you know in your innermost being that you are also gods..."

As the story is, it makes it clear that the Devil was more in favor of human individuality, respect, dignity. God was against man from the very beginning. The whole evolution that has happened in science... 'Science' in its very roots means knowledge. Anything that has evolved in the inner consciousness of man – the awakened ones, the enlightened ones who have come to know that life is eternal, it is a festival, beginningless, endless – would not have been possible without the Devil. The Devil was the first rebellion against a dictatorial God.

And I have to tell you that the word 'devil' is much more meaningful than the word 'God'. 'God' simply means nothing, but 'devil' comes from the Sanskrit root *div*. From *div* are derived 'devil' and 'day' in English; in Hindustani from *dev, devata*, which means divine; from *div, divas*, which means daybreak, the beginning of the day, the end of the night. The Devil seems to be more divine than God. God seems to be really a very mean fellow, and it is good that he is dead otherwise somebody would have to shoot him. It is good that he died by himself, and we had not to have his blood on our hands.

But once God is no longer there, your freedom becomes a tremendous responsibility. It should not fall down into licentiousness, it should rise into enlightenment. Freedom brings responsibility. And I want you to understand that responsibility does not mean duty, it means only the ability to respond. Ability to respond to what? To every situation. Moment to moment you should be so aware that you can find original responses to every original situation. Nothing in existence ever repeats.

They say history repeats itself, because man is an idiot. But existence never repeats itself, because existence is intelligence, wisdom, eternity. History will also stop repeating once there are millions of buddhas around the world, millions of people who have the sense of being alert, aware, conscious, and who feel that they have a great responsibility moment to moment – not according to any scripture but according to everyone's consciousness.

Freedom brings many fruits, and many flowers, and many gifts to you. The death of God is not something to be sorry and sad for. It is something to rejoice, something to dance, something to celebrate. At last man is free from guilt, man is free from a constant judgmental eye from the sky.

It is strange that The Holy Bible says, "Judge ye not," but God does only one thing, judge. And they have also determined a day called The Judgment Day. To man it is said, "Judge ye not" – and God is continuously judging, and is going to judge finally at The Judgement Day. What kind of contradiction…?

Just today I have received a letter from a few Christians saying that the Bible says, "Judge ye not." But I am not a Christian, and I don't have any obligation to follow the Bible. I am not a Hindu… I am not a person who belongs to any religion, so I don't have any obligation to follow the holy Bible or holy Koran, or holy Bhagavadgita. All holy scriptures as I have looked into them, are absolutely unholy.

These four or five Christians who have written a letter to me want me not to judge Christians or Catholics, because the Bible says, "Judge ye not" – and they are judging me! And their Bible says, "Judge ye not." I am not a Christian so I have no obligation to follow the Bible. They are Christians, they should not judge me. I am free to judge, and I am free to judge everybody because I don't have any prejudice against anybody. I don't belong to any organization, to any system of beliefs. A God who teaches people, "Judge ye not," himself goes on judging – and you don't see the contradiction?

Jesus says, "God is love," but there seems to be no love flowing from the skies to humanity. In three thousand years we have fought five thousand wars. What kind of God is there who allows Genghis Khan to be born? Tamerlane to be born? Nadirshah to be born? These three generations of one family killed one hundred million people, and they were never defeated.

What kind of God allows President Truman to drop atom bombs on Hiroshima and Nagasaki? What kind of God is allowing all the stupid politicians of the world to pile up nuclear weapons which will only prove to be a global death?

But as I told you, God is a sadist. He enjoys when you are suffering. He enjoys when you are in pain. He enjoys when you are poor. He enjoys when you are starving to death. His enjoyment is simply sick!

The word 'sadism' comes from a French count, de Sade; he used to torture women. He was a super-rich man, a count, and had a vast territory under his control. So any beautiful woman would be dragged to his torture chamber. You all have love chambers; he had a torture chamber – that was his love chamber. And as the woman entered she could not believe what was going to happen because all over the walls were hanging different kinds of instruments of torture. He also used to carry a box, a portable torture chamber – because who knows? He may find a woman in a hotel room and he may not have his instruments.

All those instruments... First he would force the woman to be naked – not in a loving way – he would tear off her clothes, he would scratch her body, he would start beating her...and he had all those instruments. You have heard only the word 'screwing' – he really used to use screws to make holes in the woman's body. Unless there was blood he did not get excited. When he saw the woman in utter torture, then he was in great sexual excitement, then he would make love.

And perhaps something of de Sade exists in every masochist man. Unless there is a pillow fight, unless there is some conflict before going to bed, a man seems not to be excited. A woman who beats him, hits him, throws things at him, excites him.

The only perfect couple possible in the world would be if one partner was a sadist, and the other partner was a masochist. 'Masochist' also comes from another count who enjoyed torturing himself. His name was Masoch; hence the word 'masochist'. Both were imprisoned for insanity, both were found guilty; one of torturing others, and one of torturing himself.

God must be a sadist on a far bigger scale than de Sade. He is omnipotent, omnipowerful, omnipresent – everywhere. You cannot escape him; his eyes of judgment are following you day and night, twenty-four hours, wherever you are. He is threatening you that you will fall into hellfire for eternity.

Even a man like Bertrand Russell refused to be a Christian for the simple reason – he has given many other reasons, but the first reason was, "I cannot accept a God who is so unjust." In Christianity there is only one life. Even if you live a life of one hundred years, as Bertrand Russell almost managed to live, one century... He counted very honestly the sins that Christians call sins – they are not sins, they are just natural experiences. They have been converted into sins to torture you. Making love to a woman is not sin, but it has become a sin. Both are feeling immensely guilty that they are doing something against God.

So he counted all those so-called sins which are not sins, but just for the argument's sake he counted all the sins that he had committed. And he also counted all the sins that he had dreamed about but he had not committed. Still he said, "The most strict judge cannot put me in jail for more than four and a half years, and God is going to throw me into hellfires for eternity! There seems to be no proportion."

If you go on committing sin and don't do anything else, just sin and sin and sin from the moment you are born till the moment you are in your grave, then too, an eternity of hellfire is not just, it is not justice.

God seems to enjoy hellfire. God seems to enjoy poisoning all your pleasures – you should not enjoy any of your senses. Different religions have different emphases, but the point is the same. Mohammedans are not allowed to listen to music. Strange? It is sin because you are enjoying a sense, your hearing. You are giving pleasure to your ears, so you are not to be allowed to listen to great music.

I cannot conceive in what way music can be a sin. But the idea is that enjoyment is sin, so whatever you can enjoy has to be condemned.

Jainism says you should not enjoy taste, you should eat without any taste. You are putting man into such a guilt. How can he avoid tasting? When it is sweet, it is sweet! When it is bitter, it is bitter! On his tongue there are sensitive buds which decide the taste. Unless you have plastic surgery and remove all the buds from your tongue, you cannot manage not to taste the food.

But they have poisoned your enjoyment. Just small enjoyments – eating your food with love and joy with friends is condemned. And it is not only one sense, but all five senses.

Gautam Buddha is against touching a woman. Even touch is a sin, because touching a woman is a joy. She is warmer than you, she is more fragile than you, she is more beautiful than you. And what is wrong if touching a woman gives you joy? Joy cannot be wrong. And you are not harming anybody, you are not interfering by touching the woman against her will. She enjoys being touched; you enjoy being the toucher. Why should God come in between?

But he is there always, following you as a judge. He has become your inner conscience. Your inner conscience is false! It is created by the religions. So God does not depend only on himself, he depends on the priests to create a conscience in you. It is not consciousness, it is conscience – a false entity which continuously goes on saying to you, "This is not right. The scriptures are against...God is against.... Don't do this!" And your whole nature wants to do it.

Jaina monks are not allowed even to have a bath or a shower every day, because that is enjoying the coolness of water, enjoying your body's freshness. You can see these people are criminals. The Jaina monk is not allowed even to make his teeth clean. He cannot use any toothbrush, or any toothpaste, or any mouthwash. It is so difficult to talk to a Jaina monk – his breath is so disgusting, his whole body is disgusting.

In a hot country like India you perspire...and Jaina monks have to travel on dirty, dusty paths. They cannot ride in any vehicle because that is pleasure; they have to walk. So they are walking on dusty roads in villages, and their perspiration under the hot sun, blazing hot, showering fire on the earth... They become ugly, they become really tanned. Their bodies, their skin shrinks. And dust upon dust, layer upon layer...

All the religions have shared in some way or other the desire that man's every pleasure should be poisoned. Only then will he turn towards the priest to get some advice, because he is miserable. Make him miserable, take away all the possibilities of pleasure.

I have not come across any Indian woman who knows what orgasm is. In fact, in the Hindi language there is no word equal to 'orgasm'. The Indian woman has never known orgasm. Even the Western woman has started to know about orgasm just thirty years ago. It was due to the research of psychologists, psychoanalysts and psychiatrists. Sigmund Freud, Havelock Ellis, Masters and Johnson – they opened a new door to women's pleasure.

For centuries they did not know what orgasm was, so naturally, they were disgusted with sex. They thought that the man was simply using them, because they were not getting any enjoyment out of it. But the reason was that the man has not been allowing them to have an orgasm.

In the very primitive days he must have become aware that a woman can have multiple orgasms, and a man can have only one orgasm. So a man is not competent to fulfill a woman. Either he has to call his friends, or he has to get some hormonal injections, because a woman ordinarily is capable of having six orgasms one after the other.

It is better not to let her know that she is capable of any orgasm. It can be avoided, because the woman's vagina is insensitive. It has to be insensitive because it will be giving birth to a child. If it was sensitive, the birth of a child would have immensely increased pain; it is insensitive and still there is pain.

So the woman's orgasm has nothing to do with the vagina, it is just a reproductive mechanism. Her orgasm is not dependent on a man making love through the vagina – that is good for reproduction. She has a separate part, just a very small part – the clitoris – which is not in the way of man's making love to her. Unless the man understands the physiology of the woman, which ordinarily no man understands...

Man is the only inexperienced lover in the world, because neither does he have any experience before your marriage, nor does the woman have any experience before the marriage. This is a very strange world. When two people are going to live together for their whole lives they don't have any experience, they don't know what to do.

The woman's clitoris is the organ which gives her pleasure, and it is not part of her vagina. Man's ejaculation is just two minutes or three minutes at the most. And he has to be quick, because if you are committing sin, commit it quickly. Don't do it too long, otherwise, remember hellfire.

Unless a man understands the physiology of a woman, which he has never bothered...her whole body is sexually sensitive. Man's whole body is not sexually sensitive. The man's sexuality is very local; it is just in his sexual machinery. The woman's whole body is sexual, and unless the man plays with her whole body and arouses her body – that is foreplay... No man wants to do it, because it will take too long, and one has to be quick before God comes in. So no more foreplay!

Christians in particular introduced the missionary position, in which the beauty is under and the beast is on top. The poor woman has to lie down almost dead, and only then is she considered to be a lady. Only prostitutes enjoy. No woman of honor will groan or moan, or start gibberish or screaming out of joy. So she has been told to be completely dead while the man is making love. It is one-sided love. The other side is completely dead; the other side has not been aroused.

The people who understand sexology say the woman should be on top so that she has more possibility of movement, and the man should be underneath her so he can remain silent, because his ejaculation happens in just two minutes! If he remains silent he can manage twenty minutes or thirty minutes. A woman needs at least ten minutes to become aroused. This disparity is there, and it can be fulfilled only if the man understands that the woman is not just a mechanism to be used. She is also a soul, equally alive, and has all rights to pleasure just as you have.

So foreplay is needed, and the man should be underneath and the woman should be on top. The man should lie down like a lady, and the woman should be a real rascal! Then only is there a possibility that they come to orgasm at the same time. When they both start throbbing and getting out of control, that is the moment when they know what sex contains. It is not only a reproductive organ, it is also an organ of immense pleasure. And that pleasure, according to me, gives you the first glimpse of meditation, because the mind stops, time stops. For those few moments there is no time, and there is no mind, you are just utterly silent and blissful.

I say it – it is my scientific approach to the subject – because there was no other way for man to find out that if there is no mind and no time, you enter into a blissful state. Except for sex there was no other possibility for the mind to understand that there was some way of going beyond mind, beyond time. It was certainly sex which gave the first glimpse of meditativeness. And I am being condemned all over the world because I am telling people the truth.

Nobody has come up with any other idea to explain how you have found meditation. You cannot find it by just walking on the side of the road – it is lying there and you go over and pick up meditation. Where have you found meditation? Not a single person in the whole world...and I have been discussed around the world, condemned, just because I am talking about going from sex to superconsciousness. But nobody has given any explanation why they are condemning me because of my book – which has been translated into thirty-four languages, has gone into dozens of editions, and is read by all the monks whether they are Hindu, Jaina, Christian, Buddhist. Monks are the best customers for that book.

Here there was a Jaina conference just a few months ago, and my secretary, Neelam, informed me, "It is strange. Jaina monks come and they ask for one book only, *From Sex to Superconsciousness*. Then they hide it in their clothes and just get out of the door silently so nobody finds them out."

The book, *From Sex to Superconsciousness,* is not about sex, it is about superconsciousness. But the only possible way for man to find that there is some door, some way to go beyond his thoughts into eternal silence... Even though it lasts only one moment, that moment is eternity – everything stops. You forget all the worries, all the tensions.

Have you ever heard of any man getting a heart attack while he was making love? It should have happened more often if the religions were true. God would be so angry, that at least he could give a heart attack. Hellfire will be after death; right now...

But no man has died while making love, because making love takes away your stress. It is stress that can give you a heart attack. It is stress that can drive you mad and insane. It is sex that keeps you sane, keeps you normal, keeps you within the boundaries of sanity. Otherwise you are going to be a pervert, and perversion does not give you the same key of superconsciousness.

Homosexuals cannot have the same experience that is possible in a heterosexual relationship. Nor can lesbians have the same orgasmic experience. But ten percent of American men have accepted that they have homosexual tendencies, and thousands of women have married women – lesbian couples. And this year it is expected that forty thousand babies will be born out of lesbian couples. From where are these babies coming? From artificial insemination. Now hospitals are not only carrying a blood bank, but also a semen bank. So when a lesbian couple wants a baby, the one who is ready to take the trouble for nine months, gets an injection of somebody anonymous. An injection is not a joy. An injection cannot give you any orgasm. Although doctors call it "the prick," it is not the prick.

When my personal physician, Amrito, came for the first time from England – and he is a member of the Royal College of Physicians, highly educated – he would say to me, "Now comes the prick!" Then I would start laughing, "Amrito, this is not the prick. You have been misguided." Now he silently gives me the injection without saying anything.

These forty thousand babies will be born this year in America through an injection. Now those women are completely out of the possibility of having an orgasm. And there are homosexuals all around the world, even very intelligent people.

I have chosen this title, *I Celebrate Myself* from one of the most important poets of America, Walt Whitman. But he was a homosexual – that's where he goes wrong. All his poetry becomes superficial; he knows nothing about orgasmic joy. But you will be surprised to know that even a man like Socrates was a homosexual; hence he could not become a Gautam Buddha. Howsoever intelligent, and howsoever great a logician he was, his dialogues are great but something is missing. He is not a man of great consciousness. He has become unnatural, he has gone against nature.

But religions are forcing people to go against nature. The third man in England's hierarchy of the church...the archbishop in England's church is equivalent to the Polack pope. This man has only one man between him and the archbishop, and there is every possibility that this bishop will some time become archbishop of England. He has come with the idea that celibacy simply means no heterosexual relationship, but it does not include homosexuality, it does not include masturbation, it does not include making love to an animal – sodomy, bestiality. It does not include anything. Celibacy simply prevents you from being heterosexual. Great religious leaders...!

Fifty percent of monks in monasteries are homosexuals. And there are possibilities like the monastery of Mount Athos where thousands of monks live... They have not seen any woman since they have become monks, because no woman is allowed to enter – not even a six-month-old girl is allowed into the monastery. When I heard this, I thought, "Are those monks, monks or monsters?" And they have their own church-state, so they have their own guards and police.

For one thousand years no woman has ever entered into the

monastery. And anybody who becomes a monk in the Mount Athos monastery cannot get out alive again. Only when he is dead, will his body be taken out; it is a lifelong commitment. No intelligent man can commit himself even for tomorrow. Who knows what will happen tomorrow?

That's what I call responsibility. A man who is responsible will not commit himself to anything, will not promise anything, because who knows about tomorrow? Let tomorrow come and we will see. I will respond with my totality whatever the situation, but I cannot commit myself. I have never promised anybody anything. I have never committed myself to anything in my whole life. Let the tomorrow come. One never knows, this may be my last day and I may not be there tomorrow to fulfill my promise.

Time goes on changing – I may not be the same tomorrow, you may not be the same tomorrow. Today there is great love between me and you. Tomorrow, who knows? Love disappears, not only disappears, but sometimes turns into hate.

A man of awareness lives moment to moment – that is his celebration. He enjoys everything of the world without any inhibition. Because God is dead he need not be worried. And with God, hell is dead, hellfire has been put off. With him, heaven is also dead. So don't be greedy for heaven, and don't be afraid of hell. Just live moment to moment with a dance, with a joy, with cheerfulness, with courage.

Encounter every situation with your total consciousness, without any guilt. Enjoy music, enjoy food, enjoy love – enjoy everything that is natural.

God has been against nature, God has been against enlightenment, and God has been against your experience of eternity.

God was your enemy.

It is good that he is dead.

This is the good news for this evening.

Now your questions.
The first question:
I have been surrounded since my childhood by people who wanted me to believe in God and to follow his commandments.
Why are the God believers always trying to convert others?

This is a very delicate question.

You may not immediately grasp why God believers are always trying to convert others. The reason is they have their own doubts, and by converting others they are able to repress their doubts. If they can convert many people...by converting others they are also converting themselves. When they see that one thousand people have started believing in God – "Perhaps God is. My doubt was useless." When they see that the whole world believes in God – the whole world cannot be wrong. That is the argument, very ancient, as ancient as man: the whole world cannot be wrong. And I say unto you, only single individuals, rare individuals have been right. When something is believed by the whole world, remember, it is certainly going to be wrong! The masses are living like somnambulists, sleepwalkers, in utter unconsciousness. Their belief systems cannot be right.

I have told you a small story....

One journalist died, and as journalists are pushy people he knocked immediately on the Pearly Gates. He took it for granted that he was going to Heaven and that he was going to have an interview with God. This would be the first interview ever.

Saint Peter opened the doors. He asked, "What do you want?"

He said, "An interview with God, and this is my card."

But Saint Peter said, "You cannot enter Heaven. Your name is not on the list. And anyway we don't need any journalists. We have a quota: one dozen journalists, and they are already in."

And they are useless in Heaven because nothing happens, no sensation. All the saints are almost dead – sitting on their white clouds, playing their harp, "Alleluia! Alleluia!" Now this is going to be forever, so what news...?

George Bernard Shaw exactly defined what news is: When a dog bites a man, it is not news; when a man bites a dog, it is news.

But in Heaven, there are no dogs, only dead-as-dodo saints.

"So the newspaper started," Saint Peter told him, "but only the first issue was published. There was no news for the second issue. So even those twelve journalists are just waiting for nothing.

"It is good you knock on the other door; that is Hell, and there is always great news there. Everything that you may not have even imagined is happening, because all the great intellectuals are there, all the great politicians are there, all the great criminals are there...everybody of any importance is there! So you go there."

He said, "But being a journalist, I cannot go so easily. You will have to give me at least twenty-four hours to have a look around Heaven. If I can persuade some journalist from your quota to go to Hell, are you ready to accept me?"

Saint Peter said, "It doesn't matter. If somebody is ready to go to Hell you can take his place. This is good. For twenty-four hours you can have a walk around."

The moment he entered Heaven he started spreading a lie that there was going to be a very great newspaper starting soon in Hell, and a chief editor, and an associate chief editor, assistant editors, and all kinds of journalists were needed. He went on spreading the news so it reached to all the twelve journalists.

After twenty-four hours he went to see Saint Peter, to inquire whether anybody had gone out. Saint Peter immediately closed the door and told him, "You remain in. All the twelve have gone out."

He said, "My God! All have gone out? Then I don't want to be here. Something must be right, otherwise I could not have convinced twelve people."

Saint Peter said, "Are you sane or insane? You created the lie."

He said, "I know I created the lie, but there must be something corresponding actually happening. I cannot remain here, just open the doors!"

That is the reason why every religion is interested in converting people, because every religion, every priest, every pope, every saint, every Ayatollah Khomeini, every shankaracharya, are all deep down full of doubt because belief cannot destroy doubt. Belief can only repress doubt. A blind man can believe in light, but that does not mean he knows light. All your believers are blind people who don't know anything about the truth. Hence the doubt is just repressed underneath the belief.

To keep one's belief strong enough, one needs to propagate it continuously. That's why all the religious propagandists you see are very fundamentalist, almost fanatics, fascists. Have you seen the Jehovah Witnesses? They go on shouting, beating their drums, shouting whether you listen or not. They don't look at your eyes, they just look at the ground and they go on shouting, and they go on reading passages from the Bible. Just to get rid of them, people purchase their Bibles.

Why are these people so much interested in converting people? The psychological reason is they are afraid. Their own belief is very thin; anytime doubt may arise. Doubt is very existential. Belief is only a program that has been given by your parents, and by your priests, and by your teachers, and by your society. But it is only a program.

In the Soviet Union they are giving a different program: there is no God. Every child believes that there is no God. All communists believe there is no God.

Half of the world is communist now, so half of the world for the first time believes there is no God. It is not that they know, it is not that they have explored the outer sky, or they have explored the inner consciousness and have found that there is no God. They just have been told, just as you have been told that there is God.

Every religion tries to convert people, because those who are inside the fold are full of doubt. When the fold starts growing, their doubts are settled, their belief becomes thicker, weightier – "So many people cannot be wrong."

And have you watched this? Whenever a person moves from one religion to another religion, the new religion that he has entered gives him great respect and honor. The older religion condemns him, that he has betrayed, but the new religion gives him great honor because he has confirmed their belief – "Even people belonging to other religions are coming into our fold. Our fold *must* have the truth, otherwise why are people coming?"

All these missionaries all around the world bringing people to Catholicism are just making the Catholics inside the fold believe, "You are the real religion, and other religions are just so-so."

A man of truth never tries to convert you.

A man of truth conveys his experience to you. He shares his experience with you, but that does not mean that you have to agree with him. It does not mean either that you have to disagree with him. It was his joy to share, and that's where he is finished.

No man of truth has been ever a missionary. All missionaries are trying to convince the insiders that they are right because outsiders are coming in. All missionaries are trying to convince themselves also, that their belief system must have some truth in it; otherwise why do people get converted?

So that is the reason God believers are always trying to convert other people. Otherwise, conversion is an interference into other people's freedom. You can enjoy sharing with your friends, with their consent, whatever you have experienced – not your beliefs but your experience. And if you have no experience, be honest, be truthful. Say, "I don't have any experience. I have only a bunch of beliefs others have given me, which are not my experience. I am carrying borrowed knowledge, I don't know anything on my own, hence I cannot recommend anything to you."

What am I doing here? I am not trying to convert you to any religion, or to any cult, or to any creed. I don't have any belief system, I don't have any theology, I don't have any philosophy, I don't have any religion. What I am trying to convey is my experience of truth. If it can be of any use to you, you can use it. If you see it is not of any use to you, that's perfectly all right. It is your freedom, I will not interfere in your freedom. I will not trespass your individuality. I respect you, I love you. How can I convert you?

So no man of truth, no man of compassion, no man of authentic experience is ever a converter. It is all those believers, who are afraid of their own doubt, who want to keep the insiders in, and go on bringing new people from outside. It helps the believers to have thicker beliefs, and thicker beliefs make your intelligence also retarded. The thicker the belief, the more retarded the intelligence. No belief helps your intelligence to grow, even though there is space enough to grow. When you go on pushing beliefs and hiding your doubt in your unconscious corners of darkness, you are crippling yourself. You are destroying your own buddhahood, you are destroying your own potential.

You could have been one of the enlightened ones, but you will remain just a Catholic, or a Hindu, or a Mohammedan. And these are all fictions, beautiful fictions. You can enjoy them as stories, as novels, but don't call them "holy" scriptures.

Four hundred and eighty-eight pages in the Holy Bible are pure pornography. I sometimes wonder why people go on missing those four hundred and eighty-eight pages – not one page, or two pages. I told one of my friends to pick out all those pages, and he has published a book of four hundred and eighty-eight pages taken out of the Old Testament. Every passage is so obscene, so ugly, and you go on calling it the Holy Bible. Even playboys and their magazine *Playboy,* and the playgirls and their magazine *Playgirl,* and *Penthouse* are nothing compared to the Holy Bible.

They are nothing compared to the temples of Khajuraho in India. Even Mahatma Gandhi was so ashamed that he wanted thirty temples of Khajuraho... which are great sculpture. Nowhere have men and women been sculpted so beautifully – but they are making love, they are utterly naked, and millions of statues in those thirty temples...

There used to be one hundred temples; seventy have been destroyed by the Mohammedans. Thirty were saved because they were hidden behind thick forest. Mahatma Gandhi wanted them to be covered with mud so nobody could see them.

You must have heard about the three famous monkeys of Mahatma Gandhi – he used to keep them on his table. Even though he is dead, they are still sitting on his table. Those three monkeys were sent from Japan by a friend. They are a beautiful piece of sculpture, but they are not complete. They came from China to Japan, and the original set used to be of four monkeys, not three.

The fourth monkey seems to have been taken by the friend out of the set, or perhaps...I suspect Mahatma Gandhi himself cut the fourth monkey out of the set. I have to describe the monkeys so you can understand why he should have cut...because three is not the original set.

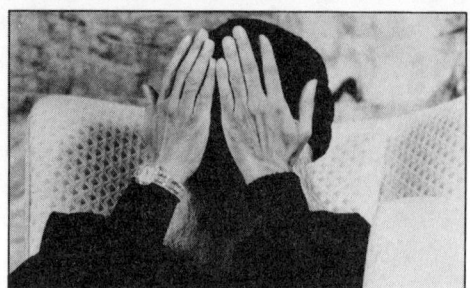

The first monkey is keeping his hands on his ears. The second monkey is keeping his hands on his eyes. The third monkey is keeping his hands on his mouth. And the fourth monkey is missing.

The fourth monkey – I know the fourth monkey. In the original set the fourth monkey was holding his hands on his genitals.

Mahatma Gandhi interpreted them – I don't agree with his interpretation. He interpreted that the monkey who is holding his hands on the ears says, "Don't listen to anything evil." And the monkey who is holding his hands on the eyes says, "Don't see anything evil." And the third monkey who has his hands on the mouth is indicating, "Don't say anything evil." Now, you can understand why the fourth monkey has been dropped – in fact he should not have been dropped if Gandhi had really been a man of truth. The fourth monkey is the logical conclusion: "Hide the origin of all evil."

But this is not my interpretation. Knowing the people, and knowing that Charles Darwin has this great idea that man has come from monkeys – and there is every possibility, because your mind still functions like a monkey. My interpretation, when I went to see Mahatma Gandhi's ashram... He was dead, but his son Ramdas was my friend, so he invited me and he showed me around. It is an ugly place – Mahatma Gandhi was a great self-torturer and he forced torture on other people.

I said, "These three monkeys...where is the fourth? – because I know the whole set."

He said, "I have never heard about the fourth." And he told me Mahatma Gandhi's interpretation.

I said, "That is not right. Looking at humanity, looking into humanity's psychology... The first monkey says, 'Don't listen to the truth because it will disturb all your consoling lies.'

"The second monkey says, 'Don't look at the truth; otherwise your God will be dead and your heaven and hell will disappear.'

"The third monkey says, 'Don't speak the truth, otherwise you will be condemned, crucified, poisoned, tortured by the whole crowd, the unconscious people. You will be condemned – don't speak the truth!'

"And the missing fourth monkey says, 'Hide your pleasures. Hide your enjoyment, don't show it to anybody.'"

People can respect you if you are miserable, but if you are happy everybody is jealous of you.

People have been asking me why my commune failed in America. It never failed. The reason it was destroyed by the violence of the American government was that it was such a successful experiment. Never has there been a commune in the whole history of man so successful.

That was the trouble. If we had failed, nobody would have bothered about us, but we succeeded. In five years we fought against the greatest power in the world – and we had no power. We were not a nation, we had no army...but we had truth on our side.

The commune was destroyed because it was successful.

The fourth monkey is saying, "Keep your pleasures, your joys, hidden. Don't let anybody know that you are a cheerful man, a blissful man, an ecstatic man, because that will destroy your very life. It is dangerous."

And looking at humanity I can say without any doubt that my interpretation is far better than Mahatma Gandhi's. He himself for his whole life was teaching celibacy. But he was an honest man, about that I have no doubt. His honesty is clear. Even at the age of seventy he was having nightmares about sex, and in his dreams he was ejaculating – at the age of seventy! This is a whole life of suppression. Otherwise by the time a man is forty-two, if he has lived his life joyfully, without guilt, without any God, without any religion, just naturally, flowing with nature with a deep relaxation, in a let-go...by the time he is forty-two he will become aware that these pleasures were very momentary. And now death is approaching, he has to find something more eternal.

These pleasures will have indicated the way to him, that if in a sexual orgasm, time and mind stop and you feel as if you are part of eternity...you disappear as an ego and you become simply one with the whole. It happens only for a moment, but it can happen...on your own if you can manage to go beyond the mind and beyond time – no need for a woman, no need for a man. Every man, every woman is capable of going beyond. Once you know it is possible, then you can manage it.

That's what meditation is – just getting beyond the mind and beyond time, and you have entered into eternal silence, into eternal life. And once you have tasted that life your whole existence becomes a celebration.

The second question:
Would You agree with Stendhal when he says, "God's only excuse is that he does not exist"?

Absolutely!

If God existed, he would have been murdered long ago. Man could not have tolerated him; he was an enemy. It is good that he does not exist, so you can go on praying... Just think....

There is a story, a very ancient story....

Once God used to live just in the marketplace, but the whole day, even in the night people were knocking on the doors and complaining about everything: "This is not the right kind of world you have created. Why is there so much sickness? If you are the creator, then why do you create bodies which are sick? Why is there old age, and why is there death?"

So people tortured him so much, the old story says, that he called a council of his angels and asked them, "I will either die out of this constant torture, or I will have to commit suicide! Can you tell me what I should do? These people don't leave me for a single moment and their demands are such that I cannot fulfill them. One woman comes and she says, 'Tomorrow, remember, no rain because I am trying to dry my wheat.' And another man says, 'Tomorrow I absolutely need rain because I am sowing my seeds.' Now what am I to do?

"And there are millions of people shouting and angry because their desire has not been fulfilled, their prayer has not been heard."

So the angels thought. One angel said, "It is good if you move to

Everest, the highest peak of the Himalayas."

God said, "You don't know it but I am omniscient, I know everything – past, present, future. Soon there will be a man who will reach to the highest peak of the Himalayas. And once one man has found me, there will be buses and airplanes, and all kinds of vehicles. And they will make roads and hotels, and again there will be the marketplace. You don't understand: it will only be a little peace for a short time. That won't do. I will have to change my place again."

So somebody suggested, "Why don't you move to the moon?"

He said, "You don't understand because you don't know the future – just after Everest they are going to go to the moon. So I will have to change again. Show me something from where I have not to change!"

Then an old angel came close to him and whispered in his ear, "The only place man may never think of is within his own heart. You just sit there..."

He has disappeared from everywhere. Perhaps you can encounter something of divineness in your own being. In your own life you may find something which is godly, but you will not find God as a person. You will find a quality, a fragrance, a presence – a certain air, a certain energy which is not yours, which belongs to the cosmos.

Stendhal is perfectly right: "God's only excuse is that he does not exist." That is saving him; otherwise there was no safety, no security.

Friedrich Nietzsche, in his *Thus Spake Zarathustra,* comes to a point where Zarathustra is coming down from his mountain cave where he has lived many, many years. And he finds on the way an old hermit's hut, and the hermit is praying to God. Early in the morning, as the sun is rising, the hermit is praying.

And Zarathustra murmurs to himself, "Is it possible that this old hermit has not heard that God is dead?"

When Zarathustra goes down he tells the crowd, "Have you heard the news that God is dead?" They all start laughing.

They say, "You must be insane. Living in a cave for many, many years alone, has made you a crackpot."

Nietzsche himself became mad in the last phase of his life, because he declared really good news but he could not manage to find something to replace God. He could not find the celebration of life, he could not find the experience of the living stream within you. He remained in a vacuum – in a vacuum you are going to be mad.

More people go mad in the West than in the East. More people commit suicide in the West than in the East. More people murder in the West than in the East. It should be otherwise – the East is so poor that people should commit suicide, should go mad...but they don't. What is happening?

The Western mind has come to know God is not there – an immense vacuum. And man cannot live without meaning, man cannot live without significance, man cannot live without joy. If God is dead, man has become absolutely empty, and man cannot live in emptiness.

He needs juices of life flowing through him. He needs to blossom into beautiful lotuses. He needs to sing songs, he needs to play music. He needs all the blessings that existence makes available to you.

The Western man is more educated, is more rich, hence his bodily needs are almost fulfilled. He looks at the sky and finds the sky is empty – there is no God. This understanding that there is no God, rather than becoming good news to the Western man has become bad news. He feels accidental, unnecessary – there is no reason why he should be here.

The East knows three religions which don't have any God – Jainism, Buddhism, Taoism – three religions which are not centered on God. And these three religions seem to be saner than the religions which have come out of Judaism – Judaism, Christianity, Mohammedanism. These three Eastern religions seem to be more sane, because from the very beginning there is no God. So they don't have to look upward in the sky, they have to look inward. That is the only place where they have to explore for truth.

Prayer is not the way; meditation is the way.

And those who have come to the ultimate experience of meditation – a Gautam Buddha, a Bodhidharma, a Mahakashyapa, a Mahavira, a Lao Tzu, a Chuang Tzu, a Ma Tzu, a Sekitō...they all don't even talk about God. That which does not exist – what is the point even to say that he does not exist? It is simply out of the question to discuss God, to discuss heaven and hell.

Hence I want you to understand that Zen has come as a flowering out of the meeting of Gautam Buddha and Lao Tzu. It is the meeting of *Dhamma* and *Tao*. It is a crossbreed of Bodhidharma and Chuang Tzu. These two religions have reached to the highest peak, and they are unorganized religions. Where they have become organized they are dead. For example, in Tibet it became organized, it became dead. In Sri Lanka it became organized, it became dead.

Wherever religion becomes organized it becomes dead because it is immediately a desire for power, a desire to dominate. It becomes politics instead of religion.

Organization destroys the individual, sacrifices the individual, and the individual is the only one who can know the highest peaks of consciousness and the depths of consciousness.

Out of the meeting of Gautam Buddha and Lao Tzu, Zen is born. Zen is neither Buddhism, nor is it Tao; it is both, just as you are both your mother and your father. You are neither – something of your father, something of your mother is flowing in you.

Zen has come to the highest point of expression. It has become almost synonymous with eternal life. Adam and Eve could not eat the fruit of the eternal life, they were expelled from the Garden of Eden. They had only eaten the fruit of knowledge. But Zen gives you the other tree, the tree of eternal life.

So in this series we will be discussing Zen as equivalent to eternal life.

God is no where.

Life is now here.

And Zen is the master key to open the doors of the mystery of life.

The sutra:
Our Beloved Master,
Sekitō said:
"My teaching, which has come down from the ancient buddhas, is not dependent on meditation or on diligent application of any kind."

The word 'meditation' here may give you a feeling of misunderstanding, of confusion, because in English there are three words: concentration, contemplation, meditation. None of these three words is capable of translating the Sanskrit word *dhyana,* which became in Buddha's language – he used Pali, a different language from Sanskrit – *zhana*. And when Bodhidharma took the message to China, from *zhana* it became *ch'ana*. And when Rinzai took the message from China to Japan, from *ch'an* or *ch'ana*, it became *zen*. It came closer to Buddha's *zhan* or *zhana*.

But there is no equivalent word in English, because even the word 'meditation' gives the idea that you are meditating *upon* something. Concentrating upon something, contemplating about something, meditating *upon* something – but *dhyan,* or *zen,* are without any object.

Zen means neither are you contemplating nor are you concentrating, nor are you meditating, because there is no object. You simply are – silent, no thought, no mind.

It is because of this Sekitō includes meditation also.

One does not need meditation or a diligent application of any kind to become the enlightened one.

But for your understanding and clarity, when I use the word 'meditation' – it is a poor word, it does not have the same quality as 'dhyan' or 'zen' – I use it because there is no other word in the English language.

And there is a reason why there is no other word – the West never came to the point of dhyana. It never came to the point where one simply is – neither doing anything outwardly nor doing anything inwardly. One simply is – a pure isness, an utter silence. That brings you to your very center, and the moment you are at the very center you start growing into a buddha, into an enlightened one. Your awareness for the first time opens its petals the way a lotus opens its petals when it is daybreak, when the sun starts rising, when the night is over.

Sekitō is right: no special discipline is needed. No special application of any kind is needed. No mind effort is needed – that's what he means by meditation. What you need is just to leave everything aside. Transcend the body, the mind, the heart. Just go on transcending till you come to a point which is the end of the road. There – you simply are.

Bashō says:
Sitting silently
doing nothing,
spring comes –
and the grass grows by itself.

You don't have to do anything, you have just to sit silently doing nothing, because any kind of doing is going to take you away from yourself. When you are not doing anything, the whole energy gathers inside; it is not invested anywhere. The moment you pass your mind, all the energy that was invested in thoughts is released. When you pass your heart, all the energy that was invested in your emotions, feelings, sentiments, is released.

Now you are becoming too full of energy. This abundance of energy gives you the first taste of existence, and as this energy becomes a pillar of tremendous height and depth, you have found the connection with the cosmos. You are no longer alone. In fact, you are no more, only existence is. Then the existence, the cosmos, the life, is a sheer dance.

I teach you to be dancers.

I teach you to be lovers.

I am absolutely life affirmative, and all your religions are life negative.

I am utterly devoted to the present moment. Don't move into the past because that is memory; there is no relevant existence to your memory anymore. Don't move into the future because that is only imagination.

Just remain here, and you will be surprised. If you are just now here, all thoughts disappear, because all thoughts are either of the past or of the future. No thought is of the present.

The present is so pure, so clean, so clear, just an opening into the cosmos. This is Zen, and this is the key to enter into life eternal. The very feel of life eternal takes all tensions, anxieties of old age, of sickness, of death and birth away from you.

You have never been born and you will never die.

It is the body that has been changing.

You have been changing houses.

But you are the reality, the truth.

The truth is not outside you, it is at the innermost hidden center.

So Zen simply means doing nothing, just being. And in that utter silence of being, you slowly slowly relax, and the spring comes and the grass grows by itself. You suddenly start blossoming – your eyes start having a new depth. Your gestures start having a new grace – your every act becomes sheer joy. It may be just chopping wood, it may be just carrying water from the well – it doesn't matter.

Once you know you are not accidental to existence, once you know you are existence itself, life takes a tremendous quantum leap. You are no longer confined to the body, you are no longer confined to the small mind. You become vast and infinite, and only in this vastness and infinity can you rejoice, can you be blissful.

And this vastness has become available to you because God is dead; otherwise he was occupying every place, he was watching you from every side. He was judging you continuously, poking his nose into your affairs, condemning you – "This is wrong, don't do it." And all his commandments were against life.

I have heard an old story....

When God made the world, he went with his commandments to the Babylonians first and asked them, "Would you like to have a commandment?"

They said, "First, we would like to know what the commandment is."

And he said, "Thou should not commit adultery."

They said, "Forget all about it. Without adultery there is no joy in life. Just take your commandments."

God was very much disappointed, "What kind of people are these?"

He went to the Egyptians...the same question.

"What are the commandments? First we have to know it before we take one" – and nobody was ready to take it.

And then he found Moses who asked a wrong question. When God said, "Would you like to have a commandment?" Moses said, "How much? How much does it cost?"

God said, "It is free."

Moses said, "Then why one? I will have ten."

But when God is no longer there, all his commandments disappear and all his holy scriptures disappear, and the world becomes one for the first time. No religions, no religious boundaries, no discrimination – without God, humanity is one.

Zen teaches you not only to be one with humanity, but to be one with the trees and the rivers, and the mountains and the sky and the stars. This whole universe is our being. We are just flowers of different colors giving a beautiful variety to existence. We are expressions of existence, unique expressions. That gives you pride, that gives you dignity. That gives you an intrinsic honor, a self-respect which you were not able to have if God was alive.

But the whole of humanity has not heard even yet. They are still praying to a fiction, and that fiction is making the whole humanity schizophrenic, neurotic, obscene, ugly.

Three rabbis were sitting on a park bench one evening....

They used to come to that park every evening – old rabbis. One was seventy-five, one was eighty-five, one was ninety-five – all retired.

The youngest rabbi who was seventy-five looked very sad. The second rabbi who was eighty-five asked him, "What is the matter? Why are you so sad this evening?"

He said, "What to do? I have to tell you so that I can be unburdened. It happened that a beautiful lady was a guest in my house, and when she was taking a bath I looked through the keyhole at her beautiful proportionate body."

Both the rabbis started laughing.

The second rabbi said, "You idiot. Everybody does that in their childhood."

But the youngest rabbi said, "You have not heard the whole story and you have interfered. I was caught red-handed by my mother."

Those two rabbis said, "We know. Everybody gets caught. This is nothing to be sad about."

But the man said, "You don't understand at all. This happened today! It is not a question of childhood."

They said, "Then it is a serious matter."

"But it is nothing," the second rabbi said. "What is happening to me, you don't know..."

His problem was that he had not made love to his wife for three days. And both the rabbis started laughing, because they both knew what his "love" was. At the age of eighty-five, one leg in the grave, one leg out... what was his love? They already knew it, so they both laughed.

He said, "Why are you laughing?"

They said, "We are laughing at your love. Don't be worried about it."

His love was, he would take the hand of the wife before going to sleep, squeeze it three times, and say goodnight. That was his love.

But wives are wives, and even this much love the wife was not allowing him for three days. She would turn and say, "I have a headache; you just go to sleep."

So he said, "For three days she has had a headache. At exactly the moment I try to make love to her, she says, 'I have a headache; you just go to sleep.'"

The third, the oldest rabbi said, "You are all idiots. You don't understand real problems. The real problem is happening to *me*. Just this morning when I was going to make love to my wife she started screaming, 'Are you a sex maniac? The whole night you have been making love again and again and again.'"

So he said to his friends, "It seems I am losing my memory. I thought it was the first time."

A repressed humanity is going to have all these problems. But who has created all these problems? Your God, your priests...they are the greatest criminals, because very piously they appear to be your well-wishers, but they have destroyed everything in you.

Zen wants you to resurrect, to take hold of your life again, which you have given to somebody else to be taken care of. Be a master, and you will start blossoming flowers of beauty and blissfulness and ecstasy, and a divine drunkenness.

> Sekitō says,
> *"When you attain the insight as attained by the Buddha, you realize that no-mind is buddha..."*

Just going beyond the mind, and you have become a buddha. It is such a small passage, so small a journey – perhaps a single step. But because you are not total, I tell you about three steps. I divide one step into three steps, because you are hesitant to take such a jump – one step. Otherwise there is only one step: from mind to no-mind. But because you hesitate to go beyond the mind, you are afraid you may go insane. That is true. If you go beyond the mind from the wrong door, you will be insane.

There are two doors to go beyond the mind: one goes below the mind, one goes beyond the mind. Both are outside the mind. If you enter from the lower door, you will be insane, and you will be lying on a psychiatrist's couch. If you enter the no-mind from the above door, you will be a buddha. No buddha has ever suffered from any madness, any neurosis, any psychosis – nothing.

> *"When you attain the insight as attained by the Buddha, you realize that no-mind is buddha and buddha is no-mind"* – they are synonymous – *"that no-mind, buddha, sentient beings, bodhi, and klesa, are of one and the same substance while they vary in names."*

Everything is made of the same stuff, the same existence, the same consciousness of no-mind; only names differ. You can call it anything – *nirvana;* you can call it salvation; you can call it liberation. But these are different names of the same space which accurately described is just no-mind, or beyond the mind. You appear in a space which has no limits, no boundaries, and suddenly you become aware that your being has been here since eternity, and it is going to be here forever.

This very no-mind is the buddha, and this very moment is the lotus paradise. You don't have to go anywhere. You have to just sink inwards to find the bottom of your being.

> *"You should know that your own no-mind essence is neither subject to annihilation nor eternally subsisting, is neither pure nor defiled."*

It is so pure that you cannot even call it pure, because it is never defiled. Anything pure can be defiled, but it is so pure you cannot even call it pure. It cannot be defiled, its purity is absolute. No dust ever gathers on the mirror of your consciousness.

This makes a tremendous point. The sinner and the saint are both capable to go into no-mind, because the sinner cannot defile his no-mind, the saint cannot purify it. It is always beyond duality.

It is so pure and so innocent – available to the sinner, available to the saint. Both have to go beyond their mind. The sinner has to go beyond the sinning mind, and the saint has to go beyond the saintly mind. But both have to go beyond the mind, and they reach to the same space of absolute purity. It is transcendental to all dualities; it simply *is*. You cannot name it, you cannot utter a single word about it.

One of the most important logicians of the West, Ludwig Wittgenstein, has written in his great work, *Tractatus Logico-Philosophicus*...he wrote in a very strange and special style, the style that has been used in the Zen people's sutras. He would only write in small stanzas and put numbers. Every stanza, every line was complete in itself, made a complete statement. So he would number – not the pages, but he would number the first sutra, the second sutra, the third sutra, the fourth sutra...

One of the maxims – sutra means maxim, the smallest condensed statement – I came across when I was a student says: That which cannot be said should not be said. A complete statement – if you cannot say anything about no-mind, then please don't say anything, because whatever you say will be wrong. Whatever you say will not be exactly what you wanted to say. So please don't say anything about that which is inexpressible.

I wrote a letter to him, but he had died. His friend sent me the reply: "If he was alive he would have accepted your amendment. He was a man of tremendous honesty and he would not have thought that you were criticizing him."

I was not criticizing. I was simply saying to him, "You are saying, 'That which cannot be said should not be said,' but you have said something about it. Remove this maxim. Even to say this much is saying something. That which cannot be said should not be said – you have said something about it." Nothing can be said about the no-mind, including this sentence: Nothing can be said about no-mind.

It is a pure experience – you can *experience* it. You can have it, you already have it. You can dance with ecstasy when you come to recognize that it has been always there, you just never looked at it. You were so occupied outside, so involved in trivia that the essential got lost. But it is there waiting.

"It remains perfectly undisturbed and self-sufficient. The same is so with the wise and the ignorant."

They are made of the same stuff: no-mind – the wise and the ignorant. The ignorant have not to become wise before they enter into no-mind. They can enter into no-mind from every place they are – the sinner, the ignorant, the wise, the knowledgeable. Wherever you are, your distance from no-mind is the same.

This is a grand rebellion against all religions. It does not say the sinner has first to become a saint, the immoral has first to become a moral person. Zen gives you a tremendous insight that wherever you are, whoever you are, whatever your actions, nothing can defile, nothing can make it disturbed. From your very space you move directly into no-mind. From different spaces you move to the same center, and you will find your being absolutely clean, utterly clean. It has never been otherwise.

"Your no-mind essence is not limited in its working, and is not included in the category of mind, consciousness, or thought.

"The three worlds of desire, form, and no-form, and the six paths of existence are no more than manifestations of your mind itself."

All your so-called disciplines, methods, yoga...all your prayers, are just gimmicks, projections of your own mind. Drop everything!

I am reminded of a great Catholic bishop....

He had a beautiful parrot who used to recite the Catholic prayer completely. It was a precious parrot. The parrot was shown to all the guests, and he would recite the whole Catholic prayer. And he was such a pious, saintly parrot. He was trained – he used to have a rosary in one hand, and he would go on saying, "Alleluia, Alleluia!" And everybody was surprised that such a pious parrot...

But he looked very sad, as every saint always looks – you cannot become pious without becoming sad. Because he was looking so sad, the bishop was always worried what to do about it, because otherwise he was absolutely normal.

One day he went to see one of the members of his congregation, a woman, who had got a parrot just that day. And the parrot owner had told her, "I don't want to sell this parrot to you. You can take any other parrot. We have got many in our shop." But she became so interested in the parrot – it was a very beautiful specimen.

She said, "I will pay anything, but only for this parrot."

The man said, "I have to tell you that this parrot comes from a very ugly place. He used to be in a whorehouse so he uses four-letter words. That is why I am trying to prevent you from taking it."

But the lady said, "I will teach him, but I will take it." He was so beautiful looking that she thought, "If he can speak four-letter words, what is the problem? Just a little training will be needed." But it was simply impossible. He would say anything in front of the guests, in front of the neighbors. He would shout anything – all kinds of obscene words.

So when the bishop came for his weekly visit, she told him her misery, "What to do? I have purchased this parrot...so beautiful."

The bishop said, "Don't be worried. I have a very pious, saintly parrot, who continuously goes on moving his beads on the rosary, has the complete prayer and recites it so perfectly. I will take your parrot and keep this parrot with my parrot in the same cage. And he is such a saintly person he will teach this parrot." So he took the parrot.

He put the parrot in the same cage, and he went in. As he came out, he could not believe his eyes. The saintly parrot had dropped his rosary and was sitting very close to the other parrot. And the bishop said, "What happened? Why have you dropped your rosary? And why are you not reciting Ave Maria or Alleluia?"

The parrot said, "I was praying for a woman, and I have got it. No more rosary, no more prayer. I have got such a beautiful girlfriend. You get lost!"

Your so-called saints and your so-called sinners are not much different – only their masks are different. And my experience is that your sinners are more innocent than your saints. I have seen criminals, I have seen murderers. I used to visit the jails, and then I was finally jailed in America. I lived as an insider in five jails, and I found such beautiful human beings, far more beautiful than the politicians, than the priests – utterly innocent people.

Zen gives equal opportunity to sinners and saints, to the good and to the bad, because its understanding is very clear. Its insight is so deep that the distance from no-mind is equal.

So it does not matter what kind of things you have been involved in. Whether you were doing things which people think are wrong, or whether you were doing things which people think are right – it does not matter! Those were all your mind phenomena. Just go beyond the mind. When the saint drops his mind, and the sinner drops his mind, they both enter into the same space, the same buddhahood.

This is the great rebellion of Zen. And this gives you a totally different kind of religiousness. This makes you dance, live with totality with no inhibition, with no guilt, because wherever you are, the moment you want to enter into your eternal life, you can take a jump. From any point in existence, from any kind of personality, you can drop that personality and move into utter silence.

No religion has that amount of guts; no religion has that amount of courage – Zen is really daring! It belongs only to the lions, not to the sheep of Jesus Christ.

"They are all like the moon reflected in water or images in the mirror."

If a saint comes in front of a mirror, the mirror does not bother that "you are a saint." A sinner comes – the mirror makes no discrimination. The sinner is equal to the saint, to the idiot, to the so-called great scholar.

The mirror mirrors equally.

The no-mind is your mirror.

In front of the mirror everyone is equal.

Zen gives you a totally new concept of spiritual communism. All religions are against communism, only Zen has the capacity to absorb communism.

You may be an atheist, it does not matter.

You may be a theist, it does not matter.

The distance from no-mind is equal.

So I never ask you who you are. Whether you are an atheist, whether you are a theist – it is your business. Whether you are a communist or an anarchist – it is your business. Whether you are a Christian or a Hindu or a Mohammedan, it does not matter. What matters to me is whatever kind of mind you have make it the jumping board and jump into the no-mind. No-mind knows no differences, it is one cosmic whole. And to me, the man of no-mind is the only religious man. All else is just pseudo.

He is saying,
"They are all like the moon reflected in water or images in the mirror. How can we speak of them as being born or as passing away?"
You are never born, you have always been here. You have always been in the space, in the time, here and now; you will never die. Death and birth, are both superficial episodes in a long eternal life – small things; they don't matter.
"When you come to this understanding you will be furnished with all the things you are in need of."
I have been telling you again and again that you don't need any morality,

you don't need any discipline. But if you come to the no-mind, all that you ever needed will be furnished. You will become immensely compassionate. You will have the grace which is almost not of this world. You will have love without any conditions. You will share your joy, your blessings, to all and sundry – not only to friends, but also to strangers. You will become just like a rain cloud which goes on showering without bothering whether it falls on the stones, or on the road, or on the roof, or in the field, or in the garden. When you have abundance, who cares? You simply go on sharing. Anybody who is receptive will take it, who is not receptive will not take it. But that is not your problem.

A buddha is choicelessly good. It is not that he is practicing a certain morality, following certain commandments. It is simply that he cannot do anything wrong. His consciousness, his light is so clear that he can see exactly what is good. He knows the good is a reward in itself, not that you will have a reward in heaven. And the bad is a punishment in itself, not that you will have a punishment in hell. So there is no heaven, no hell.

Every action brings its joy or its misery. A man with clear eyes can see. And I don't think anybody is going to choose misery, is going to choose pathology, is going to choose something ugly and obscene. If you have eyes, you will choose – the most beautiful, the most glorious, the most majestic. It will come spontaneously.

Gyodai wrote a haiku:

*For my sake,
do not light the lamp yet,
this evening of spring.*

These small haikus are as beautiful as small dewdrops on the lotus leaves in the early morning sun. They shine more than diamonds, more than pearls.

"For my sake..." It is a beautiful evening of spring. Slowly, slowly the darkness is coming. The sun is setting, the birds are returning to their trees. The fragrance of the flowers is all around. The flowers of the night are opening their petals.

Darkness has its own beauty; it is very clean, and it makes every separation disappear. Everything becomes one. Darkness has a depth which light misses. Darkness has a silence which light does not have.

So when the darkness is descending, and he can smell the night flowers opening, and the birds coming back to the trees making beautiful sounds, he says, "For my sake, do not light the lamp yet" – don't disturb this beautiful spring evening – "this evening of spring." Let me rest, let me watch this transformation from light into darkness.

Light is very superficial, darkness has depth. Light comes and goes, darkness remains.

You don't have to bring it in; you can't push it out. You cannot do anything with darkness directly, you can do only something with the light. You bring the light in – darkness disappears. You take the light out – darkness comes in. In fact it never went anywhere; it was there, the light just covered it. When the light is gone, darkness is left.

Light is momentary because it depends on fuel. And fuel – even the fuel of the sun one day is going to be finished, because it is giving so much light, radiating every moment. It is becoming poorer every moment. Scientists think that it will take at least four million years for the sun to die. But in the eternity of existence, four million years don't matter.

Every day some suns are exhausted, become old, dead, finished. The physicists say they enter into black holes, they disappear. And every moment, as suns are disappearing, new suns are being born. Science has not yet discovered white holes. I think if there are black holes there must be white holes. If black holes pull stars and planets and they disappear, they die, then perhaps on the other side is a white hole from which after some time of rest – maybe nine months in the womb – they come out, again born.

But nothing in existence dies. Everything goes on, and everything gets tired. There is a moment to live and there is a moment to die. But your essential being simply goes from action to no-action. And again when it has gathered energy, it is rejuvenated, it becomes fresh; it comes back again from a new womb.

Only a buddha never comes back. His death is final because he has no desire left. It is the desiring mind that takes you into another womb. Buddha, a man who has realized his no-mind, is completely empty of desires, ambitions. Now there is no need for him to enter into another womb and suffer nine months in a prison. Then getting out of the prison is not a pleasure either. And the whole life again starts, the whole round. The same journey, the same youth, the same romances, the same failures, the same frustrations...and the old age, and the fear of death.

The interest of Zen is how to help you to get rid of this circle of birth and death. The only way is going beyond the mind. It is the mind that contains all your ambitions, desires, tensions, anguishes, anxieties, angst. If you get out of it, you are the awakened one. You have come to the point from where you can move into the cosmos directly. You become part of the whole, or more accurately, you become the whole.

> Maneesha's question:
> Our Beloved Master,
> In his poem, "Song of Myself," Walt Whitman writes:
> "You shall possess the good of the earth and sun... You shall no longer take things at second or third hand, nor look through the eyes of the dead, nor feed on the specters in books...."
> "There was never any more inception than there is now, nor any more youth or age than there is now, and there will never be any more perfection than there is now, nor any more heaven or hell than there is now."
> Beloved Master, from the deification of a fiction to the celebration of one's self – is this not the essential difference between the old and the new man?

Maneesha, it is exactly the difference between the old man who lived under a slavery, and the new man who would have come out of the slavery of God, of churches, of religions.

The old man never really lived, he followed borrowed knowledge. He was always dictated to, dragged from this point to that point. The new man will live out of freedom, spontaneity, awareness. He will not have any scriptures, he will not have any dictators, he will not have any gods. He will be himself the ultimate consciousness. This is real growth.

And it is time, the right time! We have lived in slavery enough. Now drop it...*in toto!* Move into an open sky. Open your wings, the whole existence belongs to you.

The new man is going to be an emperor, in the sense that he will be the master himself. He will not allow any other master. He will not allow any other slavery. He will not allow nations, he will not allow races, he will not allow caste systems. He will not allow all kinds of religions and their superstitions. The new man will be absolutely clean and fresh and innocent like a child. And out of that innocence arises a divine being, the buddha.

The buddha is the new man.

It is time for Sardar Gurudayal Singh.
Put the light on!

Jerry and Judy Jam are sitting at breakfast one morning when Judy sighs and puts down her toast.

"Darling," she says, "I have been thinking about that time when you were shipwrecked. All the newspapers called you a hero because you survived alone in the Indian Ocean for three months on a life raft.

"And yet I feel, darling," continues Judy, "that you have been hiding something from me ever since. What happened?"

"Well, dear," replies Jerry, trying not to look like Mickey Mouse, "since you have been so wonderful to me, I must confess I am hiding something from you! There was a lovely girl on that raft with me. We were on that ship together when it sank. We were the only ones that survived."

"A-ha!" cries Judy.

"It was not like that, dear," explains Jerry. "It is true, she was a prostitute, but she saved my life! We had no food, no water – all we had was ourselves and our will to survive."

"I see," snaps Judy. "So what did you do?"

Jerry takes a long drink from his coffee cup and continues. "You have to understand the conditions out there, dear. We had no food, no water. All we had was our own naked bodies."

"You have already told me that!" interrupts Judy, sharply.

"We held each other tight," continues Jerry. "All we had was our bodies – naked under the burning sun."

Judy does not say a word. She just stares at him as though he is a snake.

"All right! All right!" cries Jerry, as he cracks under the strain. "You want to know the truth? We fucked! Yes! We screwed all the time! If it had not been for that wonderful girl I would never have survived! Believe me – she saved my life!"

Slowly, Judy pours herself another cup of coffee. "I don't like it," she says. "But I suppose I will have to live with it. But just one thing. Have you ever seen her again?"

"Just once, dear," replies Jerry. "I met her in Las Vegas last summer at our sales convention."

"And what was she doing?" snaps Judy, suspiciously.

"The same thing, dear," replies Jerry. "Still saving lives!"

On the Buckingham Palace lawn one afternoon, Prince Edward – the rather dim son of Queen Elizabeth – is sitting reading *Playboy* magazine. He looks up at his brother, Prince Andrew, and asks, "Hey, Andy, you've got brains: tell me – what is a *fox pass?*"

Andrew thinks for a moment, and then says, "Oh, you mean, *faux pas!* That's a French expression which means a social blunder."

Edward looks at Andrew blankly. "What do you mean, 'a social blunder'?" asks the dim prince. "Give me an example."

"Well," explains Prince Andrew, "remember last Sunday when the Archbishop of Canterbury came to lunch, and mother took him for a walk in the rose garden?"

"Yes, I remember," says Edward. "What about it?"

"Just listen," continues Andrew. "Remember the archbishop pricked his thumb on a thorn? It was bleeding a lot, so mother brought him into the palace. They went into the bathroom together, and stayed there for a long time. And when they came out, we all went for lunch. Do you remember all that, Edward?"

"Sure, I remember," replies Edward.

"Now," continues Andrew, "do you remember, as I was just passing the pudding to you, mother said, 'Archbishop, is your prick still throbbing?' And then the archbishop replied, 'No, Your Majesty, the swelling has gone down since you massaged it in the bathroom.'

"And then the pudding flew out of my hands and spattered all over everybody, and you shouted out, 'Shit!' Do you remember all that?"

"Yes, I remember!" cries Edward, excitedly.

"Well," says Prince Andrew, "when you shouted 'shit' – that was a *faux pas!*"

One afternoon on the little Greek island of Crete, the local theatrical group is performing the famous Greek drama, "Eat-a-Puss Rex." Young Spiro Sphincter, an amateur Greek actor, gets a small part in the play. He only has to come onto the stage, approach a beautiful girl lying on a bed, and say the words: "I would love to kiss your lips and steal away!"

But on the opening night Sphincter is really nervous. He comes onto the stage, his knees shaking, he stumbles over to the girl in the bed, and stutters, "I would love to kiss your...I would love to kiss your..." but his mind goes blank.

He tries again.

"I would love to kiss your..."

Suddenly, someone in the back jumps up and shouts out, "Pussy!"

Instantly, Old Mrs. Acreepolis, sitting in the audience, has a severe stroke and falls over dead.

The next day at her funeral, in The Holy Orthodox Church of the Blessed Bleeding Virgin, Bishop Kretin, who has now got only three old ladies left in his flock, swears revenge!

"We have got to stamp out this kind of filth!" cries Kretin. "I am going to put a stop to this moral decay!"

So that evening at the theater, Kretin is sitting at the side of the stage with a loaded shotgun on his knee and a stick of dynamite in his pocket, looking mean and menacing.

Sure enough, in the second act of the play, the young actor Sphincter comes bounding onto the stage, stumbles over to the girl in the bed, and announces, "I am going to kiss your...I am going to kiss your..." But again his mind goes blank.

There is a ripple of light laughter from the audience, and immediately Bishop Kretin jumps to his feet and cocks his gun.

"All right, everybody," screams Kretin, "I will blow the head off the first son-of-a-bitch who says 'pussy'!"

Nivedano...

Nivedano...

Be silent, and close your eyes.
Feel your bodies completely frozen.
This is the right moment for turning inwards.
Gather all your energy,
your total consciousness,
and rush towards the center of your being
which is just below the navel, inside.
Two inches below the navel....
Rush inside with an urgency
as if this is the last moment of your life.
Unless you have that urgency and intensity,
you can never reach to the center.
It is not far away, it is very close;
it only needs intensity and a deep feeling of urgency.

Faster and faster...
Deeper and deeper...
As you are coming closer to your center,
a great silence descends over you like soft rain.
You can feel the coolness of it.
A little more...
And suddenly you find immense peace
arising from the very center of your being,
surrounding you like incense.
Just a little more...
And you will start feeling immensely calm, quiet, tranquil, blissful.
Just one step and you are at the center.
The moment you reach to the center you are almost drunk by the divine.
You disappear.
In place of you, there is sitting the image,
the symbol of the Eastern awareness, enlightenment, Gautam the Buddha.
It is your very nature.

Everybody is by his very birth a Gautam Buddha.
Very few people go deep enough to recognize it;
they remain outside their whole life.
You are the most fortunate people on the earth,
who are trying to reach to your innermost nature.
Being the buddha simply means being alert, aware, conscious.
It means you have become only a witness.
This word 'witness' has to be remembered,
because this is the only quality that buddha is made of.
Witness that you are not the body;
witness that you are not the mind –
this is the way to transcend body and mind.
Witness, finally, that you are only a witness.
This is how one becomes a Gautam Buddha,
the highest peak of consciousness ever achieved.
A great ecstasy arises in you – you have never known it before.
You are feeling in tune with the universe;
your heartbeat has become harmonious with the heartbeat of existence.

To make this witness deeper and more clear,
Nivedano…

Relax…
but go on remembering only one thing –
that you are a witness, nothing else.
This is your transcendence.
And as your witnessing deepens,
you start melting into the universe as ice melts into the ocean.
Gautama the Buddha Auditorium is turning into an ocean of consciousness –
ten thousand buddhas have become one oceanic consciousness.
We are separate on the periphery, but we are one at the center.
The center is the center of everyone.
At this moment, rejoice…
and gather all those fragrances that are surrounding you –

the blissfulness, the ecstasy.
Drink more and more from this eternal current of your life.
And persuade the buddha to come with you –
he is your nature, he has to come with you.
He has to become your very day-to-day life;
he has to express his grace in your actions,
in your words, in your silences of the heart.
That day, you will feel the most blessed person in existence
when you disappear and only buddha remains.
These I have called the three steps of enlightenment:
The first step, the buddha comes behind you as a presence –
very solid, very tangible, you can feel it.
You can feel its fragrance, you can feel its power;
it fills you with great cheerfulness.
The second step, the buddha comes in front of you; you become the shadow.
And slowly, slowly the shadow starts disappearing.
The third step, you are no more.
Not even a shadow is left, only buddha remains –
a transparent consciousness, an eternal life.
Those who come to this experience are the real people who can celebrate life.
I celebrate myself.
And I want you all to celebrate yourself.
Become a dance, become a song.
Become a lotus, become a spring.
There is no religion and there is no God to prohibit you –
you are free from all superstitions,
you are free from all God-oriented theologies,
you are free from all rubbish
that everybody in the world is carrying within himself.
Throw it out so that your inner world is completely clean
and ready to welcome the buddha.

Nivedano…

Now come back.
But come back as a buddha,
with the same grace,
the same silence,
the same peace,
the same blissfulness.
Sit down for a few moments
just to recollect the golden path that you moved on,
the immense opening that happened at your very center.
You found yourself so close to existence that it started flowing in you.
Its dance became your dance;
its celebration became your celebration.
Its immensity, its grandeur, its splendor, became your splendor.
And see, just behind you is the buddha,
with all its transparency…utter silence….
This is the first step.
Soon you will be able to take the second step.
You will become the shadow,
and buddha will become almost your very heart, your very heartbeat.
At the third and final step you will not be any more.
You will be absent, and life will be present.
Then begins the celebration.
Unless life is a celebration you have lived in vain.
Unless life turns into a Gautam Buddha
you have been wasting a tremendous opportunity given to you by existence.

Okay, Maneesha?
Yes, Beloved Master.

CHAPTER 2
Ringing Bells In Your Heart
FEBRUARY 14, 1989

THE SUTRA

Our Beloved Master,

When Daiten first came to Sekitō, the master asked him, "What is your no-mind?"
Daiten replied, "The one who speaks is it."
At this, Sekitō shouted, "**KWATZ!**" – and left.
Ten days later, Daiten again came to Sekitō and asked, "The last answer I said to you was not no-mind. What is no-mind?"
Sekitō said, "Without raising eyebrows or moving eyeballs, bring your no-mind here."
Daiten said, "There is no no-mind to be brought."
Sekitō said, "Basically, no-mind is.
Why do you say no-mind is not?
That is the wrong statement."
At this, Daiten was greatly enlightened.

Friends,

First, a few questions.
The first question:
To us, are the words 'God' and 'no-mind' synonymous?

No, not at all. God can never be synonymous with no-mind. God is always there, far away. God has been always referred to by the word 'that' – invisible, just a fiction. No-mind has been always referred to as *this*.

No-mind is your reality, your ultimate nature; God was a mind-created lie. No-mind is your truth, your splendor, your very universe. They cannot be synonymous.

God does not exist; no-mind exists.

God is only a belief; no-mind is an experience.

God has been the cause of all your mental sickness.

No-mind is pure health, wholeness.

The moment you utter the word 'God' you immediately start thinking of him as a person, as a creator. No-mind is not a person; on the contrary, your very personality disappears, only then does no-mind start blossoming. No-mind is not a creator. It has always been here, and will remain always here; it is always now. No-mind is your eternity, your very source of life.

God was just an excuse to exploit humanity and to keep humanity in a very subtle and invisible bondage. God has been your prison; no-mind is your freedom. God has been in the hands of the priests, and the priests are doing the ugliest job in the world, because their whole business depends on a lie.

No-mind has no priests, it is simply there inside you. And once you experience it, suddenly you become aware that no-mind is not your property, it is not your monopoly. The first experience appears to be that it is *your* no-mind, but soon you become aware that the no-mind contains the whole universe, it contains the whole existence.

God has always been an outsider. You cannot create anything if you are not an outsider. The Hindus refer to God as a potter, but the potter has to be outside the pot, only then can he create it. If he is inside the pot, the pot is already created. What is he doing inside the pot? The potter has to be outside, only then can he create the pot. All religions have the same idea in different symbols – but God is an outsider.

If there is a God you are only creatures, created people. Without God you are buddhas, uncreated people. God is the heaviest burden that man has been carrying, and because of that there is no progress, there is no evolution. The heavy burden, the chains, go on pulling you backwards. They don't allow you to move faster to the higher peaks of evolution.

God has to be completely demolished from your minds. It is an absolute necessity and urgency. Once you drop God you will be surprised how many other lies have simply disappeared. He is the source, the foundation of all lies. Just watch God disappearing and you will see heaven has disappeared, hell has disappeared, fear has disappeared, dread, greed... they are simply gone. God was the source. For the first time you can breathe at ease.

God was judgmental; no-mind has no judgment.

God was continuously condemning you; no-mind is a blissful, ecstatic state.

God is just programmed into your mind.

In the Soviet Union they program differently. They program no-God, but both are programs. The atheist does not know that there is no God, nor does the theist know that there is a God. Both are belief systems contrary to each other. But that does not mean that one is right and the other is wrong. Both cannot be right, but both can be wrong – and both are wrong.

An authentic man will not accept any belief system either of atheist or of theist. He will explore on his own what the truth is; he will not like secondhand knowledge. You never think about it, but you would not like to wear somebody else's shoes. You would not like to wear somebody else's secondhand clothes. In fact your whole mind is secondhand, and not only secondhand, but your mind has been going from hand to hand to hand for millions of years. Living with this mind is not living at all.

Your mind is borrowed – your life cannot be sincere and honest. Your mind is borrowed – your morality cannot be truthful, it will only be hypocrisy. Out of a borrowed mind, how can you manage any truthfulness, any sincerity, any authenticity, any originality? God is the oldest lie, and no-mind is a fresh original experience.

God is no where; no-mind is now here.

No-mind is equivalent to life, is equivalent to existence.

God is against life, God is against existence.

Can't you see all the religions are against life? They don't want you to live. Anything that makes you joyous, anything that makes you really alive – they start crushing it, condemning it as a sin.

No-mind simply allows you to be natural. It gives you an opportunity to be natural, to be relaxed, to be at ease – no guilt, no inhibition, no suppression. Nature is accepted in its totality, it becomes your very heart, your very being.

There is no morality from outside. That outside God was creating all things from outside, imposing on you. And everybody around the world is carrying mountains of loads of beliefs, moralities, commandments. They are all inventions of the mind.

No-mind is not an invention of the mind, it is a discovery. You don't have to invent it, it is already here. You just have to be here also – and the meeting, and the transformation. And out of that meeting and transformation arises a totally new kind of morality, a new kind of spontaneity, a new kind of natural grace, a new love for existence, a new reverence for all that is here, for all that surrounds you.

But everything that comes from your very innermost being is being prevented by your God, by your priests, by your scriptures. They are your enemies. You have to take it very clearly. Unless you understand who are the obstacles, you will never reach to no-mind.

God is the biggest obstacle to no-mind.

Because of God, the God-oriented religions could not manage any kind of meditation, because meditation goes inwards, and God is outside. And because God is outside, all the God-oriented religions have invented prayers.

Prayers are for the outside God, and nobody has seen that God. A few people have pretended – either they were lying or they were hallucinating, but nobody has seen God. It is one of the most unproved hypotheses. Don't carry with you unproved hypotheses; they become very burdensome. As time passes they go on gathering more weight. The weight becomes so heavy that you stop growing. There is no space left for you to grow. All kinds of rubbish, furniture, rotten...surrounds you. You don't have any space to move.

If God is there you don't have any empty space, you don't have any empty sky. You don't have any possibility to evolve – there is no space. Where are you going to evolve? God is filling every place. That's why religions insist that he is omnipresent. If he is omnipresent, then there is no space left for you. If he is all over, then wherever you go you will be struggling against God.

No-mind is a pure space. It simply gives you an opening which goes on widening as your experience becomes ripe. Finally, you find there is only pure space all around you, infinite and eternal – and you can open your wings. It is your home – you can fly as high as you want. There is no weight dragging you downwards, dragging you backwards. The experience of weightlessness is synonymous with no-mind.

A strange Sufi story is....

A Sufi mystic was staying in a disciple's home. But he used to pray to God so loudly that the neighbors started complaining. In the middle of the night he would start shouting so loudly – you have to shout loudly if you want to reach to an invisible God. You don't know where he is. Nobody knows his telephone number, nobody knows his address. Blindly, you are just raising your hands towards the sky, which never answers because there is nobody to answer.

Looked at scientifically, people who are praying to God are absolutely insane, neurotics, because they are praying to somebody who is not there, and they are talking to somebody who has never been there. No answer ever comes.

That Sufi used to shout loudly. Finally, the disciple decided that it was better to keep him in the basement at night. So they arranged a bed in the basement of the house, so he could pray as loudly as he desired and nobody would be disturbed.

But in the middle of the night the whole neighborhood gathered, and they said, "Why have you put him on the roof of your house?"

He said, "Roof? We have put him in the basement."

But they went up to the roof and he was there praying to God so loudly. And when you are praying from the roof, naturally your sound goes on waking all the neighbors.

The disciple asked, "How did you manage to go to the roof?"

The mystic said, "I had to, because from the basement God will not hear me."

Mohammedans have great pillars around their mosque, high pillars they call *minarets*. And the priest goes to the high pillars, because if you pray from the high pillars there is a possibility God may hear you.

Hindus have in their temples – Tibetans also have them in their temples – different kinds of bells, gongs. Did you know their purpose is to attract the attention of God? So you give a good beat on the gong and God will listen to you. Then after giving the beat on the gong, or the drums, or the bells, you can pray.

In the Hindu temple the bell is where you enter. And the bigger the temple, the bigger the bell. The richer the temples, the bigger and bigger the bells...deafening sound. First you have to ring the bell to wake up God for him to listen to you. But you don't know where he is. Your gong, your bells are just resounding in the empty sky. There is nobody to be wakened.

No-mind is a reality that you can experience, but for that no prayer is needed. You don't have to look outside of you. You have to close your eyes, and you have to look inwards without any idea of what you are going to find. If you have any idea that this is what you are going to find, then most probably you will imagine, and you will think you have found it.

Go inwards without any prejudice, because all prejudices are part of the mind. Your Jesus, your Krishna, your Rama – all are part of your mind. If you carry any prejudice with you, you remain confined to the mind. If you want to transcend the mind and reach to the no-mind, which is the ultimate consciousness, pure consciousness, the very essence of existence... But for that, prayer is not of help, nor are temples of any help, nor are scriptures of any help.

No philosophy is needed, no system of beliefs is needed, no theology is needed. All that you need is to unload yourself of everything that has been forced upon you.

Unload yourself.

Unburden yourself.

Drop everything that has been given to you by your parents, by your teachers, by your priests, by your leaders.

Drop everything that has come from outside.

Throw it out!

And suddenly you will find your mind is giving way into no-mind. You have only to drop the rubbish – and God is part of the rubbish, the heaviest part.

So there is no possibility of God and no-mind being synonymous.

Here, we are searching without any belief, without any hypothesis. We are simply going into our subjectivity, into our interiority.

As far as I am concerned, this is the only temple: your body. As far as I am concerned, your subjectivity – silent, peaceful, just an empty space – is the very source you have come from, and is the very goal you are going towards.

When the source and the goal meet, you are enlightened – the whole circle, the whole pilgrimage is complete. You have left the source as ignorant, you have come back to the source again as innocent. You have again become a child.

One birth is given by your parents, another birth you have to manage by yourself. The second birth is the birth which matters. The first birth is going to end up in death. The second birth is the beginning of eternity: no death, no end, no beginning.

No-mind is the whole universe, and it is not possible to find this no-mind by worshipping, by prayer, by believing. This mind needs you to be completely cured from all past-oriented ideologies, from all organized religions, from all scriptures, from all that has been forced upon you. It is phony, it is plastic.

Real roses come on the bush from its interiority. You can hang plastic roses on the bush, but they will not be fragrant, and they will not be alive. And because they are not alive they are not going to die. They will just hang there. They are already dead; they are man-manufactured flowers.

God is a man-manufactured idea.

No-mind is not *your* idea. No-mind is not manufactured by man. No-mind is a gift of existence. You can only be grateful, you can only be in deep gratitude when you find no-mind. You will not find even a single word to say to existence. Even saying "thank you" will look very superficial.

In the West it is very formal, you even say "thank you" to your mother, you thank your father – not that you really mean it, it is just part of formality.

In the East it is totally different. I have never thanked my father, I have never thanked my mother. It is so superficial, it is so formal. When you love someone you cannot utter the words 'thank you'. It will destroy the whole beauty of the experience.

So when you come to no-mind, you are utterly dumb.

Kabir has made a statement. He says the experience of no-mind is *Gunge keri sarkara* – as if the dumb man has tasted the sugar. He cannot speak. He knows taste, but he is dumb; he cannot speak.

The experience of no-mind is inexpressible. You can have it, you can dance in celebration but you cannot say anything about it. Your dance certainly will shine with a new joy, with a new ecstasy, with a new drunkenness. Your dance will show a new radiation, a new aura around you. Your eyes will be shining. For the first time they have seen something worth seeing. Your whole being will be throbbing with joy, because you have come back to the original source.

Let gods die. Don't carry on them. People are carrying dead gods, and when somebody is dead and you go on carrying him, *you* start stinking. All religious people stink because they are carrying a dead body.

There is a beautiful Hindu mythology....

Shiva, one of the gods of the Hindus, one of the three gods, the trinity of Hinduism... Shiva's wife dies, but he won't accept the death of his wife. His mind was constantly telling him, "If you go around the country there may be somebody who can resurrect her."

He used to live in the Himalayas, so he came down with the dead body of Parvati, his wife. The very word *parvati* means daughter of the mountains...a beautiful woman, but dead. He carried the corpse around the country, asking everybody, "Is there any physician, any man of miracles?"

The body was deteriorating, and soon it started falling into pieces. The legs dropped in one place, the hands dropped into another place... Hindus have twelve holy places. Those twelve holy places in the country are the twelve places where Parvati's parts dropped. But even though parts were dropping, Shiva continued around the country until he found that the last part had dropped. It must have taken him years.

But your carrying a dead God is a longer pilgrimage – millions of years. And you go on believing that someday, somewhere, God will materialize. Meanwhile you go on carrying the corpse. The corpse is destroying you also, because it is rotten, and it is making a rotten humanity.

God is a sickness; you have simply to drop it. But the only good thing is that *you* are carrying the sickness, so *you* can drop it. It is your belief, so you can throw it out! It is not something that is a part of you, it is something that you are holding unnecessarily. It is not holding you! This is the only beautiful thing about it – that you can drop God.

One day I dropped God, and since then I have felt so weightless, so blissful. I used to carry the dead body myself, but I realized that the body was dead – no breathing, no heartbeat – it was up to me whether to carry it or drop it. And as I dropped it, for the first time I felt myself as an individual. The dead body was overwhelming me, it was covering me from all the sides. It had become my personality.

For a moment I felt naked, because the personality had dropped, the masks had dropped. But soon I knew that this nudity, this nakedness was natural. Everybody is nude behind the clothes. The moment you drop your clothes... Have you ever felt a certain freedom just on the seabeach as you drop your clothes? You suddenly feel the sun with your body, the wind blowing on your body, and a tremendous sense of freedom – just by dropping clothes, which are not of much weight.

God is very heavy. It goes on becoming heavier and heavier as time passes. A moment comes when it is heavier than you – you are crushed under the mountainous load. Unless one is free from God, one knows not what freedom is.

So God cannot be synonymous with no-mind.

No-mind is really the antidote to the disease called God.

No-mind is your freedom.

All chains dropped, all thoughts dropped, all feelings dropped...suddenly you find only the purest essence has remained. All that was covering it, layer upon layer, has been dropped. This dropping I call meditation.

Finally, only a witness, a *sakshi*, remains – just a pure awareness. This is ultimate freedom, and the authentic religion is for ultimate freedom and ultimate liberation.

God-oriented religions cannot even give you a sense of freedom, or a direction for freedom. Their whole effort is to direct your mind towards God. Fill your mind with God, repeat his name again and again so it becomes ingrained in your mind. The more ingrained it becomes, the more difficult it will be to leave it. The sooner you leave God, the better. And you will have to leave one day, so why not now! One cannot live a lie forever. Only truth can be lived forever.

You have to believe only in lies, you don't have to believe in the truth. Truth has to be discovered. I teach you purely the attitude of an agnostic – one who does not believe, who does not disbelieve, but who is a seeker, a searcher, an explorer.

Certainly the first thing to be explored is your own inner being. That is the closest life throbbing, everything else is a little far away. The man of intelligence first will look inside his own house before he goes searching on the moon and on Mars. First he will look inside to see what is there. And those who have gone inside have never come empty handed. They have come with so much bliss, so much ecstasy, with such an abundance that they start sharing, because as they share they come to understand the inner economics.

The more you share the more you have. If you don't share, you won't have even that which you had. Jesus says, "Those who have shall be given more, and those who have not, even whatsoever they have will be taken away." I cannot agree with him. I say unto you, the more you give, the more you will have; the less you give, the less you will have. If you don't give at all, you won't have anything left.

Sharing is the only compassion.

Sharing is the only service.

Sharing is the only way the awakened one lives. That is real character. That is authentic morality. That is true religiousness.

You don't have a God, but you become godly. Hence I say, the moment you drop God you are moving in the right direction of becoming godly. You will be divine in your ecstasies, in your silent spaces of the being. You will be divine – but you will be divine because you will be participating in the divine existence. Everything is sacred to the man who has come to know himself, who has discovered his hidden secret of life. Everything becomes sacred.

A story is told about the mystic Nanak....

He went to Kaaba, the holy place of the Mohammedans. It is a beautiful story.

He reached Kaaba by the evening, but his fame had already reached, so people were waiting for him. They received him, welcomed him, but he was very tired. So he said, "I would like to go to sleep, I have been walking miles and miles."

So they prepared a bed under a tree, but he turned the bed. Mohammedans don't sleep with their legs towards Kaaba, but he turned the bed so that his legs were towards Kaaba, and his head was on the opposite side.

When the head priest of Kaaba heard about it, he came running. He said, "We thought you were a great mystic, but you don't even seem to be religious. You don't understand that you are hurting our feelings. You are keeping your feet towards the most divine and the most holy land! You should turn your feet."

Nanak laughed. He said, "As far as I am concerned, wherever I turn my feet I find they are towards the holy land, because to me the whole existence is holy. Now if you think there is some place which is unholy, please turn my legs. I am willing!"

There was a silence. The priest could not say that there was some place that was unholy. But this could not be tolerated either, that this man continued to keep his feet towards Kaaba.

I think up to this point it is factual. Beyond this point it becomes more and more symbolic. But even that is significant....

Finally, the priest decided to turn his legs and turn his head towards Kaaba. But they were utterly disappointed, surprised. They could not believe their eyes. Wherever they moved Nanak's legs, Kaaba moved!

This must be symbolic, but it is significant. It is poetry, but it gives you the feeling that if everything is holy and sacred it does not matter where you keep your legs it will always be towards the sacred land. The whole existence is sacred for a mystic. Nanak showed his understanding very clearly. Only a man of no-mind can do that.

A man of no-mind knows that everywhere life is throbbing – in the trees, in the rivers, in the mountains... Even the Himalayas are still growing. It is the youngest mountain in the whole world, but really powerful because it has got the highest peaks in the world and they are still growing – one foot per year. But that means it is alive, it is not a dead mountain. It is reaching towards the stars, perhaps very slowly because it is not a small mountain. And for mountains, even to rise one foot in one year is quite fast. Looking at eternity, if the Himalayas go on growing in this way, soon they will be touching stars; it won't be long.

When you see life everywhere, in the stones – perhaps fast asleep so that you cannot feel it, perhaps a different dimension – in the trees, so that you cannot understand it... But everything is so abundantly alive, all that you need is space and perceptivity of no-mind.

God is your blindness.

No-mind is going to give you fresh eyes to look again at the universe.

The second question:
Nietzsche made the observation that when "ordinary people" are in an unpleasant situation, "they always seek to get out of it with the smallest expenditure of intelligence."
Is God simply the first and last resort of a retarded humanity?

Yes, absolutely yes. God is the invention of the retarded, of the idiots, of the imbeciles, of the people who want a shortcut so they don't have to exert any intelligence. God is the belief of the unintelligent. God is the belief of the unconscious. God is the belief of those who are still asleep and dreaming. The moment you wake up, all dreams disappear, and with the dreams your God will also disappear.

No-mind is waking up from the sleep of the mind.

No-mind is a sunrise.

Mind has been a long long dark night, and no-mind blossoms into tremendous intelligence, not intellect. Intellect is part of the mind, intelligence is part of no-mind. It is a totally different phenomenon. And when that fire of intelligence rises in you in great flames, you don't find any God anywhere, but you certainly find everything is sacred because everything is alive.

So a great reverence for life – that's what I teach you. But you will know life only when you have touched your own life. Then you will know the criterion for what is alive. Right now you don't know the criterion for what is alive.

The third question:
Through my own recent encounter with death, I came across many stories of people from diverse cultures and of different religious backgrounds, who temporarily left their bodies and appeared to observers to be dead. They reported seeing a "being of light," which was totally loving and compassionate.
Could this "being of light" be the basis on which the concept of God has been created?

No, not at all. This experience is authentic. It happens sometimes to people who have almost died – not completely, but almost. They see a luminous being. It is their own being, it is not God. In meditation you will encounter the same luminous being without dying.

Meditation is a kind of death. You are separated from the body, you are separated from the mind – that's what death does. You are separated from the body, you are separated from the mind. Suddenly you become aware of a luminous being, which you think is separate from you because you have never seen such an experience before. If you have been a meditator, you would have recognized – "This is me."

You are a light, luminous body inside this body – a flame, an eternal flame of light. But those who have almost died and come back to life, because they don't have any experience of meditation, they think they have seen something, a luminous being. They remember it vaguely, faintly, a faraway echo, but they remember it. They have seen something luminous. Naturally they cannot conceive that they have seen themselves.

God is not based on the experience of people who were almost dead and have come back again to life. But meditation knows exactly what has been happening to these people – they have encountered themselves. But because the encounter was for the first time, and so quick...just like a flash it came and went away, and they were back to life. Naturally they think they have seen some object, some person standing there with a radiant, luminous body, because they have known only objects in their lives. They have never known the subject.

A meditator will not commit such a mistake. A meditator will recognize immediately – whether alive or dead – that he is the luminous eternal light.

> The sutra:
> *Our Beloved Master,*
> *When Daiten first came to Sekitō, the master asked him, "What is your no-mind?"*
> *Daiten replied, "The one who speaks is it."*
> *At this, Sekitō shouted, **"KWATZ!"** – and left.*

Daiten is not yet enlightened, but he must have been a great scholar. He has read in the scriptures that the no-mind is the one from where all that is original comes out. When a buddha speaks, he is not speaking borrowed words. His speaking is coming from no-mind. No-mind is flowing in his words, hence the beauty.

The same ordinary words on the lips of a buddha certainly become magical, alive. Very ordinary words suddenly take a totally different flavor, a new fragrance. They start being poetic. They have around them a certain aura. That's why the words of a buddha start ringing bells in your heart.

He is not speaking strange words. You know those words, you use those words. But when a buddha speaks those same words, because they are coming from no-mind, they carry some space around them that makes the awakened one's words so authoritive. The awakened one is not authoritative. He does not command you, he does not give quotations from the scriptures to support as an evidence. He is his own authority.

I have been telling stories, and people who don't understand me have sometimes written, "Your stories go on changing. Sometimes you say something, sometimes your story completely changes..." They are only listening to the mere words, not to me. They are blind people, they cannot see that my story is a response to the people to whom I am talking. In the present moment it takes a new shape, a new meaning, a new dimension.

My stories go on changing because life goes on changing. What can I do about it? Sometimes it is spring and there are flowers all over, and sometimes it is not spring and the trees are standing naked without any leaves. What can I do? Life goes on changing. My stories are not dead, they are as alive as I am alive. They are coming from a living source.

And they have told me – great scholars and professors, linguists, those belonging to different religions – "I like your story but it is not in the scriptures at all." I said, "Then you should put it in. Your scripture is not growing, it is dead. If you like the story, if you felt there was some meaning, then put it in your scripture."

Buddha is not the end of the world. There are going to be buddhas after Gautam Buddha. There will be buddhas after me, after you, and certainly they are going to continuously improve. It is not an effort, it is a spontaneous phenomenon.

When I start the story I don't know what shape it is going to take. I am as much surprised as you are – "My God! This story is not the story I have heard before." But what can I do? It is not my mind. Mind has a memory system, so it goes on repeating the same gramophone record, and gets stuck at the same point each time. If it is an ancient gramophone record, the needle goes on stopping at the same place. You start again; again it will stop at the same place.

Once I was participating as a student in an inter-university competition for eloquence. I was the first one to speak, and the second person came from the Sanskrit University of Varanasi. It is devoted completely to Sanskrit scriptures and language. But the student must have been feeling a little inferior to the other students who came from different universities, because in the Sanskrit University they don't teach English. So he must have crammed one statement in English of Bertrand Russell, just to make an impression.

But he was nervous. As he started, after three or four lines, he said, "Bertrand Russell has said..." – in English – and then he stopped. His mind went blank. I was just sitting by his side because he was the second person to speak. The whole auditorium was full of students and professors, and there was a great silence when he stopped. I thought I should help him, so I told him, "Repeat again."

And when you have crammed something, you can repeat it only from the very beginning. So he said, "Sisters and brothers..." So the whole audience started laughing. He again repeated those three or four sentences and came to the point, "Bertrand Russell has said..." – and a fullpoint.

I said, "Repeat!" Finding no way out, he again started, "Brothers and sisters..."

And it was such a joy – for ten minutes it continued. I would say, "Repeat," and finding no way out...and I was the only help. Everybody was laughing. And he would say, "Sisters and brothers..." – and finished! Everybody was waiting for these three sentences, "Bertrand Russell has said..." – fullpoint.

After ten minutes, the chairman, the vice-chancellor of the university, himself was laughing. He told the boy, "Just sit down. Don't be worried, everything is okay. Just sit down" – he was perspiring. And the vice-chancellor said to me, "You should not have done this."

I said, "I was simply helping him. I never thought that he was a gramophone record. I thought some time he may slip ahead – 'Bertrand Russell has said...' But he proved to be a gramophone record, broken. It was not my fault. And anyway, he gave such a joyous evening. Even if you give him the first prize, I am ready, because he has given so much joy nobody can give."

Now scientists have found that your memory system functions exactly like the gramophone record. They have opened the brain for other reasons, but somehow they found that if they put an electrode on the memory point in your brain, you start saying something. And if they take the electrode away, you stop and your brain automatically reverses. Again when they put the electrode back, you start from "Brothers and sisters" – again the same. Take the electrode off, and you stop.

They have discovered that the mind has an automatic reverse system – once you have stopped, it goes back to its original place. You touch that spot again and the person starts saying the same thing. There is no reason why he is speaking – nobody has asked anything. But he is helpless – the memory starts repeating like a record.

Daiten must have been a scholar. He has quoted this sentence, not from his own experience but from scriptures.

What is he saying? When Sekitō asked him, *"What is your no-mind?"*

Daiten replied, "The one who speaks is it."

One who speaks *originally*. If one speaks only that which is borrowed, it is from the mind. But if one speaks originally, spontaneously, then it is coming from the space called no-mind. But he forgot the word 'originally'. That happens to scholars; it cannot happen to a buddha. Whatever is coming, is coming from the very source. But when you are repeating a scripture which is not your experience, there is going to be some difficulty.

If he had said, "The one who speaks spontaneously – that is the place of no-mind..." He has forgotten that one word 'original', and perhaps it was not written in the scripture itself, because no buddha has ever written a single word. All scriptures have been compiled by their disciples, sometimes after the death. Sometimes hundreds of years have passed and then disciples of disciples...generations have passed.

The four gospels of Jesus are recorded after his death, and not immediately, three hundred years afterwards. Now nobody was a witness; all the witnesses were dead. And these gospels were recorded by people who had not seen Jesus. They had not even seen Jerusalem. Now biblical research scholars have found that even the geography that they have mentioned in the four gospels is wrong. These people have never been to Israel. They have heard from others, who have heard from others, who have heard from others.

That's why I have spoken on Thomas' gospel which was written in India. He was a direct disciple of Jesus, but his gospel is not included in the Holy Bible. It was discovered just thirty years ago, but it is the most beautiful because at least Thomas was a witness. And it has tremendous beauty because it is not only that he was a witness to Jesus, here in India he went through a transformation.

He meditated, he practiced yoga, he lived like a sannyasin and moved from monastery to monastery. Buddha's air was still there. Buddha was gone five hundred years before that, but his fragrance was still alive. So in his gospel there is a certain authority which is lacking in the four gospels of the Bible. First he was a witness, he had heard Jesus, and secondly he himself had experienced the truth. The combination of both, gives a greater authority to the fifth gospel of Thomas than The Holy Bible.

Thomas is the only man in the whole world whose body has not deteriorated. His body is still in a church in Goa. Every year at Christmas time, his body is brought out of the church and his coffin is opened for any observer, for any scientist, for any researcher. Nobody has been able to figure out why it looks so fresh, as if he had died just now. There seems to have been no device used. It is not kept in a freezing temperature, it is in a hot country, but even the skin does not look as if it is dead. He looks so fresh. I have been to see the body.

Jesus' miracles may have been a myth, but this man really managed a miracle. After two thousand years he is the only person around the world whose body looks as if it has died just now – or perhaps he is fast asleep. No smell, and if it can remain for two thousand years, there is no problem for it to remain forever. Care has to be taken that nobody disturbs it.

There have been efforts to disturb it by Hindus, by Mohammedans, by people who are not Christians, because it is a great argument in favor of Christianity. But the man Thomas was not a Christian, he never knew about Christianity. He came just after Jesus was crucified. He left Jerusalem for the simple reason that Jesus must have told his close friends – and Thomas was one of those who was very close to him – about India, and about the universities of Nalanda and Takshashila, and about meditation.

So now that Jesus was crucified, he saw there was no point in being there, and he left. He came by ship, so he landed in South India. But he traveled all over India, and met all kinds of mystics who were deeply rooted in meditation. His body is a proof that he must have followed a certain method which was known to the Tibetan lamas, to the Ladakh people.

They used a certain method of meditation when the meditator was dying...at the last moment, a certain process called Bardo. It was nothing but a post-hypnotic suggestion. When a man is dying, he is in a very vulnerable state. And if he has been a meditator, then he is perfectly awake. Death is coming, but he is perfectly awake. He can be hypnotized and told, "When you leave your body, the body will remain intact as it is..." You have to continue repeating so that it enters, not only into his mind, it enters even into his bones, into his marrow, into his blood.

Bardo is a very intensive hypnosis, and it is also possible to give directions for the future to the soul that is leaving the body. Both can be done. The body can be preserved by post-hypnotic suggestion. But you cannot do it if the man has died. Then there is nobody to listen to the post-hypnotic suggestion. The man has to be alive, just on the verge of death. You give him the post-hypnotic suggestion: "Your body will remain intact, will remain intact...you go on." And if he is a meditator, even the bones, the blood, the body starts listening. The soul will leave but the body will remain completely as the soul has left it. This was one way that Bardo was used for the body.

And there was a second way. You can give suggestions to the leaving soul as to what kind of womb will be good – "Choose rightly. Don't be accidental." Millions of people are making love, and millions of people are dying. So those souls are roaming around, finding a couple who is making love. This is accidental. Because they die unconsciously, they unconsciously grope in the darkness, and whoever comes close by, just by chance they enter into that womb.

Bardo prevents the accidental. It gives the soul a right direction: "You need a certain kind of womb, so don't be in a hurry. You have been a meditator, and you have to find a mother, a father, who will allow you to meditate – not only allow you to meditate but who will help you to meditate, who are themselves meditators. So don't be in a hurry! Choose a couple."

Sometimes the man of meditation takes time to find the right womb; ordinary persons immediately enter into the womb. Bardo gives two kinds of possibilities: the body can be kept, and the soul can be given a sense of direction where to go. But this is possible only if the man has been deeply into meditation, has been practicing meditation for a long time, and was capable of remaining conscious when death comes, because death is the greatest operation.

Nature has managed it so that nobody should die consciously, just as a surgeon will not be ready to operate on you if you are conscious. First he will give you chloroform or something that makes you unconscious. Then he can operate on you because you don't know what is happening. You are so deeply asleep that things can be removed from your body, bones can be cut, replaced, anything can be done.

Death is the greatest operation, because the whole seventy years' attachment to the body has to be broken. Nature has managed – this is the wisdom of nature, the intelligence of nature – that a person who is not capable of detachment with the body, who does not know that "I am not the body," should be made unconscious. Otherwise he will be passing through tremendous anguish and anxiety.

So it is natural wisdom, but it is not applicable to the meditator. The meditator can afford to die consciously without any pain, without any anguish, without any anxiety.

> *Daiten replied, "The one who speaks is it."*
> *At this, Sekitō shouted, **"KWATZ!"** – and left.*

This shout says to Daiten, "Shut up! It is not you, it is borrowed. I can see the deadness of your statement." Shouting "Kwatz!" is saying "Shut up!" And then he left immediately, because there was no point in wasting time with this man, he was just a dead scholar.

> *Ten days later, Daiten again came to Sekitō and asked, "The last answer I said to you was not no-mind…?"*

He realized. He was sincere, at least, honest.

First he had tried to deceive Sekitō – you cannot deceive a master, that is impossible. He looks through and through you. He knows from where the answer is coming: from the mind or from the no-mind. It is so clear to a master from where the answer is coming. Any answer from the mind –

"Kwatz! Shut up!"

He must have thought about it: "Why did the master behave in such a hard way? And I was a stranger, a new person. Certainly there must be some reason why he behaved without any compassion. I must be wrong." And then in ten days' meditation he understood, "What I said was only a repetition of scriptures." So he came back.

> Ten days later, Daiten again came to Sekitō and asked, "The last answer I said to you was not no-mind. What *is* no-mind?"

...Please tell me. I don't know."

An authentic seeker begins with "I don't know, because all that I know is not mine. It does matter. I may have much knowledge, but as far as I am concerned, I don't know." This acceptance is the beginning of the search. If you know already, there is no need to search, there is no need to seek.

> Sekitō said, "Without raising eyebrows or moving eyeballs, bring your no-mind here."

Strange, but masters are strange people. They have their own ways of pushing you into the unknown territory of your own being.

> Sekitō said, "Without raising eyebrows or moving eyeballs, bring your no-mind here."
>
> Daiten said, "There is no no-mind to be brought."

In the first place, I don't know what no-mind is. In the second place, if it is no-mind how can you bring it? It is not a thing. It is not even a thought, it is pure awareness. It cannot be brought here as an object for your observation.

> Sekitō said, "Basically, no-mind is."

You cannot bring it – I can understand. It is not a thing, it is not a thought, it is only pure isness, thisness, suchness.

"Basically, no-mind is. Why do you say no-mind is not?"

It is the only isness in existence. Because you cannot bring it, you think, "It is not. That's why I cannot bring it." You cannot bring it because no-mind is the whole universe. How can you bring it? It is already here.

This very moment it is here, as it was in front of Sekitō.

"Why do you say no-mind is not? That is the wrong statement."

Just say I don't know. Say no-mind is not a thing, not a thought, hence it cannot be brought. But don't say no-mind is not. No-mind only is – pure *is*.

> At this, Daiten was greatly enlightened.

...Hearing this statement, that all that is, is no-mind. Isness and no-mind are two names of the same thing. This presence of life in the trees, in the stones, in people, in birds...this vast isness, this presence is no-mind. You don't have to bring it here, it is already here. You cannot take it anywhere else.

As far as time is concerned, it is now.

As far as space is concerned, it is here.

If you are silent, you will immediately become aware of it.

This statement made such a deep penetration into Daiten, he was greatly enlightened.

An authentic seeker, sincere seeker, who does not hide himself behind false knowledge, borrowed knowledge, who does not pretend that he knows without knowing, if he accepts "I don't know" – he is already very close to the truth. He has accepted his innocence now there is no barrier. No God, no scripture, no knowledge – he is just as close as one can be to no-mind. A little push by the master, a little statement, and he will be drowned into existence. That drowning into existence is enlightenment. Disappearing into existence is enlightenment.

I have always loved one story from China....

The emperor of China was a great painter. At his seventy-fifth birthday, he was feeling old, and perhaps the day was not far away when he would have to leave the body. So he arranged a great competition before he would leave the body: a competition for painting throughout China.

First, in every state there would be a competition, and one painting would be chosen. Then the final would be in the capital, and the emperor would choose which was the greatest painting. He himself was a competitor. He had painted a beautiful painting.

All the painters came from all over China. They all brought their great canvases that they had done. Only one man came without any painting, just paint and a brush – strange fellow!

The emperor asked, "Where is the painting?"

He said, "I don't like old things. I will paint freshly here and now. You have to give me a room, because I don't paint on canvas, I paint on the walls. Give me the biggest room in your palace and don't disturb me. And keep a guard so that nobody disturbs me. I don't know how long it will take, because it is going to be a spontaneous thing. I don't know what I am going to paint. I am just going to paint out of spontaneity, whatever happens, however long it takes."

The king said, "I am getting old, that's why I have arranged this competition. You have to be quick and fast."

He said, "No. I don't know. It may be quick. Tomorrow morning I may inform you that the painting is complete, or it may take longer. I cannot promise."

No man of understanding can ever promise anybody, because who knows about the next moment? All promising is in ignorance.

The king said, "You are a difficult person, but I can see in your eyes, and I can see in your face – perhaps you will be the greatest painter." So he gave him the biggest room in the palace – and there were many big rooms – with a plain wall so he could paint, and he closed the doors.

The painter said, "Nobody should enter, not even you, until the painting is complete. I will come out for food or anything I need." And he kept a curtain also so that even the guards could not have a look inside at what was happening behind the curtain.

It took three years for him, and the king was saying, "What are you doing? I may never be able to see your painting, I may die!"

The painter said, "It does not matter. If you die you die. If you are alive you will be able to see it. But I cannot do anything in a hurry."

The emperor had to wait.

Four years passed and the painter came out one morning and said to the emperor, "The painting is complete. You are welcome."

Such curiosity had arisen in the emperor's mind. For four years, he was thinking, "What is that guy painting?" He himself was a painter. It did not take four years for one painting. And when he came the emperor immediately followed him. They went behind the curtain.

The painting was just unbelievable; it looked so real. He had painted a huge forest, so green, lush green, almost three-dimensional. And a small path was going – you could see the path was going and going...and then it disappeared into the thickness of the jungle.

And the emperor said, "Where does this path go?"

The painter said, "Let us... Come with me. We can walk and see where the path goes, because without experience you will not know where it goes."

The story is, both went into the path – the guards were watching – and as the path turned around, they both turned around and since then nothing has been heard.

This story – in a painting you cannot enter – is a symbolic story. It says you can enter in the isness of things. The painter has made the painting so alive that branches were moving in the wind. The path was no ordinary path, and the symbolic meaning is: if you cannot enter into a painting, the painting is not worth calling a painting. But entering does not mean physical entry. Entering means you get lost completely: you are no more, only the painting is.

That's how you enter into meditation – you are no more. You come across a tremendous isness; everything disappears, you disappear, yet that isness remains. That experience of isness is enlightenment. This story simply gives a symbolic representation of enlightenment.

A painter is not worth the salt if he himself cannot disappear into his own painting. Picasso is reported to have said, "When I am painting, I am no more, only the painting is."

Nijinsky has said many times in his life – because he was asked again and again – "When I am dancing I am no more. As long as I am, the dance is superficial. When only dancing remains and I am no more, then it has a tremendous quality." It was observed by scientists, and they could see the tremendous quality. Whenever he forgot himself completely in dancing he used to jump higher than gravitation allows. Scientists were simply at a loss how to figure it out, because that much of a jump was not possible.

And even more miraculous was his coming back.... Gravitation pulls everything so fast. You see every night – you think stars are falling. All around the earth six thousand stars fall every day on the earth. They are not stars, stars are very big, a thousand times, a million times bigger than the earth. If one star falls, we are finished. Those are not stars, those are small stones which have been left hanging in space.

When the moon separated from the earth – once it was part of the earth... You have all these great oceans, the great Indian Ocean, and the Pacific, and the Atlantic. All these oceans are created because the mud and the stones and everything from these places fell out, because the earth was liquid – in the beginning it was liquid. The moon is just the combination of that whole lot that has fallen out of the earth. But it created great oceans – the Pacific is five miles deep.

But when such great lumps fell out, many small pieces also fell out. Those small pieces are just floating in space, millions of pieces of stone of different sizes. The earth's gravitation pulls these stones downwards, and at the point where the atmosphere begins...it is two hundred miles deep. Around the earth there is a thickness of two hundred miles of atmosphere, because up to that point there is air. Beyond that there is no air; it is pure space, even air is not existent. Sometimes those small stones – and there are a few big stones also...

The stone in the Mohammedans' holy place that they worship, Kaaba, is also one of the stones that has fallen from outer space, but it is a very huge stone. In every museum you can find stones which have reached to the earth. But what happens when they enter the earth's atmosphere by chance? Gravitation pulls them so fast that the friction with the air makes them turn into a fiery stone, a fire. That is why you can see them up to a point, and then suddenly they disappear. If the stone was small, then it would come to a certain point and it would be burned out. The friction of the air is such that only very big stones can come down to the earth; otherwise they disappear in the air somewhere.

Nijinsky's coming back was absolutely against gravitation. He came just

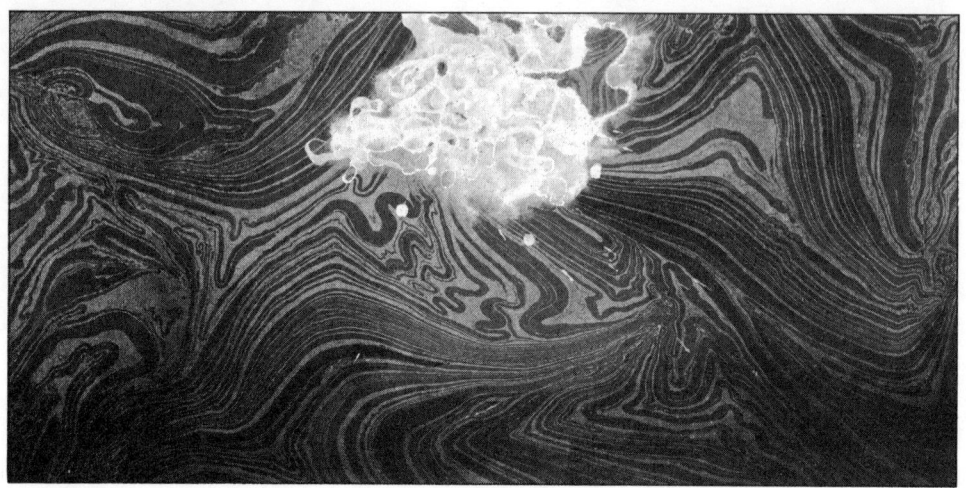

as a feather comes slowly – so slow was his movement coming back. Both the things were against gravitation: first his jump, and then his coming back like a feather as if he had no weight, gravitation cannot work on it.

And he was asked about it again and again. He said, "I have tried, but whenever I try, it does not happen so I cannot say anything about it. When I am not, when I get completely disappointed and forget all about it, that one day suddenly it happens. When I am not trying to do it, it happens. I am not, only the dance is. When *I* am not, only the dance is." Nijinsky perhaps was the greatest dancer in the world.

But this is the misfortune – that these people were born in the West. They had no idea that they were so close to no-mind. They needed a master just to give them a little push. Nijinsky would have been a Gautam Buddha, and Picasso would have been a Gautam Buddha. They have come so close. But the West has no idea how to go ahead, how to go into the painting.

Just move on on the road and get lost.

That will be your great experience – when you are lost. When you are no more, only existence is. And this existence gives you such bliss, such ecstasy, such eternity, that you are bound to feel a tremendous sacredness, a great reverence for life and this vast universe which has given birth to you.

One day it will allow you to disappear again into the oceanic consciousness. This entering into the oceanic consciousness is enlightenment.

Shiki wrote:

*The moon rises –
leaf upon leaf upon leaf
flutters down.*

He must be sitting under a tree, and it must be the time for fall.

"The moon rises…" – he is watching the moon rising.

Zen has many ways of meditation – watch the moon rising. The emphasis is on watching, not on the moon. Watch the sun rising. The emphasis is on watching, what I am calling witnessing to make it more clear – *witness* the sun is rising. And witness "leaf upon leaf upon leaf flutters down" – and you are just a witness.

On one side the sun is rising, on the other side, "leaf upon leaf upon leaf flutters down." And between these two you are just a mirror, no judgment.

He is not saying that the sunrise is beautiful, and he is not saying that the leaf upon leaf upon leaf are creating beautiful music in the air. No, he is not making any judgment. He is simply describing what he has been witnessing, just like a mirror, showing you the sun is rising, and leaf upon leaf upon leaf is fluttering down. He is just a watcher.

This is the whole secret of Zen.

Maneesha's question:
Our Beloved Master,
St. Bernard wrote: "Who is God? I can think of no better answer than: He who is."
Eckhart stated: "Thou must love God as not-God, not-spirit, not-person, not-image, but as he is – a sheer, pure, absolute One, sundered from all twoness and in whom we must eternally sink from nothingness to nothingness."
If one substituted the pronoun 'he' with 'it', would not these two Christian mystics be speaking the language of Zen?

Maneesha, you can change the 'he' into 'it', and certainly they will be speaking the language of Zen, but you cannot do that. It is their statement, not yours. They are still saying 'he'. They are not even saying 'she'; 'it' is far away – although they have come very close to the point. That's why both the saints were in trouble with the orthodox church, particularly Eckhart who was tortured, harassed, threatened to be expelled if he published his books. His books were published after his death because of these statements.

The statement is tremendously good, but still, somehow the faint image of God is present. "Who is God? I can think of no better answer than: He who is." Using the word 'he' and saying "who is," is very close; only the 'he' is standing in between.

That's what I have been telling you – even a very thin concept of God as a person is going to create enough of a barrier for you.

St. Bernard has come very close, but to be close is still to be at a distance. Closeness is a kind of distance. What does it mean? You may be one inch away, or one mile away, or one thousand miles away – you are away. Even one inch away – you are away. That one inch is as thick as the China Wall, solid rock.

When St. Bernard says, "He who is," using the word 'he', he accepts a personality, and not only a personality but a male personality. Both are wrong. Existence is neither male nor female. It expresses in the both – as female, as male, but it itself is simply pure isness. Its expression will be manifold, but its essence is the same. A woman in her interiority is as pure a consciousness as a man in his interiority.

If St. Bernard had really experienced isness, he would not have used the word 'God' or 'he'. It seems he must have been a great giant, but only intellectual. Many times philosophers have come very close, but then they go on in a round and go far away. Just coming close is not enough, but even this was condemned by the church, by the pope.

Certainly St. Bernard has some conception of a male God, and you cannot change his statement. If you change his statement, then it comes exactly to what Zen is. But then it will not be the statement of St. Bernard, it will be your statement.

So I would say that he came very close, but because of the 'God', and because the programming in his mind of the Christian God was still there, that prevented him from the quantum leap from mind to no-mind. His idea is still within the mind. He has logically and rationally worked out that if God is there he can only be described as "He who is." But this is not the exact experience.

The exact experience will not use the word 'God', will not use the word 'he'. It is male-chauvinistic, and it gives a personality to existence which it has not.

Existence is infinite, so it cannot have a personality.

It cannot be called *who*, and it cannot be called *he*.

So St. Bernard is still not enlightened – intellectually great, logically great, but existentially still a little far away from the truth.

Eckhart comes even more close, maybe just a fragment of an inch away, when he says, "Thou must love God as not-God, not-spirit, not-person, not-image, but as he is – a sheer, pure, absolute One, sundered from all twoness and in whom we must eternally sink from nothingness to nothingness." He has come very much closer than St. Bernard, and hence he was more condemned than St. Bernard, because he was destroying the whole Christian theology.

But still I say he is within the framework of the Christian God, although he seems to be a far more refined intellect than St. Bernard – a very thin barrier, a Japanese rice-paper barrier. But that is enough to keep your eyes closed.

His statement is beautiful: "Thou must love God as not-God." But why use the word 'God' at all if it is to be loved as not-God? Why not say, "Thou must love not-God, not-Spirit, not-person, not-image, but just the sheer existence, pure, absolute One, sundered from all twoness, and in it we must eternally sink from nothingness to nothingness"? But his beginning, "Thou must love God," is a Christian programming.

Zen has dropped all programming. It has dared as much as human consciousness is capable of. Now making this statement has a certain compromise with the church. "Thou must love God" – so the Christian church is satisfied that he is still talking about God, although a little crazy, because he says, you must love God as not-God. Then who is he? a woman? a man? a tree? the ocean…? What do you mean by "not-God"?

So Christianity condemned him, but because he was saying, "Thou must love God," they told him not to publish such writings while he was alive, because they would create doubt in people's minds. And they have been doing that even today.

They prevented one great French scientist, Chardin, from publishing his papers about the Peking man – he discovered the Peking man – "because your papers will go against Christianity." And because he was an ordained priest, he had to follow the orders from the Vatican. They destroyed a great man. He could have contributed much. But if you don't have any feedback, if other scientists don't know what you are writing, what you are discovering, and you don't know *their* opinions... It needs constant feedback.

Science grows, not by one scientist, it grows amongst all the scientists. There is a constant dialogue going on through papers, through conferences, through books, through periodicals...a constant dialogue is happening all around the world. That's how science tries to figure out the best hypothesis about anything.

Now preventing Chardin from publishing any paper, from attending any conference, from writing any book while he was alive – and of course when you are dead somebody else will write it, you will not... Somebody else does not have the same scientific background, nor the same discovery. And after your death what happens to your ideas will not be a feedback; you will not be able to improve upon it. They destroyed a great scientist of the same caliber as Albert Einstein.

But I am also angry at Chardin. Rather than stopping his writings and researches, why did he not resign from being a Christian priest? He resigned from science in favor of Christian superstition. Nobody has raised the question that he is also part of the whole slavery game; everybody has condemned the Vatican.

I condemn the Vatican, but I also condemn Chardin – Chardin more than the Vatican. The Vatican has been doing that for centuries – that is not new. But why was Chardin such a sheep? Why could he not gather the courage? A man of such tremendous intelligence should have left the priesthood. What was in it? A religion that prevents you from declaring truth is not worth being part of.

But he proved a coward – he stopped writing. And now a Chardin society exists in France which publishes his works and papers and his researches – but it is too late. If somebody raises a question, Chardin is not there to answer. And by the time Chardin died, other scientists had come to better hypotheses. If he had been allowed, or if he had had the guts to come out of the church, he would have managed to refine. It is a continuous growth and evolution. Science is not something static.

When Albert Einstein was asked, "If you had not discovered the theory of relativity, do you think it would ever have been discovered?" he said, "It would not have taken more than three weeks."

And finally it was found that somebody in Germany had already discovered it before Albert Einstein, but he was a lazy guy and did not publish the paper. So not *after* three weeks, but three weeks before, it had been found. Einstein was right – that when something is there, sooner or later it has to be discovered. You cannot go on missing it if there is a truth in it.

Eckhart also proved to be a little cowardly, just like Chardin. He came very close, but he continuously maintained that he loved God. Of course he has those conditions "as not-God..." Then as what? And if you are loving only the isness of existence, then why go on calling it God? Why continue that old superstition, that old lie? Just a compromise with the Vatican, just a fear that if you don't do that much you are taking a risk with your life.

I was born into Jainism, and when I started speaking against their ideologies – and when I say anything I say it with my total being – they were unable to answer me. Their highest command decided to expel me from Jainism. But I wrote to them: "You need not expel me, I expel your whole Jainism and your whole Jaina society. You need not expel me, I have already expelled you." So they were shocked, they could not figure out what to do. They could not expel me, I was already outside – what does it matter? And I don't think it has done any harm to me.

Compromise is always cowardly.

Truth never compromises.

Maneesha, both these people were very close to Zen, but both were cowards. God makes people cowards. Religion makes people cowards. Otherwise, what was the risk? Eckhart should have left Christianity, St. Bernard should have left Christianity, and then they would have been the very first Zen masters in the West. But they missed that great opportunity, that great dignity. They remained slaves of the Christian church.

I want you to be lions and not like sheep as Jesus wanted you to be. He has insulted humanity very badly.

It is time for Sardar Gurudayal Singh – a really great time.
Put on the light, because I want to see the faces of my people laughing!

Three women – Betty Boobs, Lucy Legs, and Nellie Knickers – meet at an old high-school reunion. They soon start gossiping about the men they have married, and what they are like in bed.

"My husband, Bob," says Betty Boobs, "is like a 1989 Rolls Royce – comfortable, sizeable, powerful, and very satisfying!"

"My husband, Larry," says Lucy Legs, "is like a 1970 Cadillac – still fairly comfortable and satisfying, but lacks performance sometimes. Generally, quite a good ride."

"Hmm, my husband, Norbert," says Nellie Knickers, "is like a vintage Model-T Ford."

"Really?" say the other two, staring at Nellie in amazement. "Why do you say that?"

"Well," continues Nellie, "what I mean is – he manages to rally twice a year, but he has to be started by hand!"

On the forty-second floor of the Fast Buck Brokers building, executive vice president, Bilbo Ballbag, is interviewing girls for a secretarial job.

After examining many talented and capable applicants, Bilbo finally hires Gorgeous Gloria for the job.

After two days, Gloria is bending down to get something from the bottom drawer of the filing cabinet, and Bilbo Ballbag gets an eyeful. He immediately calls her into his office.

"Look, Gloria," he says, his eyes playing with her tits, "I wonder if you would mind working with me over the weekend?"

"Sure," says Gloria, giving Bilbo a wink, "that would be great."

"Good," replies Bilbo, "we can get all this extra work done aboard my luxury sailboat!"

"Ah, dear," says Gloria, "but I get terribly seasick."

"Don't worry!" says Bilbo, perspiring as he loosens his tie. "I will take care of everything."

That evening, on his way home from work, Bilbo stops in at the drugstore. He goes up to the counter and approaches Victor Vaseline, the clerk.

"Give me a pack of Trojan condoms and a bottle of seasickness pills," says Bilbo.

"Yes, sir," says Victor, and he fumbles around under the counter, and discreetly hands Bilbo the two items. "It is none of my business, sir," continues Victor, "but if it affects you like that, why do you bother?"

Amongst the early Christians, it was rumored that the Lord and Savior, Jesus Christ, was blessed with enormous sexual machinery, which used to terrorize all his followers, men and women alike.

As the story goes: On that fateful day on Calvary Hill, Jesus had been hanging on his cross for a couple of hours, staring up at the sky, waiting for Godot.

He looks down and sees his favorite girl, Mary Magdalena, weeping in the crowd, and feels a stirring of the spirit in his loincloth.

"Mary! Mary!" Jesus calls out. "Come closer!"

Hesitantly, Mary walks out of the crowd towards the cross. She comes closer, but stops in her tracks when she sees the huge growing lump in Christ's knickers.

"Mary! Mary!" moans Jesus. "Closer, come closer!"

Mary shuffles forward nervously eyeing the ever-growing mountain in his underpants – then she stops, again.

"Mary! Mary!" gasps Jesus. "I have something from the Holy Ghost to impart to you – come closer!"

"Ah! Christ, No!" cries Mary, her eyes popping out. "Don't give me anymore of that Holy Ghost shit! I can see your resurrection from here!"

Nivedano...

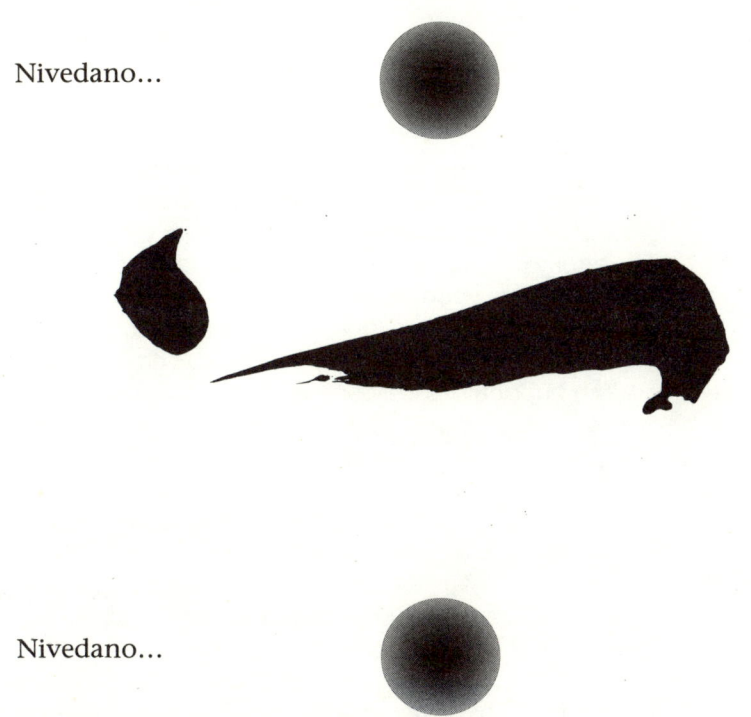

Nivedano...

Be silent...
Close your eyes,
and feel your body to be completely frozen.
This is the right moment to enter inwards.
Gather all your energy, your total consciousness,
and rush towards the center of your being,
which is just below your navel, inside – two inches below, exactly –
with an urgency, as if this is the last moment of your life.
Only those people have ever reached to their center
who had this urgency, this intensity.
Faster and faster...
Deeper and deeper...
As you come closer to your inner center,
a great silence descends over you just like soft rain with all its coolness.
And inside you, a great peace arises, a peace that passeth understanding.
A little more close –
and you feel so blessed.
A little more close,
and you are getting drunk with the divine.
Just one step and you are at the center of your being, utterly ecstatic.
As you get centered, you are no more, just a pure isness.
This isness we have called symbolically, the buddha.
This is your original being.
Centered, silent, no more your old being –
utterly naked, just a pillar of light...you are the buddha.
Everybody is born with a hidden buddha in him.
The word 'buddha' means the awakened one.
It is everybody's eternal birthright.
The buddha has only one quality: watching, witnessing.
Witness that you are not the body.
Witness that you are not the mind.
And finally, witness that you are only a witness –
just a mirror reflecting everything.
At this moment you are the most fortunate people on the earth.
Everybody is concerned with trivia;
you are entering into the essential and the eternal.
You can feel a tremendous reverence for existence,
a great joy in the sacredness of everything.
The whole universe becomes your home; you are not an outsider.

To make your witnessing deeper,
Nivedano…

Relax…
but go on remembering that you are only a witness.
As your witnessing deepens,
you start melting into an ocean of consciousness.
Ten thousand buddhas disappear into one consciousness,
into one ocean of consciousness.
Gautama the Buddha Auditorium has turned into an ocean of consciousness
without any waves and without any ripples –
utterly silent and quiet.
This is your real space, this is your no-mind.
From this no-mind you can enter into the cosmos.
This is the door, the opening.
Collect the peace,
the silence,
the blissfulness,
the ecstasy,
the divine drunkenness,
before Nivedano calls you back.
And also persuade the buddha to come behind you – he is your dhamma.
He is your nature; you have just never requested him.
And he has been waiting and waiting, hidden deep inside you.
A sincere request, a welcoming heart, and he is bound to come behind you.
This is the first step of enlightenment:
Gautam Buddha behind you as a shadow.
But the shadow is miraculous, the shadow is not dark;
the shadow is pure light, pure presence.
You can feel the warmth of it, you can almost feel the touch of it.
It surrounds you with a new fragrance,
and it gives you a totally new dimension to live.
Your everyday acts start changing their color, their approach.
Your very life becomes meditative.

At the second stage,
the buddha comes in front of you,
and you become the shadow.
To be a shadow of the buddha is a beautiful experience.
And the experience goes on becoming deeper and deeper
as the shadow disappears.
At the third and final stage, there is no more of you –
not even a shadow, only the buddha is.
This isness is the master key
to open all the doors of the mysterious existence that surrounds you.
Once you have the key, you are the master of your own being.
There is nobody above you, there is nobody below you.
For the first time
you experience a tremendous communion with the whole existence.
I call this the only authentic spirituality, the only authentic religiousness.
Now don't forget to request the buddha to come behind you…

Nivedano…

Come back…but come as a buddha,
with great grace, peace, silence.
Sit down for a few moments
just to remember the golden path that you have traveled,
the center that you have found within you,
the opening into the cosmos,
and all those fragrances from the beyond;
the silence showering on you,
and the warmth of the buddha who has come behind you.
You can feel him.
It is your very nature.
It is you in your truthfulness, in your existential experience.
If the first step is complete, the second will follow automatically.
When the second is complete, the third will follow automatically.
The day you will complete the third step

will be the most fortunate day in your life.
That day you will be awakened from a long, long sleep, a spiritual sleep.
That day you will become enlightened.
Then there is no more birth, no more death.
You have become one with the whole.
This is the only holiness I know of.
There is no other.

Okay, Maneesha?
Yes, Beloved Master.

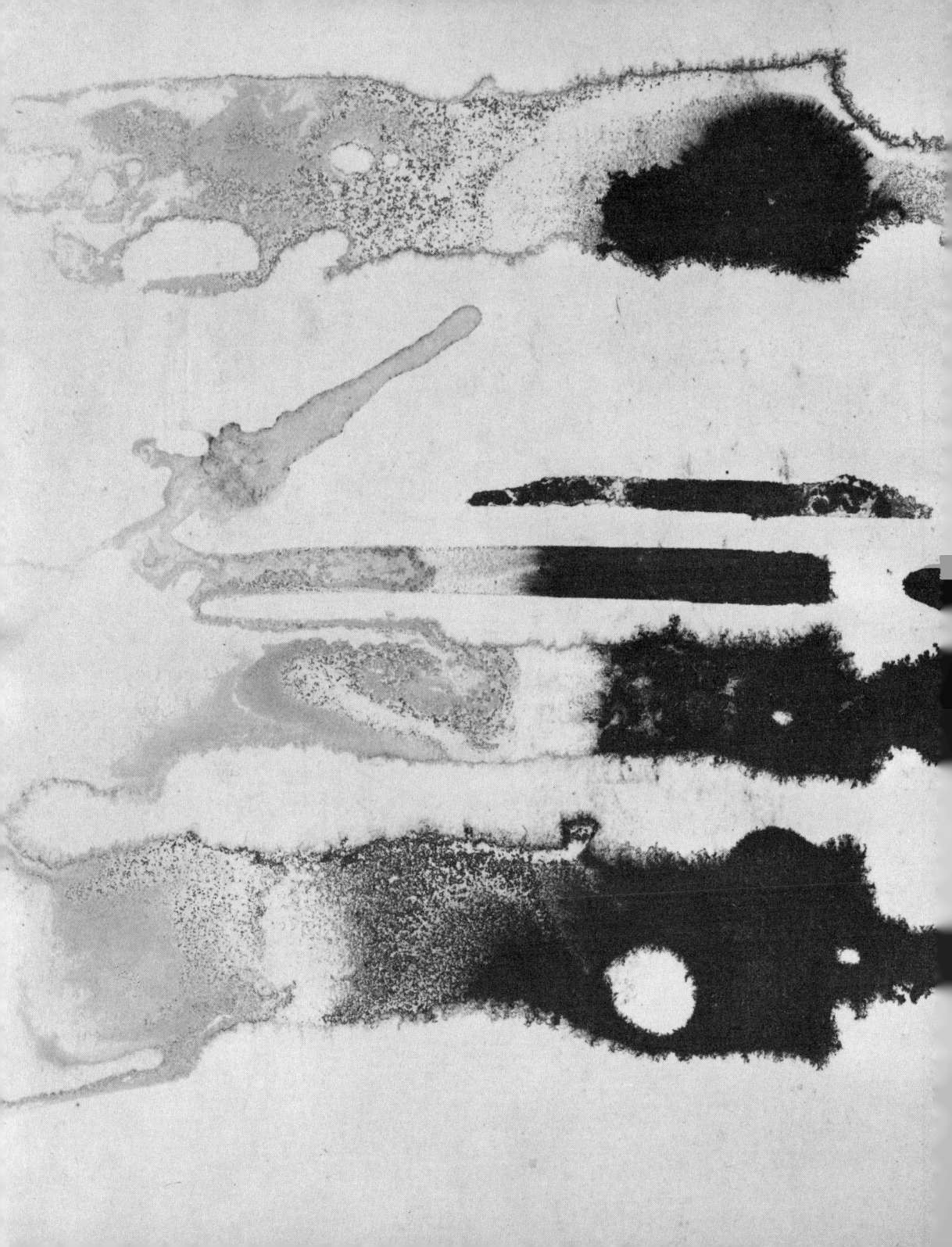

CHAPTER 3
The Paradise of Yourself
FEBRUARY 15, 1989

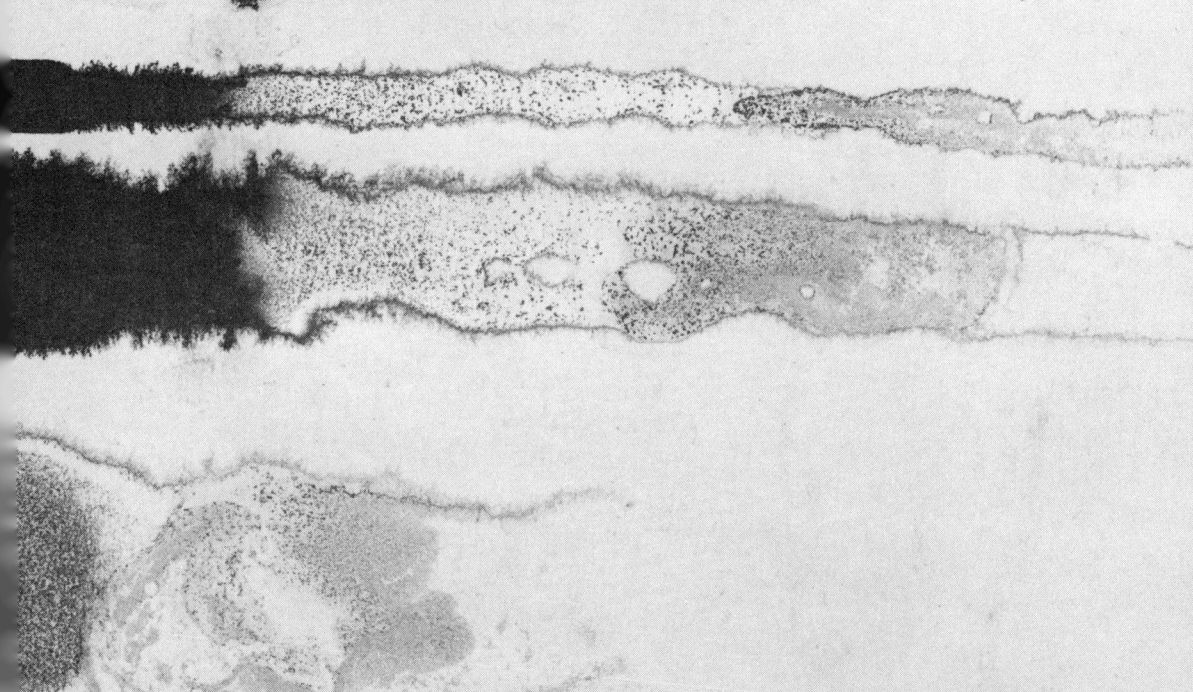

THE SUTRA

Our Beloved Master,

One time, when Daiten came to Sekitō,
the master asked him, "Are you a Zen monk
or an ordinary monk?"
Daiten replied, "I'm a Zen monk."
Sekitō asked, "What is Zen?"
Daiten replied, "It is raising eyebrows and moving eyeballs."
Sekitō said, "Excluding raising eyebrows and moving
eyeballs, bring your original face and show it to me."
Daiten said, "Please Oshō, exclude raising eyebrows
and moving eyeballs, and look at me."
Sekitō said, "I have excluded them."
Daiten said, "I have given it to you."
Sekitō said, "What is the no-mind you have given to me?"
Daiten said, "Not different from you, Oshō."
Sekitō said, "No concern about you."
Daiten said, "Really, there is not a no-mind nature."
Sekitō said, "Is there not a thing with you also?"
Daiten said, "If there is not a thing anymore, that is
the real thing."
Sekitō said, "The real thing cannot be obtained. So, that
is what you understand. Retain it firmly and keep it."
Daiten then left Sekitō and retired to Mount Reian
in southern China, where many disciples would
later gather around him.

Friends,

I have been saying for years that it is time that the politicians should be watched, and they should be looked after by psychiatrists, psychoanalysts.

Since nuclear weapons have come into existence, the politicians have become immensely powerful. Power certainly corrupts, and absolute power corrupts absolutely. It not only corrupts, it gives you a megalomania. And every politician is a split personality; he has to be. He says one thing, he does another. He always has a mask to show to the people, and his real face is always hidden. The longer he remains in power, the more possibility of his going neurotic, schizophrenic.

It was okay in the past, because all these politicians could not do much harm, but today it is absolutely different. A single politician who is mentally, psychologically sick, can destroy the whole beautiful planet. I have been waiting for psychoanalysts and psychiatrists themselves to declare this situation, and the declaration has come today.

Two psychiatrists, very famous, known worldwide, Dr. Jablow Hershmann and Dr. Julian Lieb, wrote in the *Washington Post* recently that there should be a shrink in the White House. At present there is an official physician for the president, but no psychiatrist. They said, "In this nuclear age, when the president of the U.S. can start a nuclear war, one has to make sure that he is mentally stable, and not subject to euphoria, manic depression, or suicidal tendencies."

They cited several examples. "President Nixon, before he resigned, had been miserable for months – avoiding people, taking long walks alone. He refused to talk about how he felt, and had drawn away from his family. He was not sleeping enough, and once could not sleep for four nights in a row. He was drinking too much, sometimes before lunch. He had become unpredictable: one minute close to tears, the next furious over some bit of nonsense, and an hour later on top of the world. Sometimes he seemed out of focus. He rambled or gave orders that were ridiculous. One night he walked the halls of the White House talking to the portraits on the walls. He hinted of suicide.

"Such episodes," say Hershmann and Lieb, "are usually kept under wraps, but we have begun to realize how widespread the phenomenon is – from the periodic inertia of Ronald Reagan, to the latest revelations about Lyndon Johnson, to the details of incapacitating conditions suffered by Woodrow Wilson and Franklin Roosevelt."

It would be a good sign if every president, not only the American president, but every prime minister – whoever has the power to destroy this world – had a personal psychiatrist looking after him. But that is not enough. Man is body – the personal physician can look after it. Man is mind – the psychiatrist can look after it. But man is something more too. So what these two psychiatrists, Hershmann and Lieb, are suggesting is an incomplete cure.

Every president, every prime minister, every king around the world, should also have a master of meditation. Only then we can be safe, and this planet can be safe.

Psychiatry can only help to keep the mind normal, at the most, but its limit is the mind. But man's existence is far bigger, it is beyond the mind. That beyond has to be understood also, and that beyond only can create right sanity. That beyond can make you peaceful and silent, creative, celebrating. Once you know something of the beyond, you are no longer suicidal, and you are no longer murderous.

Nuclear weapons will disappear from the world if we can make the politicians understand the absolute necessity. Just as they do not feel embarrassed by having a personal physician, they should not be embarrassed by having a personal psychiatrist, and they should not be embarrassed by having a personal master of meditation. These have become absolute necessities.

If we want the world to survive, the politicians have to be kept under control by intelligent people, by people who know the secrets of life, of eternity, and the people who can impart that energy, that understanding, that experience of the innermost being. This is the only possibility, otherwise there is no hope for humanity, and no hope for life – no hope for Gautam Buddhas, people rising to the highest peak of consciousness, to the deepest depth of consciousness.

And this planet is special. It is a very small planet, but it is absolutely unique because it has life, consciousness, *and* the opportunity for evolving into Gautam Buddhas. It should be saved at any cost. We cannot afford a global suicide.

I thank Dr. Hershmann and Dr. Lieb for their suggestions, but I would like them to know that their suggestions are incomplete because more psychiatrists go mad than any other profession – four times more. More psychiatrists commit suicide than any other profession. More psychiatrists are vulnerable to all kinds of mind sicknesses, because the psychiatrist is not a meditator. This is our whole inner poverty.

The psychiatrist knows about the mind, but mind is not in itself the eternal source of life. It can slip at any moment into neurosis. At any moment it can become megalomaniac. A little power…

I am also worried about the psychiatrists who will be looking after the presidents and the prime ministers. They themselves may turn out to be megalomaniacs because they now have great power!

So their suggestion is good, but it has to be supported by a master of meditation who can look after the president or prime minister, and also can look after the psychiatrist. Do you understand what I mean?

It is absolutely urgent because we don't have much time before somebody goes crazy. Any moment the destruction of the earth is imminent.

The questions from sannyasins.
The first question:
I heard You say existence is non-judgmental, but our minds are full of judgments. Where do they come from? Are they also related to the idea of God?

Existence is non-judgmental.

That is one of the greatest contributions of Zen to humanity: that you need not be a saint to be awakened. You can be awakened from any angle, from any dimension of life.

It is almost like somebody is dreaming that he is murdering someone, and somebody else is dreaming a very sweet dream that he is serving the poor people. Somebody is dreaming that he is very virtuous, a saint, and somebody is dreaming that he is a murderer, the worst kind of criminal.

Do you think the saintly dreamer will wake up sooner, and the sinner and the criminal will take a little longer time to wake up? They will both wake up exactly at the same time, by the same method. Just throw one bucket full of ice-cold water on both and they will jump out of their beds. It does not matter whether they were dreaming of sin or they were dreaming of virtue.

Zen's understanding is – and I absolutely support it, it is my own experience – that you can wake up wherever you are, whatever you are doing; your actions, your personality, your character, don't count at all. This is a tremendous declaration because all religions have been telling you, "First you have to become a saint, then only can you enter into the paradise of God."

Zen gives you a tremendous equality. It does not matter what you are doing, it does not matter how you are behaving, it does not matter what is your personality – polished, crude, uncultured... You can wake up by the same method, meditation, directly, without changing anything in your character, in your actions.

And existence in this way is non-judgmental. It gives life to the sinner, it gives life to the saint, without any discrimination. It gives love, showers silence over all, without any discrimination.

Your question is, where do these judgments come from? Fundamentally, originally, they come from the fiction of God. But a fiction cannot do anything, the fiction has to hire living people. They come from your priesthood, from your popes, your shankaracharyas, your imams, your Ayatollah Khomeiniacs.

Just now, one Mohammedan has written a book about the holy Koran. It has been banned by Rajiv Gandhi – and he has not read it – because the Mohammedan pressure in India is of immense importance. They vote in a solid block and they are second to Hindus – they create fear. They asked that the book should be banned. It is being banned in many countries which are Mohammedan.

Ayatollah Khomeini came on the radio in Iran and declared that wherever this man is, he has to be immediately killed, murdered – not only the person who has written the book, but the person who has published it, and the person who has printed it, and the person who has the sole agency to sell it. All four have to be butchered wherever they are. And it is the duty of every Mohammedan to finish them off as quickly as possible and burn all the copies of the book. Not a single copy should remain anywhere in existence. And that man has done an immense job of analysis.

This you call a world which is democratic?

This you call a world where there is freedom of speech?

These priests are the source, the immediate source. In the name of God they have made your minds judgmental. Without understanding anything, you are carrying judgments in your mind.

The moment you see something, immediately a judgment arises. You don't have to make the judgment it has become almost automatic. You see a rose and suddenly you watch a judgment arising: "This is beautiful." But the moment you say, "This is beautiful," the judgment is hiding the rose. The judgment is coming from past experiences of roses. But this is a new rose, you have never met it before, it has never before been on the earth. For the first and last time it has come into expression. You may have seen roses, but this one is not the same. All your judgments about other roses are figments of your memory.

The robotlike arises in you: "This is beautiful" – not that you have understood its beauty, not that you are existentially in direct contact with its beauty, not that your eyes are absolutely pure and rejoicing the beauty of the rose.

The judgment comes and you destroy the rose.

The judgment stands between you and the rose, and you are lost into past memories of roses that you have seen before. But this is not one that you have ever come across.

Any judgment is past oriented, and existence is always herenow, life is always herenow. All judgments are coming from your past experiences, your education, your religion, your parents – which may be dead, but their judgments are being carried by your mind and they will be given as a heritage to your children. Generation after generation, every disease is being transferred as a heritage.

Only a non-judgmental mind has intelligence, because it is spontaneously responding to reality.

I want you to drop God.

I want you to drop your scriptures.

I want you to drop your parents.

I want you to drop everything that has been given to you with all good intentions – that does not matter. Those good intentions don't have any weight but they have made you judgmental.

So immediately, without knowing, without understanding, without experiencing, you come to a judgment. The judgment comes immediately, so quickly that if you are not alert enough you are not going to be able to get rid of them. They are just waiting there in your mind, in your storage of the memory. The moment you see something, the moment you hear something, immediately comes the judgment: "It is right, it is wrong. It is according to my mind, hence I agree with it."

But if you are agreeing according to your mind you are not agreeing, you are simply getting your mind to become stronger.

The function of the master is a very delicate one. He has to take away all your mind, slowly slowly, so that a certain pure space exists in your mind. Then only have you the eyes to see, and the ears to hear. Then everything goes deep, without any obstacles, to your very center of being.

Everything in existence is nourishing.

Everything in existence has its own purpose, it is fulfilling its own job. That which you deny according to your borrowed knowledge is needed by existence, otherwise it would not have been there. Anything that is happening anywhere must have some support from existence, otherwise it will simply drop dead.

Life needs variety. Just think of a world where everybody is a saint – it will be the worst world, the most boring. And the boredom will become so heavy that it will create only one desire: how to finish yourself, because you cannot finish all the saints. Only you can commit suicide to get out of that boredom. If all the people were of the same size and had the same faces… howsoever beautiful the faces, howsoever beautiful the personalities, if they were all the same, carbon copies of carbon copies, you would be utterly bored. Knowing one woman you would know all women, finished – there is no opportunity to have another experience. Knowing one man you would have known all men.

And that is not right because every man is different and every woman is different. Every rose is different from other roses, every flower is different from other flowers.

Just now, as I was getting ready to come here, taking my bath, and the cuckoos in my garden were really going cuckoo! But I wondered that every cuckoo has its own song to sing. I could make out clearly how many cuckoos there were. Their song was different, their sound was different.

Existence takes care of variety.

Sinners are also needed in this world – they make life more cheerful. Saints are also needed as an example that you should not follow them. They are as dead as dodos. They are good examples to avoid. Sinners are nice people. I have never seen a sinner sad and I have never seen a saint joyful. It is strange, it should have been otherwise if religions were true. But religions are not true.

Sinners have a quality of innocence which saints don't have. They are very calculating, very cunning. What they are doing in their saintliness is just purchasing some good land, some good house, some bank account in the other world. They are so greedy that they are not satisfied with this beautiful planet and this beautiful dance of life. Sinners are non-greedy people, they rejoice in small things – a beautiful woman, delicious food, just a little drink; and they are so happy to dance and sing and celebrate. These are the real salt of the earth. They are needed. And saints are needed so that you can avoid them.

But remember, everything in this world has its own place and has its own dignity, and by your judgment you are destroying the dignity of someone, you are interfering into somebody's territory.

A man who is full of judgment becomes ugly, become unbearable. A man without judgment is always welcomed by everyone because he will never interfere into your territory, he will never trespass your spirituality and your dignity.

All your judgments are coming from the priesthood in the name of God. God cannot do it by himself because he is a lie; he does not exist, he has never existed. But priests go on supporting the lie, it is their very profession. If God is exposed completely then the priests have no way to continue their exploitation of humanity. They are selling God to almost the whole of humanity – a God which does not exist.

I have heard about a shop in New York which was advertising: "We have manufactured invisible hairpins."

Certainly there were queues of women. Invisible hairpins? No woman can resist the temptation.

One woman looked into the box when she got it – of course the invisible pins you cannot see – seeing the box empty, she asked the salesman, "Are you sure that there are invisible hairpins inside?"

He said, "To be frank with you, we have run out of invisible hairpins for almost two weeks, but the empty boxes are selling. But the truth is, there are no invisible pins, and only empty boxes were selling from the very beginning."

You can sell invisible pins to people...and God is the most invisible thing in the world. Perhaps some day we may invent invisible pins, but God cannot be manufactured. And a God manufactured by us will not be much of a God. We would like to change the model every year, and those who are super-rich would like to change every six months.

But because God is nowhere to be found, the priests can go on thriving on the business. They know perfectly well – they are the only people who know – that God does not exist. But they cannot say it because what will happen to their whole profession? A millions-of-years-old profession, supporting millions of priests around the world – and they are the highest people everywhere. They don't want to lose it, they don't want to miss their whole business.

So they go on creating more commandments, more judgments, they go on creating more theological fictions and they go on feeding your mind. Their whole purpose is your mind should be full of all kinds of rubbish so you cannot have any space to be intelligent. Because if you can have an empty mind the no-mind is not far away. The empty mind becomes the door to no-mind. When the empty mind becomes a stepping-stone to no-mind, it creates no problems, no obstacles.

So your mind has to be filled with the holy Koran, with the holy Bible, with the holy Gita, and there are thousands of scriptures. You can choose whatever kind of rubbish you want – it comes in all sizes and all shapes. There is immense choice. There are three hundred religions on the earth. You can't imagine a new religion, they have exhausted all possibilities. Three hundred religions about one God – you can choose. You are free to choose but you are not free *not* to choose.

And that's what I am teaching you: don't choose.

Explore, discover, don't decide before you have realized. And realization, liberation, freedom, will give you an insight into everything. You will feel compassionate and loving to the whole life that surrounds you, non-judgmental.

I have told you the story of a Zen master....

A thief entered his house without knowing that it was a Zen master's house – it contained nothing. The Zen master felt very embarrassed. The night was cold and he had only one blanket that he used in the day to cover his body, and in the night to cover his body to go asleep. That was all that he had, and the whole house was empty.

He felt so compassionate towards the thief that when the thief was going out he threw the blanket on his shoulders and told him: "Please accept it. You came without informing me. If you had just informed me at least three days before, I would have gathered something for you. I feel for the first time really poor. I cannot give you anything; this house is empty."

And the thief was very much afraid of this man. He was standing naked in the cold winter night and he had given his only possession, the blanket. But the man was strange, he was saying to him, "You should first inform me and then you can come. But give me a little time so I can beg from people and keep something for you. This is not right for you to come so suddenly without any information."

The man certainly was strange. The thief had come across hundreds of people – everybody was angry, everybody was handing him over to the police. He had suffered in jails so many times. Everybody was abusive, everybody was insulting. Out of jail, life was difficult. Nobody was ready to give him a job, so finally, he had to commit another crime just to enter into jail because that became his home. At least he had food, shelter, clothes.

This man was strange. He became afraid of this man – he rushed out of the door.

And the Zen monk shouted, "Stop! That's not right, come back. First give me a 'thank you' so that you don't feel guilty that you have stolen anything – I have given it to you.

"And then close the doors. You have opened the doors, at least this is your responsibility to close the doors. I am naked, the door is open, and the cold wind is blowing…and you don't have any compassion."

So he gave him a "thank you," and while he was leaving and closing the door, the saint said, "Perhaps some day this 'thank you' will save you, this closing the door will be of much help to you."

He could not understand what help it could be.... But that night, looking from the window to the full moon in the sky, the Zen master wrote a small haiku which said:

I am so poor.
I would have loved
to give this moon to that thief,
but I don't possess it.

Two years afterwards the thief was caught again in a very dangerous case – perhaps he would get a life-long imprisonment.

The judge asked him, "Can you bring anybody as a witness that you are not a criminal? We don't have any evidence, only circumstantial evidence, that you have committed a crime. If you can produce a man of dignity to support you in that you are a man who is not capable of doing such a crime…"

He remembered the Zen master because that was the only person who could support him. He told the judge the name of the Zen master.

The judge said, "You are referring to a Zen master – I know him. If he says you are not a criminal the case is finished."

And the Zen master came and he said, "This man you are saying is a criminal – this man is so nice. When I gave him a blanket he thanked me, and when I told him to close the door, he closed the door. He is so obedient, such a nice person. The blanket was not much, it had holes, it was old, but he received it as if I was giving him an empire. He was so grateful – just leave him." The case was dropped. The Zen master was well known, even to the emperor.

The thief followed the Zen monk, and the Zen monk asked him, "Where are you going?"

The thief said, "I am not going anywhere, I am coming with you. I have found a man who has no judgments and who has returned my dignity to me. For the first time I feel I am a human being and there is someone who loves me, there is someone who feels for me, and there is someone who has compassion even for a man who has never done anything good."

The Zen master said, "Don't judge yourself."

This is the trouble. People judge others and they judge themselves too. When they judge themselves they feel guilty; when they judge others they take people's dignity and honor. This judgmental mind is a double-edged sword, it cuts both the ways. It cuts you, it cuts others. It has destroyed the whole humanity.

Drop this judgmental mind, and with this judgmental mind you will drop all your religions, all your moralities. You will become an innocent child, rejoicing in everybody and his uniqueness.

The second question:
It seems that many of us are still plagued with guilt, even though we have been in Your surgery a long time. No matter what it is, we feel guilty if we do, guilty if we don't – a no-win situation. And the deeper it is, the more subtle and elusive it seems to be.
Will we ever be freed from this insidious emotional blackmail? Is this the surgery You have been doing in these discourses on God?

What do you think?
By killing God I am killing your guilt.

I have no concern with God because he does not exist. But I have to be very discreet not to kill your guilt directly, because you will stand in defense. So I kill the gods – that is my indirect way to kill your guilt. Otherwise I have no concern with God. Without God you cannot be guilty, and that is certainly my concern.

I am operating on God – that is an indirect way of operating on you. It is a very strange kind of surgery in which God is to be cut into pieces so that your clinging to God disappears and your clinging to God's commandments disappears. When there is no God, suddenly you will drop all morality, and all so-called duties, virtues. Suddenly you will become a pagan.

I love the pagan.

I want the world back in the hands of the pagans.

All the religions have destroyed the pagans because they were the people without any judgment, without any God, without any morality…just simple, innocent, flowing with nature, in a deep let-go. So whatever was spontaneous they were doing, whatever was coming from their nature they were following. There was no question of guilt, there was no situation like a no-win situation.

The pagan was always victorious. Whatever he was doing or not doing, he had his dignity, his honor. I want you to be pagans, that is the first step to being a buddha. I have chosen Zorba as an example of a pagan, and that is the very foundation. On that foundation you can make a shrine for the buddha. But without the foundation, the buddha is hanging in the air like a balloon. You can worship it, but you cannot be nourished by it unless your roots are deep into the earth. Your branches cannot grow into the sky, you cannot touch the stars without deep roots in the earth. First you have to be very earthly, earthbound, then only will you start growing towards the stars.

Without roots in the earth you become simply a star gazer, you don't grow towards stars. You simply look at the buddha, you worship, you pray. But neither is worship going to help nor is prayer going to help. What is going to help is a real foundation, and that real foundation is to be without God, to be without scriptures, to be without discipline, to be without any commandments. Be a free man, don't be a spiritually enslaved person.

Once you have attained freedom from all these fictions, mythologies, you will feel so great, so fresh, so young, and so alive, that the dance will come by itself. So abundantly rich in your innermost being…because your innermost being is the place from where you are joined with the cosmos. Your roots in the cosmos grow from your innermost center. Once you have accepted existence as it is, you have accepted yourself also as you are.

If you want to improve on existence, on other people, you cannot be at ease with yourself. Your own judgments will kill you. You have never thought about it…whenever you are judging somebody, you are judging yourself also; if you condemn somebody as a thief, you are condemning yourself also. You may have have done many kinds of stealing – you may have stolen thoughts from other people, you may have stolen hypotheses from other people.

It is not only money, anything that you take from others without being grateful to the person, without his knowledge, is stealing. Money is the most ordinary thing in the world, there are far higher values. When you imitate you are stealing. If you imitate Jesus, if you imitate Buddha, what are you doing? – you are stealing their personality. You are a thief of the worst kind and you cannot feel at ease.

People cannot accept themselves because they cannot accept others as they are. I have never judged in my life. I have loved all kinds of people; just their uniqueness makes them more loveable. And because I have loved all kinds of people without discrimination, I have no way of feeling guilt, I have no way of rejecting myself. I have loved myself immensely.

These both go together: if you judge others you will feel guilty, and you will be judging yourself also continuously – whether it is right or wrong. Both have to be dropped together because they are two sides of the same phenomenon. And it is so easy. Don't ask me how long it will take – that is a cunning way of postponing. It does not take time, it needs understanding. And that understanding is possible now, this very moment. You drop all your judgments – you drop all your guilt. They go together down the drain.

Then you will live like a healthy animal, and out of your health and out of your healthy animal will arise the greatest experience possible. As you become natural you are coming closer to the experience of the buddha.

Only Zorbas can be buddhas.

Gautam Buddha himself was a Zorba. Buddhists don't understand it. For twenty-nine years of his life – the first part of his life – he had as many beautiful women as any man in the whole of history. He had all kinds of comforts and luxuries that were available in those days. He lived in so much luxury, so much drinking, dancing, singing – that was his whole life for twenty-nine years. What does not normally happen to you even by the time you are eighty years, happened to him by the age of twenty-nine.

He became fed up – everything was repetition. Because he was surrounded with so many women he became fed up with women. You don't become fed up because of your wife. Your wife is a protection, she does not allow you to look this way or that way, she keeps you looking straight forward, looking ahead – four feet ahead, not above! And you don't want to create unnecessary trouble for yourself, so you have to follow. And because she is imposing certain moralities on you she has to follow those moralities herself; otherwise she will not be able to impose them.

It is a very complex system. The husband becomes the prison to the wife, the wife becomes the prison to the husband. Both are slaves and both are masters; both are prisoners and both are jailers – and both want to get rid! But both have values – that marriages are made in Heaven, and what God has put together you should not put asunder.

Now, no marriage I have seen happens in Heaven. God himself does not have a wife and he has escaped from women as far away – perhaps millions of light-years away...no possibility of finding any woman. But the desire is there so he comes once in a while to create a Jesus Christ. Once in a while, he has to be forgiven...poor fellow is living with a Holy Ghost. I have been trying to find whether this Holy Ghost is a man or a woman; perhaps he is capable of functioning in both the ways!

I have heard a story....

When Henry Ford died...and he was a perfectionist and a great man, one of the greatest, richest people. He came from a poor family and all that he created was by his own effort with his own intelligence.

So when he met God in Heaven, God asked Henry Ford – because he was the right person to ask – "What do you think of my creation? You are a perfectionist, I know. You have created the best cars and you went on improving and improving and improving. What do you think about my creation?"

He said, "Your creation needs tremendous improvement."

God said, "For example?"

He said, "For example you have put the pleasure center of men and women at the wrong places. The woman's pleasure center is between two exhaust pipes!"

He was a manufacturer of cars, and he seems to have been right: "What kind of dirty fellow are you? The pleasure center is at the dirtiest place. Could you not put it somewhere else? – in the hands...?"

And I think his criticism is right.

God was just shocked – he used to think that Henry Ford was a Christian!

But when you force judgment on people, these people are going to force judgment on God if by chance they meet him.

The judgmental mind is going to judge everybody, it is going to judge the person himself. Everything becomes miserable, everything seems to be wrong, everything seems to be negative. He always goes on counting the thorns in a rosebush and never looks at the flower. There is no time to look at the flower, counting the thorns takes his whole life. He always looks at the dark side of things. If you ask him, he will say, "It is a miserable world. Between two nights there is only one day!"

His whole perception is to condemn and he feels good in condemning. But he does not know that when he is condemning others he is also condemning himself. Deep down he will feel guilty.

Don't postpone. Don't ask me how long it is going to take – it depends on you. If you are miserable and feeling caught in a no-win situation, then why carry it? If I could drop it, why can you not drop it? I am not a messiah, or a prophet, or an incarnation of God. I don't have any miracle powers with me, I am just as human as you are. If I could do it, who is preventing you?

Perhaps you have started enjoying your misery. Perhaps you have become habituated and it seems that if you drop your misery you will be empty. Yes, you will be empty, but just in the interim period which is very small. For a moment you will feel all is lost, but soon you will see your emptiness starts becoming filled with a totally new energy that you have been repressing by your judgments, and guilt, and morality, and religion, and God.

Suddenly you will feel from your own very sources new, fresh waters of life are rising like fountains. Soon you will find yourself filled with tremendous contentment, filled with light, joy, blissfulness – not only filled but overflowing. Such an abundance is possible, but you have to take the risk to be empty. And it is not much because what you are losing is only misery, guilt, sadness, suffering, hellfire; what you are dropping out is not worth keeping in.

And once you are clean, you are ready for existence to assert itself with all its grace and beauty, with all its wisdom and enlightenment. But for a moment you will have to be empty.

Before the new enters, the old has to go.

Before the truth enters, the false has to fall out.

And you have certainly been blackmailed. The whole of humanity has been blackmailed, and the blackmailing continues. From the very childhood it starts and it goes on even when you are going into your grave and the priest is giving a sermon. From birth to death the priest is blackmailing you in the name of God, in the name of great things. The politician is blackmailing you in the name of nationalism, patriotism. Your own parents are blackmailing you in the name of obedience and respect for the elders.

Once I participated in an all-India seminar of professors arranged by the federal government under the auspices of the education ministry. All the professors were discussing only one thing – after one professor, another, another, another – that the problem was that students don't have any respect, and something had to be done about it. It seemed everybody was in absolute agreement.

When it came for me to speak, I said, "All these people are talking nonsense."

The education minister was shocked, and all the professors who had fallen asleep woke up. I said, "It is not that students are not respectful, the problem is that the professors are not worthy of respect. You are taking the whole problem from the wrong side; that's why you cannot solve it.

"And I am saying it from my own experience. I have been a professor for nine years and nobody has been disrespectful to me. Because I respect my students, how can they disrespect me? I respect them, I love them, I give them freedom. I tell them: If you want to leave the class you can leave silently without disturbing anybody. Don't ask me; you don't need to. Whenever you want to come into the class you can come. Don't ask me because your asking me disturbs me and disturbs the class."

When I first entered the university I could not believe my eyes: the girls were sitting on one side, the boys were sitting on the other side, and in between there was a big gap. I said, "What is the matter? To whom am I going to talk? To this gap? And I don't have the kind of eyes that go this way…"

(The Master spreads his arms out, indicating to both sides of the auditorium.)

"So if you want me to teach, you have all to bring your desks into the middle and be together, because I hate to see you throwing letters – it is ugly. Why not sit beside the girl and enjoy the warmth and share your love? You are old enough – you don't need any control. I don't think you are cannibals and that you will eat the girl or do something…so get mixed up immediately!"

They looked at each other thinking, "This is a very strange situation. Every professor functions like a constable, keeps us apart, and this fellow seems to be strange…"

I said, "Be quick, otherwise I will leave the class and I will never come again!"

Unwillingly they had to pull their desks together. With great embarrassment they went to the girls who they had been throwing stones at, whose bicycles they had been puncturing. The girls were very much…and I said, "Be close to each other. Why are you shrinking to this side and the girl is shrinking to that side? That gap between you has to be filled. Be together!"

They reported to the vice-chancellor: "What are we supposed to do?

Another professor comes and he says 'What is happening? Put your desks separate! Who has done this?' We are continually carrying the desks from side to side."

So the vice-chancellor called me and he said, "This is not right on your part."

I said, "Have you ever been young?"

He said, "Yes."

I said, "Then be frank. Have you ever loved a girl when you were a student?"

He looked all around to see that nobody was listening...I said, "There is nobody. Only I am here, and you can be truthful."

He said, "Yes."

I asked him, "Have you ever punctured their bicycles, thrown stones?"

He said, "Yes."

I said, "Then you understand everything. You are creating an unnatural situation. Now my students will not puncture anybody's cycle, they will not throw stones – they don't have to. And this is absolutely natural. They are sexually mature – they became mature long ago when they were fourteen and thirteen. Now they are twenty-two, twenty-four, twenty-five. You have been torturing them for ten years continuously, blackmailing them against biology, against existence, against nature. This is the time they should have as many experiences as possible before they choose a woman or a husband."

You go shopping...even for small things you go to many shops to check the price, to see the product. You are going to live with a woman or a man your whole life and you have not been shopping...? First do the shopping. Just go around and have as many experiences as possible. If you are intelligent, all these experiences will make you richer. Then you will be capable of finding a woman or a man with whom you can be in deep love and friendship.

There is no need for divorces. Divorces will be very few if we give children enough experience. Then they will know that there are slight differences between man and man, woman and woman. And they will also come to know with what kind of woman, with what kind of man they feel the most at ease, at home. You don't give any opportunity. This is sheer blackmail.

Your parents are responsible, your God is responsible, your priests are responsible, your teachers are responsible – your whole society is responsible. But ultimately *you* are responsible. Why are you living in this prison when the doors are open? Get out! And don't ask me how long it will take.

It depends on you whether you run out of the prison, or walk in such a way that you will be caught again and put back into your cell.

A small child was late to school one rainy day, and his teacher asked him, "Johnny, you are always late. Again you are late?"

He said, "What can I do? It was so slippery that I would go one step ahead, and I would slip two steps backwards."

The teacher said, "If you are right, then how did you manage to come here? One step ahead two steps backwards...you could never have come here."

He said, "You don't understand. Then I started walking towards my house! Finally, I got to school."

So it all depends on you – it is a very slippery way. If you really want, this moment it can happen. But if you postpone, then perhaps never. Now or never.

The sutra:
Our Beloved Master,
One time, when Daiten came to Sekitō, the master asked him, "Are you a Zen monk or an ordinary monk?"
Daiten replied, "I am a Zen monk."
Sekitō asked, "What is Zen?"
Daiten replied, "It is raising eyebrows and moving eyeballs."

There is a certain ancient method coming from Taoism to Zen – it can give you a very empty mind. If you just close your eyes and move your eyeballs, soon you will see you are getting dizzy just as the whirling Dervishes in Sufism get dizzy, just by whirling. But when the Sufi Dervish gets dizzy he starts feeling the center of the cyclone. His whole body is moving, but there is something at the very center which is unmoving – that is his very being.

For Mevlana Jalaluddin Rumi it took thirty-six hours of continuous whirling. He went on and went on and went on. And that is the whole secret of it – that you should not stop because you are feeling tired, you should go on and on till you fall. Not that you have to manage to fall, you just go on doing the whirling. A time is bound to come when you cannot manage *not* falling. You will fall down almost dead. I say almost – the whole body is utterly tired. But there you can see the difference, because the whole body is so tired and so dead, it wants to go back to the earth just to rest. You will see inside you there is still a center full of light, full of energy, not tired at all. Contrast is needed to see that center.

Zen has a far more simple method. There is no need to stand and whirl.

You just sit down and roll your eyes, your eyeballs, faster and faster, and soon you will see your whole head is whirling. A moment comes when this very whirling of the head inside gives you the passage which leads to your very center below your navel.

In Zen they call it *hara* – it is your very life source. You must have heard that in Japan, suicide is called *hara-kiri*. If you push a knife in just two inches below your navel, it will hit the hara center which is your life source. So without a single drop of blood, the person dies because he has hit the life center and opened the door for life to fly out into existence. They have found the best method to commit suicide. But how did they find it? They found it through meditation. The same center is your birth, and the same center is your death.

So when you are whirling your head, you will find a passage which is not touched at all by your whirling – either by whirling the body, or just by moving your eyeballs. Both do the same function – you reach to your life center.

Perhaps this Zen monk had been using that method for meditation. So he said,

"It is raising eyebrows and moving eyeballs."

Sekitō said, "Excluding raising eyebrows and moving eyeballs, bring your original face and show it to me."

"Neither eyebrows nor eyeballs contain your original face, the buddha, the awakened one. So leave them aside, these are unnecessary things, non-essential. *Bring your original face to me.*"

Daiten said, "Please Oshō, exclude raising eyebrows and moving eyeballs and look at me."

Daiten was certainly very close to enlightenment. He is saying to Sekitō, "Please Oshō – Oh, great master – *exclude raising eyebrows and moving eyeballs and look at me. This is my original face.*"

Sekitō said, "I have excluded them."

Daiten said, "I have given it to you."

"If you have excluded the eyebrows and the eyeballs I have given my original face to you."

These dialogues are so valuable, so mysterious. But once you have got the knack to understand them they give you such tremendous keys to open the mysteries of life.

Daiten said, "I have given it to you."

Sekitō said, "What is the no-mind you have given to me?"

Daiten said, "Not different from you, Oshō."

It is the same: you have it; I have also got it. There is no need for any explanation, there is no need for any answer from you. It is the same –

"Not different from you, Oshō."

Sekitō said, "No concern about you."

Daiten said, "Really, there is not a no-mind nature."

He is saying, "Once I have found my original face, I am no more. And when I am no more, my mind is no more, my no-mind is also no more. In fact, my individuality has melted into the cosmic whole. Don't ask me personal questions, I am no more a person, only a presence."

Sekitō said, "Is there not a thing with you also?"

"Are you sure that you don't have anything left that needs to be dissolved?"

Daiten said, "If there is not a thing anymore, that is the real *thing."*

When you don't have anything you have the *real* thing, the very essence of existence, the very essence of life. When you lose yourself you have found really yourself for the first time. This is the mystery of existence.

By losing you find.

By dissolving you arise.

By disappearing you find yourself becoming the whole – not disappearing but expanding to infinity.

A great statement from Daiten:

"If there is not a thing anymore, that is the real *thing."*

Sekitō said, "The real thing cannot be obtained."

"The real thing cannot be obtained" means that the real thing is always there. So there is no question of achieving it, obtaining it, finding it, reaching it, realizing it. All these words are meaningless. It is already there; you have never lost it.

"The real thing cannot be obtained. So that is what you understand. Retain it firmly and keep it."

Daiten then left Sekitō and retired to Mount Reian in southern China, where many disciples would later gather around him.

He became a master in his own right, not saying a single word when Sekitō said, "If you understand this, then *retain it firmly and keep it."* He has given him the seal of enlightenment: "You understand it, you are very clear about it. I have tried to trap you into some question, but you always managed to get out of it. So now that you have got it, retain it, keep it."

Daiten did not say a single word. In deep silence, in deep gratitude – which is beyond words – he simply left and moved to a mountain in southern China where many disciples would later gather around him.

You are life, eternal life.

You are existence, infinite existence.

You are pure no-mind.

Just misguided, misdirected, you have forgotten yourself. All that is needed is, in the words of Gautam Buddha, *"Sammasati* – just remember your self." You don't have to go anywhere, just a remembering of a forgotten language, a remembering what you already are. It is not a realization because you have never been otherwise.

You don't have to go to any Kaaba or to any Jerusalem or to any Kashi, you have just to remember, in a silent state, your authentic being. And suddenly, all that you thought was important becomes false. All that you thought – power, prestige, money, respectability...just disappear like dreams of no meaning at all. Suddenly, with an easy heart, you start living life in a totally new way out of your spontaneity, out of your simplicity, out of your innocence.

Then whatever you do is good; then whatever you do is beautiful. Then whatever you do is coming out of your ultimate purity which has never been contaminated. Then your grace is the same as that of Buddha, and your clarity is the same as all the buddhas. You are fully awake, the night is over, the dreams are finished, the sun is rising. And the inner sun only starts rising, it never sets again.

Busōn wrote:

A flash of lightning!
The sound of the dew
dripping down the bamboos.

These small pieces of a meditative mind – "A flash of lightning!" Visualize, you can see it – "A flash of lightning! The sound of the dew dripping down the bamboos." Listen quietly and you will hear the sound of the dew dripping from the bamboos.

A man of utter silence comes to know so many things which are happening around you, but you are so much occupied. Have you ever heard the sound of dripping dew from the bamboos? You are so much occupied, you are so full of thoughts that these subtle experiences around you which have tremendous beauty just escape you, just pass by your side. But you are occupied, you don't look at them. Your ears, your eyes, your mind – everything is full. There is no space for any new experience to enter in you.

Meditation makes you spacious, it cleanses all your senses. It makes your sensitivity so sharp that the smallest fragrance passing by your side, and you will immediately get it. Just a small sound, even the sound of silence, will be heard so loudly and so clear.

We are living in trivia, and all that is great in existence we are missing. Only a man of no-mind, a man of enlightenment, knows what beauty is, what joy is, what ecstasy is. And the moment you know what ecstasy is, you know you don't need any God, you don't need any commandment, you don't need any discipline. Everything comes out of your no-mind, fresh. You live for the first time in freedom without bondage.

I define sannyas as living in freedom without bondage, living in freedom from every commandment, from every discipline, from every

105

morality, from every religion.

This life in freedom is the only authentic life there is.

And this is eternal – no beginning no end.

Maneesha's question:
Our Beloved Master,
In his book, Perennial Philosophy, *Aldous Huxley writes: "Religions that make no appeal to emotions have very few adherents."*
Looking at how many Christians there are in the world as compared with those drawn to Zen, it would seem true.
Are people attached to the idea of a God because it excites the emotions? That may include fear as well as love, but at least one feels something, and is for the time being taken out of oneself.

No, Maneesha. Aldous Huxley is a great thinker, but he is not an awakened buddha. What he is saying is logically true, but not existentially true.

Religions that make no appeal to emotions have very few adherents, but those are the only religions there are. The religions that attract people and appeal to their emotions are not religions but mock religions, pseudo-religions, fake.

Authentic religion goes beyond emotions, feelings, sentiments, thoughts – that is your whole mind. But inauthentic religions which are more interested in exploiting people than freeing them, making them slaves rather than awakened, are bound to appeal to your emotions. Obviously, these religions have many more followers than Zen. But these religions are not religions, that's why so many people are attracted towards them.

When the masses are attracted to anything you can be certain something is wrong, because the masses consist of the retarded people; their mental age is not more than ten. So there are traps for them. There are religions which conceive of God as a female, a beautiful woman. Suddenly you start feeling emotions arising – God must be the most beautiful woman in the whole existence; you become possessed with romance.

That's where Sufis get stuck – they conceive of God as a beautiful woman. They are the lovers, and God is the beloved; they are male, and God is female. Now, they are simply transferring all their biology, moving it from ordinary women made of bones and flesh and blood and mucus...and perhaps false teeth, and false hair, and rubber breasts...!

The scriptures don't talk about rubber breasts, false teeth, plastic surgery, false hair, but when the scriptures were written these things were not available. So they have talked only about the bones, and the flesh, and the blood, and the mucus. God must be a golden woman – no perspiration, no need for deodorants. God must be eternally young.

This is transferring your biology to a fake idea, a fiction. But this is not religion. This is driving you mad, because if you want to love you have to understand that the real women exist here, not in heaven. And what is the problem?

I have always wondered... The people who have written scriptures – and I have listened to great saints in this country – continuously talk about women as flesh, and bones, and blood, and nothing else. And I always wondered what they think about their own bodies? Are they made of gold? Or platinum? Not a single scripture talks about a man's body, only a woman's body.

My understanding is that these people are still deep down hankering for women. To repress that hankering they go on condemning the woman. They are not condemning for you, they are condemning for themselves so that they can repress the desire for a woman.

Now this is a transfer – that God becomes a woman. I will give you another case which will be more simple....

Meera, one of the most famous Indian women saints, thinks of God as a man, a young man, Krishna. She is the beloved and he is the lover. She sleeps with a statue of Krishna in her bed.

She got married – she belonged to a royal family so she got married to the prince of another royal family of Rajasthan. But the prince was utterly disgusted because she told him on the first night, "My husband is Krishna. Don't touch my body, it will be sacrilegious. Only Krishna can make love to me, not you."

Certainly the prince was absolutely angry, and never went again into the room where Meera used to live, sing songs and dance in front of Krishna. Her whole idea about Krishna was that he was a real man in the sky, and it was only a question of a few years before she would meet him. But preparation was needed – she had to make a heart-to-heart contact.

It is all repressed sexuality....

The more she avoided a man, the more her love for Krishna grew, because sexual energy needs some expression in some way.

She left the palace, started dancing in the streets and singing songs of Krishna. You have to just look into the songs and you will see how sex is dominant, predominant: "When you come I will be waiting for you in my bed. When are you coming? The night is beautiful, the night flowers have blossomed, all lovers have reached to their beloveds, and I am waiting alone – when are you coming?"

These are subtle expressions of sexuality, sensuality. Her songs are very sensual. She had poured all her sensuality and all her sexuality into her songs, and Krishna became her hallucination. She dreamt of Krishna, she sang of Krishna, she danced with Krishna – she kept Krishna close to her heart.

She was worshipped by people as a great saint, but those who understand a little bit of psychology would have suggested, "You need psychiatric treatment, you are simply sick."

These people have attracted many people, obviously. You already have your sexuality...just a little turn.... You already have your emotions and feelings...just a little turn.... It is all a mind game.

So Catholics can number six hundred million people, but Zen is only for the chosen few, the very elite. Its appeal is not for the masses; its appeal is only for the very intelligent who can look beyond the mind where there is no feeling, no thought, no sentiment. You have simply gone beyond your body chemistry, biology, physiology. You have entered into a space which can only be called no-mind.

So, Maneesha, it is true that the religions that make no appeal to the emotions, have very few adherents, but they are the only religions worth calling religions. And the religions which attract millions of people...you can see it – the lower and more pseudo the religion, the more people will be attracted to it. Now, what has the Catholic religion in it except fictions? Just take out those fictions and nothing remains. There is nothing essential.

Biblical scholars are continuously pointing out that the miracles told about Jesus are not true. They never happened because no contemporary source even reports them. And the miracles were such that they could not have gone unreported. It is a very simple thing. A man just puts his hands on a blind man's eyes and he starts seeing; a man turns water into wine; a man makes dead people come back to life again...do you think such a man will go unreported? And he was not a Christian, so you cannot say that because he was Christian, Jews have not reported him. He was born a Jew, he lived a Jew, he died a Jew. Jesus never knew that he was a Christian.

Christianity was born three hundred years after Jesus' death. He never knew that people would know him as Christ. *Christ* is the Greek word for messiah; *messiah* is the Hebrew word.

Christianity seems to be the lowest religion, hence it attracts the greatest mass. As religions go higher, less and less people are attracted, because less and less people can understand it.

Intelligence is not widespread. How many people can understand the theory of relativity by Albert Einstein? When he was alive it was a well-known fact that there were only twelve people around the world who could understand what he meant by relativity.

Bertrand Russell, one of the greatest philosophers of this century, wrote a book on Albert Einstein. He called it *The ABC of Relativity.* And when he met Albert Einstein, Einstein asked, "Why have you written the ABC, why not the whole thing?"

Russell said, "I only understand the very beginning. I can't claim that I understand the whole implications of your theory. I have written the ABC because that's what I understand. Some day somebody will write the XYZ... perhaps you can write it."

Twelve persons only around the world – does that make the theory of relativity wrong? And six hundred million Catholics "know" that Jesus is born of a virgin woman – only stupid people can believe that. That Jesus walks on water – only stupid people can believe that. All these fictions have been created to attract the masses.

I have heard about one archbishop of England who was visiting Jerusalem. And he had two old friends, both of whom were very learned rabbis. So he informed them, "I am coming and I want to see every place where Jesus has been."

Obviously he was interested to see the Sea of Galilee where Jesus used to walk on water. The two rabbis took him in a boat to the place where he used to walk. The archbishop asked, "Can you also walk... because you are great rabbis?"

They said, "Of course."

He could not believe it. He said, "Then just give me a little example, just a few steps."

So one rabbi got down from the right side and went walking on water – the archbishop could not believe it – and he came back.

Those two old rabbis said to him, "Can you do it? We don't believe in Christ; you believe in Christ. If your faith is enough you can walk."

Now it was a question of faith. Faith was at stake. The archbishop was hesitating and trembling inside. But in front of these two rabbis, to be defeated would not be right. So he said, "Okay, I can. I have faith. If you people who don't believe in Jesus Christ can walk, why cannot I?"

And he went from the left side of the boat and immediately started drowning and shouting, "Save me! Help!"

So the two rabbis pulled him back. They said, "What happened?"

He said, "I don't know, but I have faith."

"Your faith does not seem to be worth much," those two rabbis said.

Finally, the rabbi who had gone out said to the other rabbi, "Should we tell the boy the right thing?"

The archbishop heard their whispering. He said, "What are you whispering?"

They said, "The truth is, you got out from the wrong side. On this side, the right side, there are stones just below the water. The water is just covering them by one inch, not more than that. Jesus used to walk here, and every Jew can walk who knows these rocks. It is not faith, it is rocks!"

Just take away all the miracles – and what remains of Jesus? Take away the virgin birth – what remains of Jesus? Take away his claim which is absolutely pathological: "I am the only begotten son of God" – what remains of Jesus? Just an ordinary carpenter's son riding on a donkey – a laughingstock!

So the Vatican has just now informed all the churches not to pay any attention to the biblical scholars. Because if you pay attention to them they will destroy your whole religion. This *is* their whole religion.

But Gautam Buddha has not done any miracles, so you cannot destroy Gautam Buddha so easily. He is not born out of a virgin, and he is not the only begotten son of God. Any non-essential is not there so you cannot take away anything. But certainly he becomes more difficult for the masses to understand.

His approach can be understood by the very intelligent people. So even in India...he was born in India, but his religion disappeared from India. These masses of India could not follow him. He did not give them what Maneesha calls "something." He gave them nothing, because nothing is the pure space.

Something is bound to be *something* in the mind.

Nothing is the beyond-mind.

Gautam Buddha disappeared after his death very quickly. For two thousand five hundred years there has not been a single Buddhist in India. Even in the temple which the king Ashoka built as a memorial at the side of the bodhi tree where Gautam Buddha became enlightened, the priest is a brahmin. There was no Buddhist even to be at the memorial to take care of the temple.

That brahmin does not believe in Buddha. He was paid and he is still being paid by Buddhists from outside India. He does not believe in Buddha, but he takes care. His family has been taking care of the temple for hundreds of years, generation after generation – just a caretaker. He does not believe in Buddha, he does not think that he is the right person to belong to.

But Buddhism spread in China and Japan, in Tibet and Ceylon, in Korea and Taiwan – it reached faraway places. In Mongolia, in Afghanistan, in a few states which now belong to the Soviet Union, Buddhist statues and temples have been discovered. Its spread is wide, but the reason for its spread is that the Buddhists who went to these places started compromising.

Buddha was a non-compromising man. No man of truth can be compromising – it does not matter. What matters is truth in its purity. But how many people are able to rise to that height, to that consciousness, to understand? Surely very few people.

So all the Buddhists around the whole continent of Asia are not true Buddhists, they have compromised with their local religion, they are mixed. If Buddha comes back he will simply deny all these Buddhists because they are doing something which he was against, absolutely against. And they are all doing all those things just as a compromise.

Only Zen has not compromised – that's why my respect for Zen. It has remained a very small thin stream of masters. It never became a mass religion – it cannot. The day it becomes a mass religion it will not be a religion anymore. My love for it, my respect for it is because it is absolutely non-compromising, it is not interested in gathering crowds. It is interested only in the highest evolved human beings. That is my interest also. That's why you cannot see masses coming to me.

The day masses start coming to me I will not come. I hate the unconscious masses. They have been the cause of killing people like Socrates, killing people like al-Hillaj Mansoor, killing people like Jesus. There is every possibility that Gautam Buddha also was killed by being given poison. They have tried to kill Mahavira – many attempts.

The masses are against the truth because truth is going to shatter all their lies. What Maneesha is calling "something" – that something is a lie, a consolation.

No man who loves the truth is going to console you.

He is going to destroy all your consolations. He is there to take away all your lies so you can rise to the ultimate peak of consciousness. But that peak comes to you when you are no more.

When there is nothing inside you, then the whole existence simply starts showering on you flowers of peace, love, silence, ecstasy, a divine drunkenness.

Aldous Huxley is not right because he does not understand the difference between an authentic religion and a fake religion. He is a man of rational and logical understanding, but not a man who can be called meditative. It is because of this he started taking LSD. He wrote a book called *Heaven and Hell* in which he preaches that LSD gives you real samadhi, real enlightenment.

A chemical can give you enlightenment...? And after six hours, eight hours, twenty-four hours, enlightenment disappears and you are again your old fucking self!

This is the right time for Sardar Gurudayal Singh. Put on the lights!

One night, the German Zen master, Stonehead Niskriya, decides that he wants to get a date....

It is very difficult for Zen masters to get a date. He used to have a girlfriend... When I was telling you that I cannot see this way...

(With crossed arms raised high, the Master indicates to both sides of the auditorium, simultaneously.)

...that girlfriend used to see this way! She always missed the Zen master Niskriya, so she never knew who he is. But even she escaped. So he went to Germany – you can see, here he could not find a single girl...! So he went to Germany and picked up a punk girl. Even that punk girl has escaped! That's why Niskriya is missing from his place. He has a fever!

Somebody has to have some compassion on him. He was thinking to go to Goa – not for Goa, but just to find another punk. So this story comes right on time....

One night, the German Zen master, Stonehead Niskriya, decides that he wants to get a date. But recently, he has had trouble getting any women to go out with him because they are afraid of his fierce appearance and his Zen stick.

So Stonehead has an idea. He disguises himself in a big overcoat, a black hat and sunglasses.

Then he goes into Zorba's and sits down next to Ma Papaya Pineapple. They begin to talk. Stonehead buys her a piece of *piesta,* and one thing leads to another, and finally Stonehead invites Papaya back to his room.

Papaya thinks this guy looks a bit weird wearing sunglasses at night, but thinks to herself, "Ah! What the hell! My chakras are open this week!" And they go off together.

When they get to his room, Stonehead turns off all the lights. "Well,

Papaya," he says, "I only like to do it in the dark. Is that okay with you?"

"Sure," says Papaya, and they begin to get undressed.

Papaya is sitting on the edge of the bed in total darkness, and Stonehead is standing next to her. When he bends over to take off his socks, Papaya reaches out in the dark and touches Stonehead's shiny, bald head, hovering near her face.

"Wow!" exclaims Papaya in shock. "You had better be careful with *that* thing!"

An international team of eminent zoologists gathers in Africa to do research on the life cycle of the elephant in the wild. When one year is over, all the scientists publish their reports.

The Englishman's report is titled: "The African Elephant at Teatime."

The American's report is titled: "Fast-food Cheeseburgers and the Modern African Elephant."

The Italian report is titled: "Fitting an Elephant into a Ferrari."

The French report is titled: "The Seventy-two Love Positions of the African Elephant."

The Russian report is titled: "How to Hide Your Elephant from the KGB."

The German report is published in five volumes entitled: "An Introduction to the African Elephant's Left Testicle."

And, finally, the Polish report is titled: "Elephants? What Elephants?"

Young Father Fever is having problems again. So he goes for some fatherly advice from his superior, Father Fornicate.

"Tell me, my son," says Father Fornicate, "are you still having trouble with those nasty fantasies? You know, things like crotchless panties, French ticklers and hot buttered nuns?"

"No, no!" cries young Fever, "this time it is the big 'M' – you know, masturbation!"

"Ah! Masturbation!" replies Father Fornicate, crossing his legs and gritting his teeth. "Yes! One of my favorite subjects! What do you want to know about it?"

"Well," replies Fever, perspiring, "is it as bad as they say?"

"My boy," intones Fornicate, uncrossing his legs and adjusting his robe, "it used to be believed that masturbation led to insanity and blindness. But that is no longer thought to be true."

"I am not worried about *that*," says Father Fever, trembling. "I read in the latest Vatican report that masturbation can be the cause of a serious reduction in hearing – even deafness!"

Father Fornicate leans forward and says, *"What?"*

Nivedano...

Nivedano...

Be silent...
Close your eyes
and feel your body to be completely frozen.
This is the right moment to turn inwards.
Gather all your energy,
your total consciousness,
and rush towards your center of being –
it is just below your navel, two inches below exactly, inside –
with an urgency as if it is your last moment of life.
Without such urgency and intensity,
nobody has ever reached the center of his being.

Faster and faster...
Deeper and deeper...
As you are coming closer to your center,
a great silence descends over you just like soft rain.
You can feel the coolness of it.
A little more close and you find a great peace
arising from your own life sources,
and surrounding you like fragrance.
Even the night is helping you.
The whole existence is helping you.
Not only are you meditating,
the whole existence is meditating with you.
Just one step more and you are at the center of your being,
utterly drunk with the divine,
an authentic ecstasy which is not produced by any drug like LSD,
but is part of your opening of the inner lotus.
Once it is with you, it is forever
and it transforms your whole life, your activities, your responses.
At the center, with this ecstasy you are no more, only a pure space.
This pure space we have personified as Gautam the Buddha.
It simply means the awakened consciousness.
The face of the buddha is everybody's original face.
In this space suddenly you find you are no more
but buddha is your original face.
You are no more but life is, eternal life –
without beginning, without end.
You are no more, but existence is.
And this isness brings you tremendous liberation.
This isness is the only salvation.
Nobody else can give it to you, you already have it.
All that is needed is a remembrance, it is a forgotten language.
You got too much occupied with trivia and forgot the essential.
At this moment you are the most blessed people on the earth
just because you are traveling inwards,
whereas everybody is going outwards.
One thing to remember: buddha consists of only one quality –
awareness, watchfulness, remembrance, witnessing.
You can call it anything, but I prefer the word 'witnessing',
to make it clear to you what it means.

Witness that you are not the body.
Witness that you are not the mind.
Witness that you are only a witness,
just a pure mirror reflecting,
responding to every situation.

To make this witnessing deeper and clearer, Nivedano...

Relax...
but go on remembering only one thing: witnessing.
Witnessing is the whole secret of meditation,
the master key to all the mysteries of existence and life.
As your witnessing deepens you start melting.
Your separation disappears, all boundaries are dissolved,
Gautama the Buddha Auditorium becomes an ocean of consciousness.
Ten thousand buddhas have become one solid consciousness,
one oceanic consciousness.
Collect all the experiences that are happening within you,
the silence, the peace, the bliss, the ecstasy, the divine drunkenness,
and persuade your buddha to come with you, to follow you.
These are the three steps of enlightenment:
the first step, buddha comes following you like a shadow –
it is your nature, your eternal nature.
The second step, buddha comes ahead of you;
you become the shadow.
And the third step, you disappear into the buddha.
Not even a shadow is left of you.
Only buddha is, only life is, only existence is.
This brings you immortality, eternity.
It makes you whole with the cosmos, one with the whole.
It is the ultimate sanity
and the ultimate health
and the ultimate holiness.
This is Zen.

Nivedano…

Come back, but come back as buddhas –
very silent, very peaceful, with a great grace.
Sit down for a few moments
just to remember the golden path that you have traveled,
and all the flowers that have showered on you
of silence, peace, joy, ecstasy,
and the opening into the eternal, into the ultimate, into the absolute cosmos.
Take care of the buddha who is just behind you as a silent presence.
But you can touch it. It is tangible, you can feel its warmth.
It will transform your ordinary acts into extraordinary responses.
It will bring to you a choiceless awareness
where you simply do spontaneously what is good…
a totally new kind of morality that springs out of your spontaneity,
a totally new kind of life that is lived moment to moment
with absolute dedication to existence.
A new freedom, a new sky to open your wings,
and a new celebration without any reason, without any cause.
Just overflowing energy,
overflowing juices of life,
overflowing ecstasies,
overflowing songs and dances.
To transform life into a celebration is the only authentic science of religion.
I celebrate myself and I want you to learn the art of celebrating yourself –
for no reason, for no cause.
Just to be is enough, more than enough.
To be part of the whole
is such a great metamorphosis that you cannot resist –
you have to dance, you have to sing,
you have to express your joy, your blissfulness.
You have to share it.
Sharing your blissfulness is the only charity.
Sharing your joy is the only gratitude.

Existence has given you too much, share it.
The more you share the more you will have it.
The less you share the less you will have it.
If you don't share it you won't have it at all.

Okay, Maneesha?
Yes, Beloved Master.

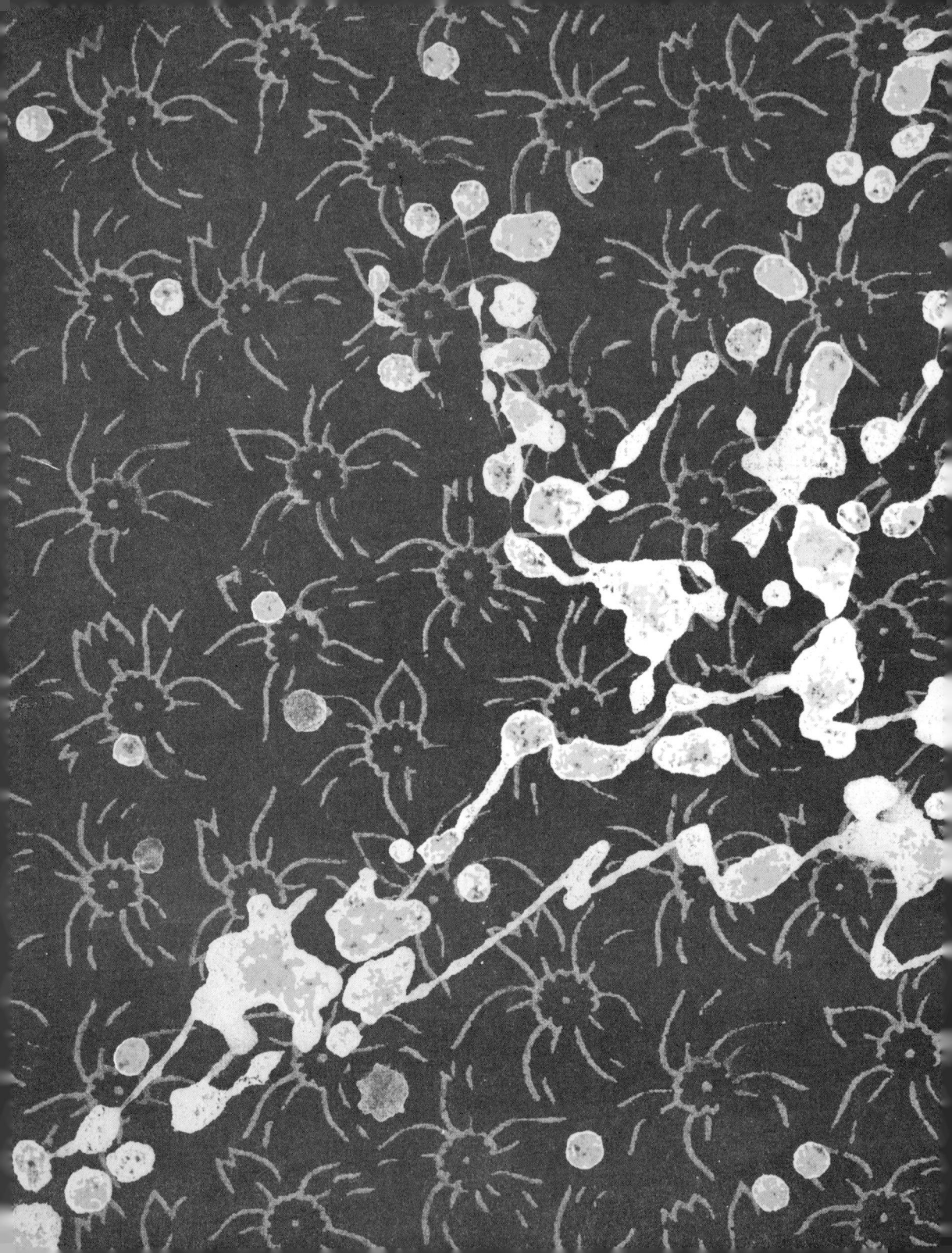

CHAPTER 4
Showering Invisible Flowers
FEBRUARY 16, 1989

THE SUTRA

Sekitō's "Song of the Grass Hut."

Our Beloved Master,

I make a grass hut in which inside there is no worldly treasure. I eat and sleep naturally and easily. When I made the hut, the reeds were new. When the hut gets torn, I cover it with reeds again. The person living in the hut is always there. He does not belong to inside or outside. I do not live where ordinary people live; I do not love what ordinary people love. Although the hut is small, it contains the dharma world.
A man of Zen understands it well. Bodhisattvas of the supreme vehicle have no doubt about it, but the mediocre are bound to be dubious.
If I were asked whether this hut breaks down or not, I would say that the subject is originally both in the breakable and unbreakable. I don't live in the north or south or the west or east. The foundation of the hut is the most solid. Under the green pine tree, in the hut's bright window – even a golden palace can't compare. If I cover myself with the old quilt, everything settles. Then I don't understand anything.
Living in this hut, I stop looking for any solutions. Who would put them proudly in the show window for the people to buy? When evening comes and the sun is setting, I come back to the hut. My being is so vast that there are no divisions.
Meeting with the intimate teachings of the ancestral master, I made a hut with grasses and don't think of leaving.
I just let the hundred years go as they pass by.
If I move with my hands open, there is no problem.
A thousand words, ten thousand solutions, only keep you in ignorance. If you want to know the immortal person in the hut, why do you go away from this skin bag?

Friends,

I hope that the Prime Minister of India, Rajiv Gandhi, will cancel the ban on Salman Rushdie's book *The Satanic Verses*. It is absolutely innocent. These people who are trying to destroy the book, to ban the book, perhaps have not read it.

Rudolph Salman Rushdie was born in India as a Mohammedan, then he moved to England, and has become a worldwide literary figure. Being born in India, he has every right of an Indian citizen too. The Indian constitution gives to every individual freedom of speech and freedom of expression as a fundamental human right.

Salman Rushdie's book has only one mention of Mohammed, which is not at all condemnatory. It is a factual thing that he describes, and it has already been accepted by the Mohammedan theologians for centuries.

The incident is concerning the earlier version of the Koran, in which Mohammed accepted three female deities. Later on he canceled those verses concerning the female deities, and declared that those verses were inspired by the devil. Now it is a well-known fact that Mohammed changed those verses. If Salmon Rushdie writes about it, it is not condemnatory, he is simply stating a fact which has been accepted.

But the anger is coming because the world will know that even Mohammed was capable of being deceived by the devil. What about the other verses? If he had not said it, those verses would have remained in the Koran.

But Salman Rushdie is not responsible for it. Mohammed himself has to take the responsibility, and Mohammedans have to accept the fact that he was capable of being deceived. Now this is hurting them. But Salman Rushdie is not responsible for it. He has simply picked up theological information and written it into his book *The Satanic Verses.*

In Pakistan already five people have been killed because they were surrounding the American Embassy. The book has been published in England and now it is going to be published in America. And they were demanding from the American Embassy that it should not be published in America, "otherwise we will destroy you." Just to protect them from these fanatical Mohammedans, who know nothing about the book but have just heard the rumor, the police had to fire at and kill five Mohammedans, and it is a Mohammedan state.

India is a democratic secular country. Rajiv Gandhi's banning the book simply shows fear. And the fear of Rajiv Gandhi should not be against the constitution of India, against the laws of India. The ban should be immediately removed. That's why I said perhaps he has not read the book himself, otherwise he would see that it is a beautiful fiction.

And now even Mohammedan scholars are coming out in favor of Salman Rushdie. Of course, they are all outside Iran.

The so-called religious leaders are the worst kind. They would have killed anybody who would have raised the question. And I doubt whether they have read the books that they are condemning or not. I suspect that the book contains nothing, nothing that should cause four persons to be murdered as a punishment. It is against Islamic law and it is against Iran's constitution.

Iran should be condemned from all corners of the world, whether one is a Mohammedan or not. It is taking away a human right, and that too, unnecessarily, because Salman Rushdie's book contains nothing condemnatory about Mohammed. Just stating a historical fact which has been accepted for fourteen hundred years by Mohammedan scholars is not a crime. And his coming to the radio and declaring: "It is the duty of every Mohammedan around the world to kill these four persons – Salman Rushdie, the writer, the publisher of the book, the printer of the book, and the sole agent of the book. These four persons have to be killed without any mercy..."

Salman Rushdie is hiding in England, and has canceled his tour of America to promote the book and its publication there.

I was waiting to tell Rajiv Gandhi, waiting until some Mohammedan scholars would raise their voices. And all around the world voices are being raised.

I have received this news report:

Eminent Muslims, including the former chief justice of Madras High Court, Justice Ismail, have unequivocally condemned Ayatollah Khomeini's "death sentence" on author Salman Rushdie and all those associated with the publication of his book, The Satanic Verses, *describing it as against all law including Islamic law.*

Islamic scholars stated that the sentence was dubious on theological, not to mention legal grounds.

Hesham El-Essawy, spokesman for Britain's estimated one million Muslims, said, "Anyone carrying out Khomeini's order would be guilty of murder. We very much regret and denounce Khomeini's statement. Threats like this, or any violent response, is not the correct religious response. It is a very dangerous development and will give Rushdie sympathy where it is not deserved."

British MP's have also called for the British government to formally protest to Iran.

One has to be very aware about the fanatic and fascist attitudes of religious leaders. A great consciousness is needed, particularly for those who are in power, that they don't misuse it. Banning Salman Rushdie's book is a misuse of power, and I condemn it with my whole heart.

I have nothing to do with the book, or with Islam, or with the writer. My concern is that these things become precedents for destroying freedom of speech, freedom of expression, which are necessary foundations for a cultured society, for a humane society.

I hope that Rajiv Gandhi comes to his senses and takes the ban away. And the same should be done around the world by all the political leaders, otherwise all creativeness in poets, in novelists, is bound to be destroyed. And they are the very salt of the earth, they are the only people who are creating something. Religious leaders who ban creative works have not contributed anything to the world, to its beauty, to its truth, to its culture, to its civilization. They have only destroyed. But they destroy in the name of God, and the poor God cannot even say anything because he does not exist.

The second thing I was going to say to you before I take the questions from the sannyasins is that I came to know this day that Chinese sannyasins are a little bit upset because I may have told you that a few of the Zen masters are Japanese, and their disturbance is that they are Chinese.

I am not a very informed person. I don't speak out of information, I speak out of my transformation. I know that Zen belongs to no country, so to me it does not matter whether they were Chinese, or Japanese, or Indians. At least Zen should not be confined to any country, to any race, to any language. It belongs to the whole universe. So what is the fuss all about?

I have never read the sutras. Maneesha finds the sutras; I simply speak spontaneously. My concern is Zen, not China or Japan. And you will see Sekitō himself says, "I don't belong to the east, I don't belong to the west, I don't belong to the south, I don't belong to the north." If Zen is also to be confined to a race, to a language, to a certain part of the earth, then it is not Zen.

So you have to be very clear. Neither am I a scholar, nor am I knowledgeable, informative. What I am saying is my moment-to-moment response. And my consideration for Zen is that it belongs to the whole universe.

So don't be bothered. It is good that you got upset. I love upsetting people. And do you see the trivia you get upset about? What does it matter where Sekitō was born – China or Japan?

I don't belong to India, I belong to this vast universe, and I want you also to belong to this vastness. Why be confined into small prisons created by politicians and priests?

The whole effort here is to bring you back to the vastness and infinity and eternity of the universe. And still you think about China and Japan and India? Then in China there are many states, and in every state there are many districts, and in many districts there are even smaller units...

A Zen master is simply a Zen master. He belongs to Zen, not to China, not to Japan, not to India. I would like you also to be clear about it. These boundaries have to be dropped. Why cling to such small meaningless, mediocre things? Why not open up yourself to the whole universe, this vast sky, the beyond? Zen belongs to the beyond.

Don't be mediocre. I don't want my sannyasins to be mediocres. I want my sannyasins to be universal citizens.

The first question:
Now being free from the concept of God, is our newly found dignity that You spoke of the other day not prone to become entangled in the ego?

You will not be entangled in the ego, because the ego is part of your mind, just as God is part of your mind. Both are fictions; they both are relatives. The moment you drop God... If you have guts to drop God, you certainly will have guts to drop the ego – that is a smaller God within you.

And once the bigger brother is dead, the little cousin-brother will die. First you have to kill the big brother; it is his reflection in you. Your God is an egoist, an arch-egoist, and he gives you the idea of the ego.

Don't get confused between dignity and ego. Dignity is very humble, very simple, very innocent; it belongs to the trees. When they blossom in spring, you just look and watch their pride, their dignity. Just watch when a peacock is dancing. Those psychedelic colors, and the beautiful dance...do you think there is any ego? But there is certainly dignity.

Dignity is a totally different phenomenon, it is self-respect. Ego is domination over others. Dignity is just standing on your own feet, independence, freedom; it is not domination over others. The moment you start thinking of dominating, you are falling into the trap of the ego. And God is the greatest ego because he created everything, he dominates everything. He is present everywhere, he is all-powerful. And his reflection in the priests... The pope claims that he is infallible. Now this is ego.

A man of dignity, a man of self-respect will not say such things. Certainly he will walk straight with his head raised in dignity. He will not walk like a slave, surrendered, subdued. He will walk like a lion and roar like a lion. But that is your intrinsic energy, your intrinsic power.

The power that depends on others creates the ego. The power that comes from within your own sources of life creates dignity. Meditation brings tremendous dignity, a great grace, but not even a shadow of ego is found in it.

If you are capable of murdering God, you will certainly be capable of murdering his image in you. In fact, the moment God is no longer there, you will suddenly be surprised. Where has the ego gone? If the moon is not there, the reflection in the lake of the moon will disappear.

To me, egos are reflections of one moon in different ponds, in different lakes, in different oceans, in different rivers – millions of reflections. But just remove the moon and all the reflections are removed. You don't have to remove every reflection. It will take millennia to remove all those reflections. And in fact, if the moon remains, you cannot remove the reflections.

So I am hitting directly on God's head. Zen masters have been hitting on poor disciples' heads. I am hitting to the very source from where your ego is arising. God removed, you will not find the ego at all, it is a reflection.

The Bible says, God created man in his own image. This causes ego. You are the highest creature in existence because God created you in his own image, and he created all the animals for you to eat. These are your religions, scriptures which are telling you to destroy the ecology of existence, which are telling you to destroy beautiful animals which bring grace and joy all around you. But God himself says in your holy scriptures, "I have created everything for your use." He is giving you the first incentive for the ego.

Once God is removed, you will simply find your ego is gone. It was the shadow, the reflection of God. And then you will find a totally new phenomenon, a dignity which is not a domination over others, which is not superiority over others. It is simply the joy that existence loves you, that existence creates you, that existence needs you, that you are not accidental. This gives you dignity, this gives you honor, and it is not dependent on others. It comes from your own innermost experience of your being.

The moment you find yourself existential, that you belong to the whole cosmos, and the whole cosmos belongs to you, there arises a tremendous splendor in your being – Himalayan peaks of consciousness, Pacific depths of consciousness. That brings you the lion's roar.

You realize for the first time you are not a slave.

You realize for the first time you are not a created creature.

You realize for the first time that existence is your home, you are not an outsider, and existence is nourishing you every moment.

There must be a certain purpose, a certain destiny that existence is seeking through you to reach, a certain height of consciousness, a certain height of love, a certain height of compassion, understanding, wisdom, enlightenment. Existence is trying in every possible way to create a buddha in your very innermost being. The moment you are a buddha, there is dignity without any superiority.

There is dignity in a roseflower. Do you think it has any power over anybody? It is so delicate, so vulnerable, but it has tremendous dignity. When it is dancing in the sun, in the rain, in the wind, it knows existence has created in him one of the most beautiful things.

Dignity arises out of meditation; ego arises out of mind.

So don't be worried about it – meditation will take care.

You will not become egoist, that's an impossibility.

The second question:
In the first lecture of the series, God is Dead, Now Zen is the Only Living Truth, *You said: "Existence needs you." For me this is like a new belief because I don't know this.*

I have not told you to believe it; I have not told you to disbelieve it. It is my experience. I am sharing it with you. You don't have to believe it, you don't have to disbelieve it. You have to inquire into it. You have to go to the same depths, to the same heights from where I am speaking, to the same center of your being. Then you will understand it, not believe it. You will *know* it. Existence needs you, otherwise you wouldn't be here. Why should you be here? Why should existence bother to keep you alive eternally?

But if you start believing in my statements, you are misunderstanding me. I am not here to create any belief system in you. Whatever I say is not to be believed or disbelieved. It has to be simply understood and inquired into. Search inside yourself for what I am saying to see whether it is true or not. Put it to the test. I know that when you put it to the test, you will come to experience it.

I am not converting you towards any theology, belief, any philosophy. I don't do that kind of dirty work. There are enough missionaries around the world doing that. I destroy your beliefs, and you start believing in me?

Please, don't believe in me! Belief in anyone is ignorance – I am included in it. Just listen to me, and then put whatever you hear and understand to a fire test. Go into the exploration. I don't want you to believe, because I know what I am saying is truth. You don't have to believe it, you have just to inquire and you will find it.

The people who tell you to believe – for example Jesus, who goes on saying to people, "Believe in me," is not certain about his truth. If he was certain about his truth, he would never have insisted on belief. He would have said, "Explore. Inquire. Search." I am simply giving you an incentive, a sense of direction where to go. Then find yourself. Because it is truth you have to find, and you will find it. Only lies have to be believed.

So all those messiahs and prophets and incarnations of God who have talked you into beliefs, are destroying your truth. They are taking you away from your innermost realization. They are taking you away from your own buddhahood, from your own nature, from your own truth.

My effort is totally against all the messiahs, and all the avataras, all the tirthankaras, all the prophets, and all the messengers. My work is not only totally different, but absolutely against them. They were creating beliefs. I am destroying beliefs, because I know the truth. And I know that if you inquire – I am absolutely certain – you will find it.

So why should I insist on belief? Only people who are not certain about their own experience, who are concerned that if you go deeper inside you may not find what they are saying, insist on believing.

So you never go. Once you believe in a thing, all search stops. That's why I want you to be open, no belief system. Just inquire into your own consciousness, and all that is truthful, all that is beautiful, you are going to find it. You will realize, when you are centered in your being, that existence needs you, because you are nothing but projections of existence, hands of existence reaching for the stars.

Evolution of consciousness is just the greatest ambition of existence, and it has trusted you with a tremendous responsibility.

Rise above the mind which is a social product. Rise above everything that others have forced upon you, and be authentically yourself. Try to find what it is that you are in your innermost being which never changes. The body goes on changing from childhood to youth, from youth to middle age, from middle age to old age, from old age to death.

The mind moves even faster. Every moment it is changing. In the morning it is one thing, in the evening it is something else. But behind mind and body there is some space which is absolutely eternal and remains the same whether your body is that of a child or of an old man, whether you are alive or dead. It does not matter to your innermost consciousness. That is the only truth, and realizing it you will see how much existence needs you.

You are its greatest potentials on the way to become Gautam Buddhas.

Now the sutras:
Sekitō's "Song of the Grass Hut."
Our Beloved Master,
I make a grass hut in which inside there is no worldly treasure. I eat and sleep naturally and easily. When I made the hut, the reeds were new. When the hut gets torn, I cover it with reeds again. The person living in the hut is always there.

He is talking about the body; the hut is only a symbol. The person living in there is always there. That will give you the clue that the hut is just a symbol; otherwise sometimes the person will have to go out to find food, to find water. But the person remains there always.

He does not belong to inside or outside.
…How can he belong to China or Japan?
I do not live where ordinary people live…
Where do ordinary people live? – in the body, in the mind. Sekitō is saying,
I do not live where ordinary people live; I do not love what ordinary people love.
What is the love of ordinary people? – money, power, prestige.

Sekitō is saying, "I also love, but not the way the ordinary people love, and not the objects that ordinary people love. I love their subjectivity. I love their subjectivity because I know my own subjectivity. Just as I am there always, they are also always there. They may know it, they may not know it. I don't love their bodies, I don't love their minds, but I love that which is behind and beyond their bodies and their minds.

"I don't love the way they love. They always love with conditions and conditions and conditions. They destroy their love because of so many conditions attached to it. I simply love because it is my nature to love. I have come to the point from where love is overflowing. There is no condition attached to it."

If you receive Sekitō's love, or my love, you are obliging me and Sekitō. You could have refused. It was within your power, but you received it with joy. You are not to be grateful to me or to Sekitō. I have to be grateful to you. I was too full of love, and you came on the way and unburdened me. I have to be obliged to you, and I have a deep gratitude towards you.

Although the hut is small, it contains the dharma world.
The hut is small in the sense that it is within you, but the moment you realize – not as a concept in the mind, but as an actual experience beyond the mind – you suddenly see that the smallest center of your being contains the whole *dharma* world, the whole world of nature, the whole existence.

A small seed contains so much, it can make the whole earth green.

Your smallest center contains so much that the whole universe can be filled by it. Once you know it, you know it; it is without limits and without boundaries.

A man of Zen understands it well –
that although the hut is small, it contains the whole existence.

Bodhisattvas of the supreme vehicle have no doubt about it, but the mediocre are bound to be dubious.
And the world is full of mediocre people.

Just today somebody has written an article against me – as an example of a mediocre mind – because I sent the telegram to Rajiv Gandhi.

It said, "If you are honest and truthful, then throw away all your weapons, arms, into the ocean, and let your armies be dissolved. Put all those people into the fields, into the orchards, into farms, into gardens, to create and to work."

The telegram was in response to his address of an international gathering of scientists, and he was telling them that there was no need for nations, there was no need for boundaries, there was no need for arms, there was no need for wars. My telegram was simply to provoke him and focus his mind – "Can you do it? And if you cannot do it, you don't have the right to tell others to do it."

I was simply making it clear to him that he is not capable of doing it. Nobody else is capable of doing it for the simple reason of the fear of being invaded. But if you are not capable of doing it, you should understand nobody is capable of doing it. Then don't talk nonsense.

My telegram was not an appeal to him to throw away the arms into the ocean and dissolve the armies. I was trying to check upon his intelligence. He has not answered, because he knows perfectly well this cannot be done.

He was simply imitating Mahatma Gandhi. Mahatma Gandhi had said it to Louis Fischer, an American writer who was living with Gandhi and working out and preparing a biography of Mahatma Gandhi.

Louis Fischer asked Mahatma Gandhi, "When India becomes independent" – it was before independence – "what are you going to do with the arms, because you are nonviolent, and you preach nonviolence? What are you going to do with your armies? What will happen to your factories which produce a tremendous amount of arms?"

And without any hesitation Mahatma Gandhi said, "I will throw all these arms into the ocean, and I will make all the armies retire and go back to work. We don't need armies, we need more people, strong people to create more food, more clothes."

The obvious question was, and Louis Fischer asked it, "What will happen if some foreign country invades you?"

And Mahatma Gandhi, without any hesitation, again said, "We will receive them as our guests, and we will tell them, 'If you want to live in this country, you are welcome.'"

Rajiv Gandhi was simply imitating Mahatma Gandhi. It is very good to use sweet words, but the point is that even Mahatma Gandhi did not prove true to his own promises. He was the first man to bless three airplanes full of bombs who were going to attack Pakistan. They came over the house where he was staying in New Delhi, Birla House, with one of the most super-rich families in India. He talked about poverty, and he lived in Birla House which is a palace....

The three airplanes, before going to Pakistan, came as close to the house as possible to receive the blessings of Mahatma Gandhi. And he came out of the house and he blessed – "Go away and be victorious." Seeing his hand raised as he was standing in the garden of Birla House, those three airplanes were the first to attack Pakistan. And this was the man who just a few years back was talking about throwing arms into the sea and receiving invaders as guests.

So I was simply provoking Rajiv Gandhi to come to his senses: "Don't talk nonsense." I have every right as a citizen of this country to ask that the prime minister of this country does not talk nonsense. If he is honest, he should answer me and offer an apology for those things he said to the international conference of the scientists – or he should do what he has said!

Now this man has written a whole article against me saying that I am suggesting to Rajiv Gandhi to throw away all the arms and dissolve the armies. "Then what will happen if somebody attacks?" – this man asks me – "Have you gone mad?"

I have returned him the answer to first think about Mahatma Gandhi. Was he mad? And you are a dim-witted fellow that you could not understand the telegram. You are a mediocre. You don't have even the capacity to understand that the telegram was not an appeal, it was a response to Rajiv Gandhi's absolutely nonsense words to the international conference.

And he contradicted himself just after four days. Then he was addressing Hindu chauvinists. Then he said, "We should save our national heritage." And just four days before that he was saying, "All boundaries of nations should dissolve." From where has the national heritage come now? And if you are going to save your national heritage, why should others dissolve their national heritage? – "We should be patriotic!"

Politicians have so many masks. I was just trying to pull his mask and let him see his original face. But this idiot who has written the article did not understand the meaning of the telegram. It was against Mahatma Gandhi, it was against Rajiv Gandhi. It was against all the politicians who say one thing and always do just the opposite.

But this is how it has been since man started growing on this planet. The mediocre are bound to be dubious, they cannot understand. Only bodhisattvas, the potential buddhas...that is the meaning of the word *bodhisattvas*. You are all bodhisattvas, potential buddhas in the seed, in the essence.

So when you go to your very center in meditation, I start calling you buddhas. Particularly, at that moment you are a buddha. You will again fall and become a bodhisattva, but slowly slowly, you will start feeling the difference between a bodhisattva and a buddha. I want this distance to disappear. The bodhisattva turns into a buddha, dissolves into the buddha. Only buddhas know exactly what is the truth. And only they are capable of not misunderstanding.

If I were asked, says Sekitō, *whether this hut breaks down or not, I would say that the subject is originally both in the breakable and unbreakable.*

Now you can understand clearly, he is not referring to any hut. He is saying, "Whether this hut breaks down or not, does not matter." One who is living in it, the subject, your interiormost consciousness which is living in the body, is not affected whether the hut is breakable or unbreakable.

Even in your death you never die.

Even in your birth you are never born.

You have always been here. Birth and death have happened many times, just small episodes in an eternity-to-eternity long life.

I don't live in the north or south or the west or east.

Where is China? Now where should I put this fellow Sekitō? When I don't find any place, I put people in Japan, because that is the most crowded place in the world – no land! So I go on increasing the crowd there.

So don't be worried. Japan has to be worried, why should you be worried? I hope sooner or later, the emperor of Japan is going to object saying, "You are sending too many people to Japan, and we are already so crowded."

Tokyo is the most crowded city in the world. Now they are creating artificial islands because there is nowhere to go. It is a small country, and had an immense increase of population after the second world war. That always happens after war, because nature immediately replaces. Seeing Hiroshima and Nagasaki and that so many people have died, nature immediately rushes and starts bringing more and more children. It is a well-known fact that after every war there is a boom of children. They suddenly go on and on. It is very difficult to stop them.

So Japan had a great boom of children. And Japanese children are really beautiful. What happens to them afterwards is a tragedy. The Japanese children are so beautiful. I don't think anywhere else such beautiful children are born – just like Japanese dolls. But something goes wrong. When they grow up, then all that beauty simply disappears. Then they look like rats, but very dangerous rats. I have always wondered what happens – such beautiful children suddenly disappear.

I love Japan because of those children. And I love Japan because of the second birth, when a man again becomes a child – those are the Zen masters.

So forgive me please. A man of Zen belongs to the universe, not to the south or the west or the east or to the north.

The foundation of the hut is the most solid. Under the green pine tree, in the hut's bright window – even a golden palace can't compare.

I am reminded of an ancient parable....

A poor man in his hut...it is the middle of the night, and the hut is so small that only the husband and wife can sleep in it. That's enough space, that is all.

And somebody knocks on the door....

It is raining so much, and the dark night – perhaps somebody has forgotten the way. Deep in the forest they lived.

So the husband told the wife, who was near the door, "Open the door."

The wife said, "But there is no space."

The husband said, "It is not a palace, it is a poor man's hut; there is always space. Only in palaces is it very difficult to find space."

The wife said, "You always say strange things. In the middle of the night that fellow must be drenched with water. It is pouring, and you want him to come in?"

He said, "Yes, you just open the door. Nobody should go away from my door!"

So the woman reluctantly opens the door, and then asks, "What should we do?"

He said, "There is no problem. We were lying down, now we will sit. For three persons it is enough space to sit, and we will talk. We have not seen anybody coming from the city for many days, so he may have some news, and he will gossip. And the night is not long – half is already gone, half will also go."

So the man comes in and they sit. The man looks around and sees that he has intruded upon their privacy – there is no space. But there is no way of going out, there is too much rain and it is too dark, and he has forgotten the way.

So he said, "Forgive me."

They said, "There is no problem. It is not a palace, it is a poor man's hut. There is always enough space."

So they started talking, and suddenly another man knocked on the door. And this stranger inside was sitting close to the door, so the man, the owner said, "Open the door."

The stranger said, "What? There is no space!"

The man said, "If I had listened to my wife, who said there is no space, *you* would not have been in. Just open the door. There is enough space, we just have to sit a little closer. And you, who have been given space, should not object."

Reluctantly that man opened the door and another man came in.

And he said, "Forgive me, but there is nowhere to go. The light from your hut has been my only safety. I have been walking all the way just looking at your hut – a small light from the window. So forgive me for intruding."

The man said, "You are not intruding. We can sit closely and it will be warmer also. You are drenched and you must be feeling cold. So the more people who are inside, the warmer it will become. Sit down and be close."

Now this new stranger is sitting closest to the door, and a donkey comes and knocks on the door by his head.

The man said, "Please open the door, because I know that donkey loves me. He always comes. And when there is trouble, the poor fellow has nowhere to go. Just open the door."

The second stranger who was sitting by the side of the door said, "What? For a donkey…? Where is the space?"

The man said, "This has been the problem, and I have been creating space. We will create space, don't be worried. We are sitting, we will stand, and the donkey can be in the center. And he is such a lovely philosophical-minded fellow – we will all enjoy him."

Those strangers said, "You are a very strange fellow."

He said, "I am. Otherwise you would not have been in. My wife is absolutely rational, she would not have allowed anybody. So please open the door. It is my hut and you should not forget you are only a guest. Another guest has come. Just open the door."

So he has to open it, but very reluctantly, angry that a donkey was being brought in. And the donkey entered and stood in between, and all those people stood up.

"Now," the man asked, "do you see how a poor man's hut is so spacious?"

"It is not a question of the hut, it is a question of the heart. If you have space in the heart, you have space in the hut. In the palaces there is no space in the heart, that's why there are empty palaces, but no space. Doors would not have been opened for you. This poor donkey has no chance of entering into a palace, but a poor man's hut respects everybody."

So he says,

The foundation of the hut is the most solid. Under the green pine tree, in the hut's bright window – even a golden palace can't compare.

The foundation is on a rock. You know Sekitō – he used to remain on a rock, that's why he became famous as Stonehead. A completely shaven head that looked like a stone, and he was always sitting on a stone. And it was the master Nangaku who ordered his people to make a hut for him –

around him, because he was a strange fellow, he would not even move.

So the foundation was really strong. It was a flat rock, and he remained sitting while Nangaku's people were making the hut around him. He did not say anything – whether to make it or not to make it, he did not take any note.

A man reported to Nangaku: "That fellow is very strange. We are making a hut around him, and he does not even inquire what we are doing."

Nangaku said, "I know him. Even when he was not enlightened he was very strange. And now that he is enlightened, he is the strangest man. But you finish the job; don't be bothered by him, and don't be afraid of him. He is a very soft-hearted man, just his head is like a stone, hard."

He is right. If you are really alive, then even a small hut with a window goes on giving you a sunset, a sunrise, the moon and the whole sky full of stars, a beautiful pine tree and the fragrance of the pine filling into the hut. Who cares about palaces?

He is saying that a man of consciousness is in a palace everywhere. His palace is this whole sky. His foundation is absolutely solid, his center is absolutely solid. Now it doesn't matter where he is. Wherever he is, he is the emperor. Wherever he is, he is in the palace.

If I cover myself with the old quilt, everything settles.
There is no sun, there is no moon, there is no sky, there are no stars – everything simply disappears, there is no world. The moment I cover myself with the old quilt…

…everything settles. Then I don't understand anything.

This is the beauty of a Zen master – he can accept his ignorance. He can accept that "I don't know anything."

Out of this not-knowing arises tremendous wisdom.

Out of this ignorance arises innocence.

Out of this not-knowing, this darkness of not-knowing, comes a fresh sunrise. This not-knowing is not the mediocre man's not-knowing. This not-knowing is beyond the mind.

Mind can be a knower, it can be a non-knower – those are possibilities of the mind. But beyond the mind you can only say, "I am." Or perhaps even "I" is not needed, perhaps "am" is also not needed; only existence is.

It is a tautology to say "existence is," because isness is what is meant by existence. So just isness, a pure isness without any disturbance of knowledge, information… But the purity of it and the beauty of it is beyond limits. Its abundant blossoming of all the qualities that man has always cherished, hoped, dreamed, have become realities. But they are coming from an innocence.

All those flowers, all those lotuses are blossoming out of not-knowing.

A mirror does not know anything, but when you come in front of the mirror, it immediately responds, reflects. A Zen master functions in the same way. You put a question to him...he is not filled with knowledge or readymade answers. You put a question to him, and just like a mirror he reflects your question. The answer is coming out of not-knowing. It is not from scriptures, it is from absolute awareness and spontaneity.

Living in this hut, I stop looking for any solutions.
The man who has gone beyond has no doubts, has no beliefs, has no questions, has no answers. He simply is, and this isness is the ultimate blossoming of your potentialities.

Who would put them proudly in the show window for the people to buy?
A man who has become a buddha, a man who is enlightened can share with you all that he has, but he has nothing to sell.

All the religions are selling. They are selling God, they are selling beautiful places in paradise, they are selling bank accounts in paradise. They are selling everything and pocketing the money from you. And you are not getting anything, and you don't know anything about what is going to happen after death. You don't have even a receipt to show to God: "I have deposited so much money with the priest. Where is my bank account? He has not given me even the number of the bank account." And one never knows.

One thing is certain that everything you give to the priest goes into his pocket. It never reaches beyond that. And how can the priest manage? He himself does not know the address of God. Where has he to send it?

He is simply selling things which don't exist. But because he is giving you hope and consolation for after death, you feel it is good to purchase something for the long journey after death. One never knows, he may be right. At least it is a great consolation that you are prepared. You have done the homework, and you can go into the darkness of death. It is a tunnel, whether it will end anywhere or not you have no idea. But at least while you were alive you dropped the fear of death. The priest was giving you the consolation; you were giving your money.

God is for sale. All churches, all denominations, all religions are selling God. They are the most dangerous people in the sense that they are giving you hopes which will never be fulfilled, and they are giving you consolations you will be utterly disappointed in.

Hence, I don't want to give you any hope, any promise. I simply want you to explore on your own. If you can find something, good. If you can't find something, I am helpless. But I know if you search deeply enough you are bound to find. If I have found it, if Sekitō has found it, then there is no problem for anybody. Every human being is born as a bodhisattva. It is only a question of turning the seed into a plant, and then the roses will come on their own.

When evening comes and the sun is setting, I come back to the hut. My being is so vast that there are no divisions. Meeting with the intimate teachings of the ancestral master, I made a hut with grasses and don't think of leaving. I just let the hundred years go as they pass by.

He lived one hundred years – the whole century.

But he is saying, "I don't go anywhere or leave the hut. I am utterly contented. There is no need to go anywhere in search. I have found it; it is within me." So a hundred years have passed by the side, but Sekitō remains almost a child. Those years have not been a corruptive influence on him. He has remained a tabula rasa, nothing is written on his slate. Utterly empty, nobody special, but hundreds of people managed to reach, finding his slippery path.

A certain magnetism arises with enlightenment, and those who are searching, knowingly or unknowingly, are pulled, sometimes in spite of themselves. They don't want, but something is more forceful than their wanting or not wanting. Some challenge is coming from some direction, and they start moving.

You can see people here from all over the earth, from every nook and corner, and I am the most condemned man, the most notorious man around the world. Why should you be here? All the governments are against me, all the religions are against me, all the nations are against me, but it does not prevent you. Something far more powerful is pulling you. You had to come; it was impossible to resist. And once you have come, it is very difficult to go away.

Even if you go away, you will be carrying me with you – not in the luggage but in your heart, because luggage gets lost many times. Don't trust luggage. And I don't like to be in a suitcase. I don't have any!

Avirbhava has all the suitcases. She carries things for me in her suitcases – eighteen in total. I wonder where she lives in the room when there are eighteen suitcases. Perhaps keeping her feet in one suitcase and her head in another…! Yes?

(The Master turns towards Avirbhava who shrieks in surprise and squirms in her seat. Eyebrows raised and chuckling, He enjoys the situation for some seconds before continuing reading the sutra.)

If I move with my hands open, there is no problem. A thousand words, ten *thousand solutions, only keep you in ignorance. If you want to know the immortal person in the hut, why do you go away from this skin bag?*

Your skin bag, your body, your hut, contains the buddha. If you really want to live without any problems and without any solutions, without any questions and without any answers – just a pure innocent life, undisturbed by anything – then don't go anywhere else. In this very bag of skin, in this very body is the buddha, and in this very place is the lotus paradise.

Sekitō's statements are tremendously beautiful. It is absolutely right to call them Sekitō's "Song of the Grass Hut." It is a song, and sung with great dignity and with great joy.

Issa wrote:

> *I have nothing at all –*
> *but this tranquility!*
> *This coolness!*

Perhaps he was writing for you. Just watch this tranquility, this coolness – I have nothing at all. But to have such tranquility and such coolness, you don't need anything. You have all! You have the whole universe within you – in the dewdrop the whole ocean, in the seed the whole greenery of the earth.

"I have nothing at all" – Issa is right. He does not possess anything, but a great tranquility surrounds him, and this coolness that penetrates deep into the very center of your being.

That tranquility is present here, and that coolness is possible to be felt by you.

Issa has put the whole of Zen into a small haiku.

*I have nothing at all –
but this tranquility!
This coolness!*

Maneesha's question:
*Our Beloved Master,
Alan Watts had a novel idea for how Easter should be spent. "Every Easter Sunday should be celebrated with a solemn and reverent burning of the Holy Scriptures," he suggested, "for the whole meaning of the resurrection and ascension of Christ into heaven – which is within you – is that God-manhood is to be discovered here and now, inwardly, not in the letter of the Bible."*

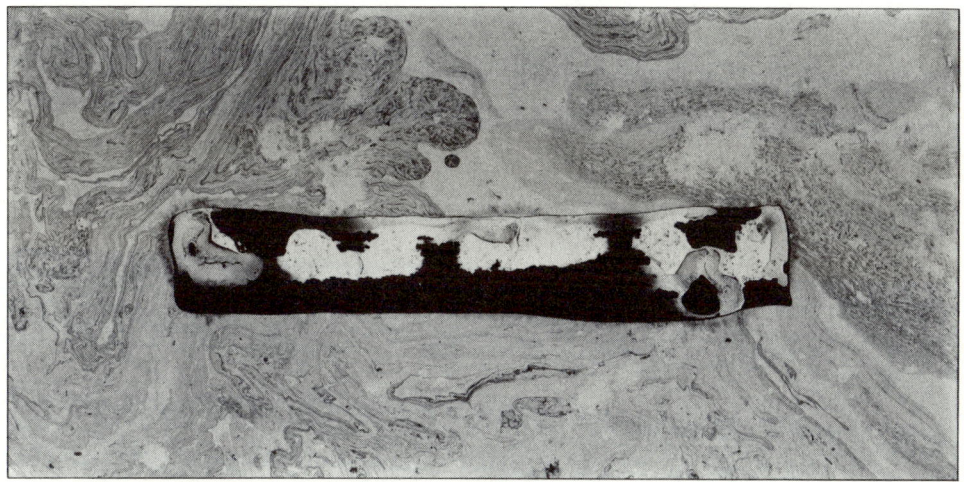

What do You think of his idea?

Just great!

Maneesha, it is time for Sardar Gurudayal Singh. Put on the lights! I want to see my people laughing, celebrating.

In Leningrad, in Soviet Russia, the Jehovah's Witnesses have been allowed to build their own special church called The Kingdom Hall. At the first service, there is a lot of hooting, shouting, fainting, preaching and sermonizing before the service finally comes to an end.

Perspiring, Old Grandma Botovitch, shuffles up to the front of The Kingdom Hall. She prostrates herself under a huge statue of Jesus nailed to the cross, and then lifts her head and plants a big wet kiss on Christ's feet.

Officer Molotov, of the KGB, has been watching Grandma Botovitch closely from behind a curtain. He marches over to the old woman and says, "Would you kiss the feet of our great leader, Mikhail Gorbachev, like that?"

"Sure," replies Grandma. "If you nailed him up like this!"

The pub door swings open and Chicken Chopper walks in with an unlit cigarette hanging from his mouth. He goes over to the bar where Dick Puller is smoking a cigar and drinking a beer.

"Have you got a light?" asks Chicken. "Fuck off!" says Dick Puller.

"Hey!" says Chicken. "I only asked for a light!"

"I heard you," snaps Dick. "Fuck off!"

"Hey!" cries Chicken. "Why won't you give me a light then?"

"Because if I do," replies Dick, "you will buy me a drink. Then I will have to buy you a drink. And then we will both get drunk. And then we will both become friends. And then I will invite you over to my house. And then it will be too late for you to go home, won't it?"

"Gee! I guess so," replies Chicken.

"Yes! That's right," snaps Dick Puller. "And then you will want me to give you a bed at my house – won't you?"

"Well, yes," replies Chicken, "maybe."

"And my daughter is a real beauty," continues Dick, "so you will want to sleep with her, won't you?"

"Yes, sure!" exclaims Chicken.

"And then," continues Dick, "you will make her pregnant, won't you?"

"Yes!" cries Chicken.

"But you won't marry her, will you?" asks Dick.

"Ah yes I will!" cries Chicken Chopper. "I will marry her!"

"Ah no you won't," says Dick, "because I am not giving you a light!"

Two Englishmen, Charles and Henry, are getting drunk at their local pub, The Duke and Tart, in London one evening. They see Paddy and Sean, the two Irishmen, at the other end of the bar, and decide to pick a fight with them.

"Just watch this, Charles," says Henry. "I will make that Irish idiot so pissed off that he will have to hit me, and start a fight."

So Henry wanders over to Paddy and says in a superior tone, "Listen here, my good man, do you know Saint Patrick?"

"Yes sir, certainly," says Paddy, putting down his beer glass. "Well, I don't actually know him personally, but I do know *of* him, certainly sir!"

"Well, then," continues the Englishman, "you must know that he was a pooftah – or to put it more bluntly, a bloody homosexual!"

"Ah! No, sir," replies Paddy, politely, "I did not know that. That's certainly interesting though – a pooftah, you say?"

"And not only that," continues Henry, still trying to provoke him, "but Saint Patrick was a shithead, as well!"

"Really?" replies Paddy. "That is amazing. Well, you live and learn, don't you, sir?"

Henry gives up and goes back to the other end of the bar. But Charles, seeing Henry's failure, jumps to his feet and says, "Leave it to me! I will get him going!"

So Charles staggers over to Paddy and says, "Listen here, you idiot, do you know that Saint Patrick was an Englishman?"

"Yes, sir, I do," replies Paddy, "your friend just told me!"

Nivedano...

Nivedano...

Be silent...
close your eyes,
and feel your body to be completely frozen.
This is the right moment.
Everything is tranquil,
a great coolness surrounds you.
You can move inwards very easily.
Gather all your energies, your total consciousness,
and with an urgency as if this is going to be your last moment of life,
rush towards your center of being.
It is just exactly two inches below the navel inside you.

Faster and faster...
Deeper and deeper...
As you start coming close to the center of your being,
a great silence descends over you like soft rain.
A little closer, and peace starts growing in you – very luminous.
This peace has been called by the mystics,
"the peace that passeth understanding,"
because it is beyond mind.
A little closer,
and you start becoming drunk with the divine.
The final step into the very center –
and you are pure ecstasy,
a dance without movement,
a song without words,
a music without sounds.

This is your original being.
Zen calls it the original face
which you have been carrying eternally with you.
It resembles symbolically the face of Gautam the Buddha.
Not knowing it, you are only a bodhisattva.
Knowing it, you are a buddha.
At this moment you are a buddha.
Buddha has only one quality –
that of witnessing.
Witness that you are not the body.
Witness that you are not the mind.

And finally, witness that you are only a witness.

This is the whole secret of meditation,
the master key of Zen,
which can open all the mysteries of existence,
all the doors upon doors, skies upon skies.
There is no end to it, only a beginning.
Gautam Buddha is reported to have said,
"Ignorance has no beginning but an end.
Enlightenment has a beginning but no end" –
a very significant statement.
Let it sink deep in you.
This moment you are so vulnerable you can allow it to sink in you.
It will blossom into tremendous experiences.
I repeat it: Ignorance has no beginning but an end.
Enlightenment has a beginning but no end.
You are at the beginning point.
From now on starts a journey into the infinite,
into the eternal,
into the ultimate,
into the absolute.

To make the witnessing more clear,
Nivedano…

Relax…
but go on remembering that you are not the body,
you are not the mind,
you are only a witness.
And as the witnessing will start becoming deeper and deeper,
you will suddenly feel a great melting of consciousness,
all boundaries disappearing.

Gautama the Buddha Auditorium becomes an ocean of consciousness.

Ten thousand buddhas dissolve into one consciousness,
an oceanic consciousness without any ripples or waves.
The whole existence starts rejoicing with you.
It starts showering invisible flowers over you.

At this moment you are the most blessed people on the earth,
because all the others are concerned only with the trivia.
You are working and searching for the essential, for the eternal.
All are concerned with lies and consolations about God.
You are working and trying with intensity to find the truth.
The truth is that existence is enough unto itself,
it needs no God.
It certainly needs every living being to rise to such heights as Gautam Buddha.
Collect all these flowers,
these fragrances from the beyond.
You have to bring them with you.
And persuade Gautam Buddha –
it is your birthright, it is your nature –
to come behind you.
He will come first as a shadow,
but the shadow will be very solid,
a foundation for enlightenment.
It will have immense warmth surrounding you,
it will be almost tangible.
On the second step, the buddha comes in front of you –
you become the shadow.
Your shadow is just a shadow,
it starts disappearing in the light and radiance of the buddha.
At the third stage,
the final stage where you become enlightened,
you disappear.
You have been just a shadow,
a fake personality, a mask.
You disappear completely,
only the buddha remains.
This remaining consciousness is your essential being.
It is your existential truth,
it is your life.
To know this,

every moment becomes a celebration.
I celebrate myself,
and I hope soon the day will come you will be celebrating yourself.
And when thousands and thousands of people around the earth
are celebrating, singing, dancing, ecstatic,
drunk with the divine,
there is no possibility of any global suicide.
With such festivity and with such laughter,
with such sanity and health,
with such naturalness and spontaneity,
how can there be a war?
The third world war is not going to happen!
I predict it!
It is not going to happen, because of you,
because of my people around the earth!
They are the only hope.
Only millions of buddhas are capable of creating the atmosphere
for peace, for love, for compassion, for celebration.
Life is not given to you to murder, to destroy.
Life has been given to you to create,
and to rejoice, and to celebrate.
When you cry and weep,
when you are miserable,
you are alone.
When you celebrate,
the whole existence participates with you.
Only in celebration do we meet the ultimate, the eternal.
Only in celebration do we go beyond the circle of birth and death.

Nivedano…

Come back…
but come back as buddhas,
carrying with you all the peace the silence, the grace.

And sit down just for a few seconds
to remember the golden path that you have followed,
all the experiences that you have encountered,
and the buddha that has come with you.
Feel the warmth, the radiance, the light, just behind you.
The day will come soon –
soon the spring will be here –
and buddha will not be a shadow to you,
you will become a shadow to buddha.
And once you are a shadow then the final step is very easy.
The shadow disappears in the light,
in the luminosity of the buddha, the awakened one.
The third step happens so spontaneously.
You are no more, only existence is.
This brings you to the celebration I have been talking about.
Unless you are full of songs, full of dances,
overflowing life, abundance of love and compassion,
you have not lived at all.
You were simply slowly dying, dying, dying.
I want you to live intensely, totally,
because only those who live intensely and totally are transformed.
Only they know what is the ultimate secret of life.

Okay, Maneesha?
Yes, Beloved Master.

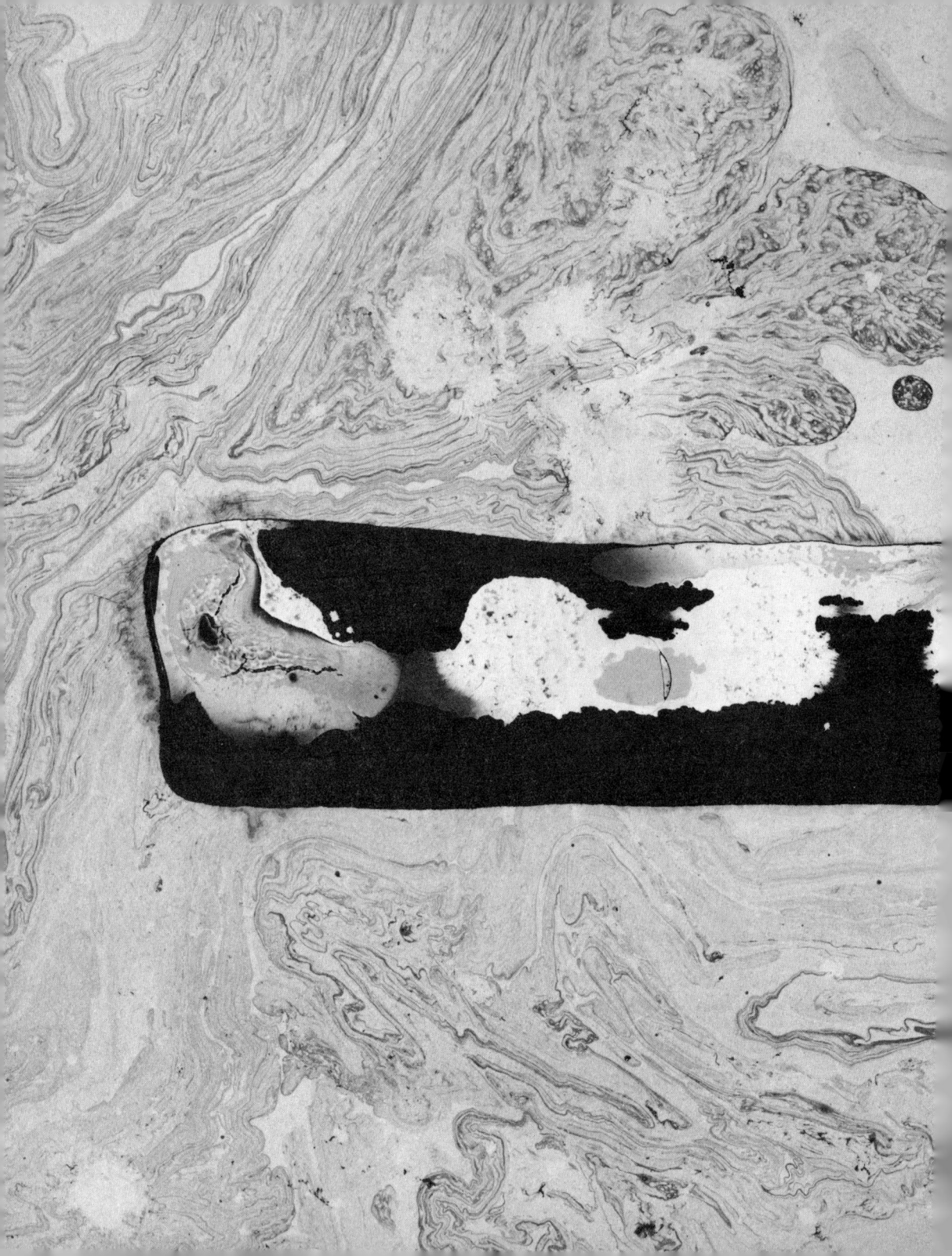

CHAPTER 5
Don't Knock – Wait!
FEBRUARY 17, 1989

THE SUTRA

Our Beloved Master,

osetsu, after becoming a monk under Ma Tzu, came to Sekitō and said, "If you settle this with one word, I will stay here. If not, I will leave."
Sekitō, knowing that this man had promise, made a gesture, but Gosetsu did not get it. So Gosetsu took his leave and made for the gate, when Sekitō called to him "Teacher!"
Gosetsu turned around, and Sekitō said, "From birth to old age, it is only the fellow there and nothing else – don't look anywhere further."
At this, Gosetsu was greatly enlightened.
He stepped on his stick to break it and stayed there.
Once, Sekitō said to his assembled monks, "Even if language is used, it is irrelevant."
Hearing this, Yakusan said, "Even if language is not used, it is irrelevant."
Sekitō said, "Here, even a needle cannot get through."
Yakusan said, "Here, it is like planting a flower on a rock."
Sekitō indicated his approval of what Yakusan said.

Friends,

I have been telling you that God has been the greatest poison to humanity and its evolution towards ultimate peaks of consciousness. Ayatollah Khomeini has supported what I have been telling to you, by declaring a death sentence on Salman Rushdie and three others for simply publishing a factual statement. No law of any country supports it. No constitution in the world supports it. But this has been the attitude of the priests all down history.

A second ayatollah – *ayatollah* simply means a religious leader – not Khomeini, but another ayatollah, and there are two thousand ayatollahs in Iran, has come up with a better support to my argument. Now he has declared that if Salman Rushdie's head is presented to him, he is going to give two point six million dollars if the person who presents it happens to be an Iranian. If it is a non-Iranian, then one million dollars.

From every Mohammedan country, including Pakistan, death squads have moved into England to kill those four people – and if not four, at least Salman Rushdie for writing the novel – and to bring his head to Iran.

Now this will show you why I have been condemning all God-oriented religions, because finally the God-oriented religion is in the hands of the priests. God does not exist, the priest exists. And the priest does not know any civilization, any culture. Murdering a man is not an argument, it is really accepting defeat. A cultured society needs dialogue. If you have something against Rushdie, you have every right to say it and criticize him – that is human. If you feel he is wrong, you have all the freedom to criticize him.

But religions don't believe in dialogues, they believe in murder, in the sword – that is their argument. To me, it is their defeat.

These people have been keeping the world retarded. A few people from India, and from other countries who have condemned Ayatollah Khomeini and the other ayatollah, have been receiving anonymous phone calls, that they will be killed also.

Here in India, one of my friends, Madhu Mehta, made a statement condemning Ayatollah Khomeini. He is a man of immense intelligence, culture, education. He leads a certain movement called the Hindustani Andolan, the movement for a new language which will not be Hindi, the language of the Hindus, and which will not be Urdu, the language of the Mohammedans, but a combination of both, Hindustani. Of course, he has no support. Neither are Mohammedans ready to support him, nor are Hindus ready to support him, but he goes on. For years he has been working on it.

That seems to be the simplest solution – for India to have a national language, otherwise this country is not going to have a national language, ever. For forty years – more than forty years – the constitution has declared Hindi the national language. But the government has not been able to implement it because the Mohammedans are against it and think Urdu should be the language. And there are thirty-two languages accepted by the constitution as state languages. They all are claiming that they should have the right to be the national language. Now thirty-two languages fighting amongst each other...there seems to be no way.

Madhu Mehta has received an anonymous phone call that he also will be killed and that anybody who says anything against Ayatollah Khomeini will be murdered. Are we living in the twentieth century, or some thousand years back where only killing and murder was the argument? – whoever kills, whoever wins in killing is the right person.

It is very easy to kill a Gautam Buddha. Any idiot can do it, in fact, only an idiot can do it. But that does not prove that the idiot's idea of religiousness is correct, nor does the death of a Gautam Buddha prove that his philosophy is wrong. In fact, it just does the opposite. It proves that the unconscious and retarded humanity, for which all the religions are responsible, have a tremendous poverty of philosophy, of argument, of a cultural and civilized dialogue. And it goes back, as far back you can see.

Socrates is poisoned – that was not an argument against his philosophy – poisoned by the masses. The reason? The reason was: "He is destroying our religion and our morality, and corrupting the youth." Socrates was one of the most intelligent persons who has ever walked on this earth. And anybody who has intelligence is not going to support a God-oriented religion, or a God-dictated morality, because it is coming from the priests, not from the God. The priest is interested in keeping the whole of humanity as retarded as possible. That's what makes him powerful, holier, higher and more superior.

There are two ways to become superior: one is to evolve your consciousness and become a buddha; another is to keep the whole of humanity retarded so you appear higher to them.

I am reminded of a small anecdote about one of the most significant emperors of India, Akbar. He was a Mohammedan but not a fanatic, and he gathered into his court all kinds of religious people, from different religious sources. He had in his court all the intelligent people of the country without any discrimination of religion or caste.

One day he came to the court and asked all his wise people of the court, "I am trying to solve a problem and I need your help." And then he drew a line on the wall and asked those people, "Can you make it smaller without touching it?"

Obviously, you cannot make a line smaller without touching it, so they were all at a loss. But every court in the past used to have a man of immense sense of humor, so that the court keeps balanced, it does not become serious, tense, stressed.

Birbal was Akbar's man of a sense of humor. He stood up finally, and he went to the wall and drew a bigger line underneath the line that Akbar had drawn, and made it small without touching it.

The priests have been trying in every way to keep humanity at the lowest intelligence. This is their way of keeping themselves holier and higher.

If everybody starts growing in consciousness, intelligence, awareness, that is going to destroy all fictions about God, heaven and hell, and that is going to destroy all the business that the priests are doing all around the world. Millions and millions of priests are just parasites. Unless we get rid of the priests, it is very difficult to get rid of God – they are both very deeply connected. It is easy to get rid of God if there is no priest, because God does not exist, and the priest exists.

It is the priests who have programmed your minds as Christians, as Hindus, as Mohammedans, in the name of God. And it has been going on for centuries.

As far as I am concerned, I don't think humanity has a mental age of more than seven years.

In America, where our commune was destroyed by the fundamentalist Christians – Ronald Reagan himself is a fundamentalist Christian, a fanatic. And the only reason to destroy the commune was that they could not tolerate a Godless commune living so happily, so joyously, singing songs and dancing and celebrating without any fear, without any inhibition, without any guilt.

The Attorney General, Ed Meese, admitted it before a press conference. When they had already deported me, he accepted that I had not committed any crime, but I had to be deported. He said, "Our priority was to destroy the commune, but without deporting Osho we would not have been able to destroy the commune."

Why was it a priority for them to destroy the commune and to propose thirty-four absolutely imaginary crimes against me?

In fact, they were committing the crime against five thousand people who had simply escaped from centuries-old slavery and declared their dignity and freedom. This was intolerable. People declaring their independence and freedom, their dignity and their prestige and their pride, their individuality – this could not be tolerated by any fanatical so-called religious person.

I had said at a press conference that in Oregon, where the commune was situated, people are retarded. All the politicians were angry; the whole of Oregon was angry. And finally, the University of Oregon decided to take a survey – because that is the only civilized way to prove me either right or wrong. And their conclusions are immensely valuable.

They surveyed cross sections of society in Oregon, and they surveyed the commune. They were puzzled. They found that the average mental age of Oregonians was seven years, and the average mental age of the sannyasins was fourteen years – double that of any Oregonian. And I don't think that if we take into account the whole of humanity, the mental age will be more than seven. It will be less than seven years, because millions of people are far more retarded than the Oregonians. When the average is taken, it may come to three and a half at the most.

People have been kept in this slavery just for a few people to enjoy the superiority. Obviously these people who have enjoyed superiority – the brahmins, the priests, the ayatollahs, the imams, the rabbis, the popes – will not easily allow human beings to declare their independence.

You have to understand deeply. My whole work here is to make you declare freedom and total independence from all prisons – religious, national, racial. Only that is going to give you a life of celebration. Your freedom will give you the space to dance, to sing, to celebrate. My vision of religiousness is that of sheer celebration, a tremendous joy in life, in love, in creative actions. This is my manifesto, the Manifesto of Zen.

Unless humanity is taken out of their prison cells – we are living in the dark ages – every vested interest is going to be against me, it is going to be against you. Every manifesto of freedom will be crushed.

It is not accidental that Socrates is poisoned, that al-Hillaj Mansoor is murdered, that Jesus is crucified, that Sarmad is killed, that many attempts were made on the life of Mahavira, that many attempts were made on the life of Gautam Buddha, and finally, he died from food poisoning. There is every suspicion that it was deliberate poisoning. Gautam Buddha was certainly a religious man. As he was dying he told his disciples, in particular Ananda – he called him close and whispered to him, "It does not matter that I am dying. I am concerned about the man who has given me the food that has poisoned me. You have to protect him, otherwise the people who love me will kill him.

"So spread the idea around my disciples, and my lovers, and my sympathizers, that two persons are the most blessed: the one who for the first time gives nourishment to the enlightened one – of course, that is the mother – and the second is the one who gives him his last food. These two persons are the very blessed ones. Create this rumor, so that the person who has poisoned me should not suffer unnecessarily."

This is the way of a religious man – a great concern even for the murderer. Unless we fill this earth with such people, humanity is not going to have all the great experiences which every human being has the birthright to attain.

Everybody is prohibited from making this earth a lotus paradise, and from experiencing in his own body the very consciousness of a Gautam Buddha. All religions are against you because they are against freedom, and they are against human culture, civilization. They are against any kind of dialogue. Murder is their argument.

This simply shows the poverty of all religions, and this also shows that humanity has to revolt against these religions, these churches, these temples, these mosques. A great revolt, a rebellion can only give you the opportunity to grow, otherwise you simply grow old, you don't grow up. And remember the difference between the two.

Growing old is not of any worth; every animal does it, it needs no intelligence. Growing up is a totally different experience. Growing old is horizontal; growing up is vertical, it leads you to heights, it leads you to depths.

And strangely enough, you will be surprised to know that time is horizontal. One moment passes, another moment comes, another moment, another moment...in a line, a horizontal line. Time is horizontal, and mind is also horizontal. One thought is followed by another thought, and by another thought, and by another thought, but in a line, in a row, a procession, or just a traffic – but it is going horizontal.

Meditation is vertical, it is going beyond mind and beyond time. And perhaps, ultimately you will find that time and mind are equivalent, two names of the same phenomenon – the horizontal procession of thoughts, of moments. Meditation is to stop time and mind both, and suddenly you start rising up in eternity. Eternity is not part of time, and eternity is not a thought; it is an experience.

It is a difficult task to get rid of God and God-oriented religions, and the priests who are supporting this lie by threatening people with murder. These murderers should be exposed, and they should be dethroned. The basic need is a deep understanding of your own divinity. Then there is no need for an external God, and then there is no need for any mediators between you and God.

Meditation is a rebellion, perhaps the most fundamental rebellion against all fictions, against all lies, and against all those who are living on those fictions and lies.

I teach you rebellion, I teach you revolt.

I teach you freedom of your individuality. Destroy all kinds of prisons, destroy all kinds of lies – and you can destroy them only by meditation. Rise beyond time and mind, and you will find not only that you are divine, but the whole existence is divine, life is divine. And you enter into a totally new dimension that has been completely blocked by scriptures, by priests, by God, by heaven and hell, by all kinds of fear, by all kinds of greed.

It is a very unnatural phenomenon that a person goes on growing physically but his mind is stuck somewhere below seven years. It cannot be natural! The mind is kept retarded, otherwise just as your body grows, your physiology grows, your mental age will follow simultaneously. When you are seventy years old, your mental age *must* be seventy years old. But it is seven years old....

According to me, if this is possible then the opposite is also possible. If a man of seventy years' age of the body has only the mental age of a seven-year-old child, then the reverse is also possible. A man of seventy may have the mental age of seven hundred years.

Once Emerson was asked, "What is your age?"

And he said, "Three hundred and sixty years."

The man who had asked could not believe it. Three hundred and sixty years...? He said, "I did not hear, please repeat what you have said."

Emerson said, "You have heard it: three hundred and sixty years."

The man said, "I cannot believe it. You must be joking...you don't look more than sixty years."

Emerson said, "Yes, my body is only sixty years old, but my consciousness is six times more than sixty. I count my age according to my intelligence, not according to my body, because I am not the body, I am my intelligence."

Religions have kept you chained, because a man of intelligence is not going to believe in any lies. So intelligence has to be crippled, and all the religions have been involved in this crippling process.

In Japan, there is a certain method, which is ugly to me, but which is very much appreciated by the Japanese people. There are four-hundred-year-old trees which are only six inches high. They look very ancient, but their height is only six inches. And the strategy that has been used is the strategy that has been used against every human being by your religions, by your God and God-oriented theologies.

The trick is very simple. For four hundred years a family, generation after generation, keeps a tree. It is kept in a pot which has no bottom, so they can go on cutting the roots from the bottom. If you don't allow the roots to grow, the tree cannot go high. They don't touch the rest of the tree; it simply becomes older and older and older. But the tree does not reach to the height which was its potential, because the roots are being continuously cut.

Intelligence is *your* root.

They show those trees as if it is an art.

To me, it is against nature, against those poor trees. You have not allowed them to grow. And perhaps if those trees have a certain kind of mind, a certain kind of intelligence, they will think, "This is how we are: six inches high." They will not be able to discover at all that they have been kept imprisoned by cutting their roots – because they don't see the roots.

You don't see your roots in existence.

Only a meditator comes to see his roots in existence. Those roots have been cut completely, continuously, century after century, generation after generation, by the priest. You have been kept retarded in intelligence.

People ask me why the masses don't come to me. They cannot understand me. Only very intelligent people who have a certain individuality and a certain sense of freedom, can understand me. The masses can only murder me. Only the intelligent, the elite...

To understand me you will have to go through a transformation, you will have to look into your roots: Who has been cutting those roots? Who are these rats who have been cutting your roots? All your rabbis, all your bishops, all your ayatollahs, all your shankaracharyas...they are the rats who are cutting your roots. And they don't give you a chance to have a fuller life. Otherwise every person will have a tremendous life of such great fulfillment that who cares about what happens after death? One has lived so totally, loved so totally that who cares about what happens after death?

There are only two possibilities: either you die, then there is no problem, or you continue to live. And you know how to live, you know how to be total, so you will live more totally without the body. You will have the whole sky available to you. So whether you are atheist or theist does not matter. What matters is to live life so totally that death becomes absolutely unimportant, because only two alternatives are left: either you will die...so what is the problem?

Do you think you had any problem before you were born? Just think of that. You had no problem, you were not there. So how can the problem exist without you? Do you remember any problem before you were born?

I say to you, that is one side; the other side is death. You won't have any problem if you really die. If you don't die, you will have all the opportunities, more than you have now. But you have to discipline yourself for living so abundantly that if you survive death, you will be able to live more abundantly because you will have more space to dance, more space to celebrate.

As far as I am concerned, I know there is no death. But I don't want you to believe it, I want you to experience it.

The religions have been creating all kinds of devices to keep you blind and in darkness.

An ancient saying describing a philosopher says: A philosopher is a man who is blind, in a dark house where there is no light, and he is searching for a black cat which is not there.

This is not the description or the definition only of a philosopher. This is exactly the description and definition of all human beings. Religion has kept them blind, in utter darkness, telling them lies, and telling them to find it: a black cat that is not there! All religions are telling you to find God, and you don't have eyes, and you don't have any light, and God does not exist. God is the cat!

And you go on groping and stumbling. The more you grope, the more you stumble; the more fractured you are, the more despair and anxiety and anguish that perhaps others have caught the cat and you have not fulfilled the promise. Your hands are empty and death is coming every moment closer and closer. Naturally the whole of humanity has lost the sense of humor. People smile only a lipstick smile; it does not go beyond the lipstick. And lipstick makes women so ugly – anything fake makes people ugly.

Even my sannyasins, when they go back to the West, start painting their lips. When they come back, it takes a few days to clean that dirt that they have been putting on their lips. I can't conceive that any man of intelligence could kiss a woman who has lipstick! That lipstick is almost a China Wall – you don't reach the woman at all. At least I am certain about me. The moment I see lipstick, I know that this woman is phony. Avoid it; it has no soul, it is just a mask.

Just a few days ago, a very rich young Indian woman – because Indian women don't use lipstick unless they are very rich and convent educated – came because she is the owner of a magazine and a newspaper. She wanted to write a story about me, and she wanted a photograph with me.

And Anando was telling me – Anando is my legal secretary – she was telling me that she is a very beautiful woman. When I saw her, I saw only the red lipstick and nothing else. I tried to avoid her face, and I told Anando, "You were telling me this woman is beautiful? Have you not seen her lipstick?"

No falsity can be beautiful, only authenticity, sincerity. As you are, in your utter nudity, you have a beauty, you have an individuality.

But all the religions are creating hypocrites. Not only is their God a lie, but they have caused the whole of humanity to be in deep hypocrisy. Pretend – that is their preaching. Exhibit that you are a moralist, that you are a puritan, that you are a saint. They have not allowed you any transformation. They have only given you masks, personalities, and they have deprived you of the individuality which is your eternal right.

Declare your eternal right, and that right will destroy the gods and the priests, because they are conspiring together against the whole of humanity.

Your God is not a creator of life, he is the enemy of life, because life is truth and God is a lie! But he continues to live because of the priesthood. That's why the priesthood has no evidence, no argument for God, only murder!

Now this nonsense that a man who has not done any harm to anybody, but has simply stated a fact that Mohammed himself had accepted...that the devil inspired him to write a few verses describing three female deities. If the prophets of God cannot even understand who is inspiring them – whether it is God or the devil – then they are not worth calling prophets of God. And what is the certainty about these prophets' other statements? Perhaps they are also dictated by the devil!

And it is a strategy, the same as I told you about this American TV preacher Bakker, who has been one of the most famous TV preachers. This is a new kind of priesthood arising in America. Millions of people used to listen to him every Sunday. He was talking about celibacy, and he was found red-handed in a sexual relationship with a woman. And then it was discovered that he was also having homosexual relations with his assistant. And because he was caught red-handed – it is very easy to throw the blame on the devil – he immediately said, "I was forced by the devil!"

It is strange. He had been having these love affairs his whole life, and he did not tell anybody in all these sermons – every Sunday for years – "I am being forced by the devil..." Suddenly, now that he is caught...if he had not been caught, he would have remained the representative of God.

But strange, when I saw this, that the man was now blaming the devil...! That the devil was forcing him to make love to his secretary, to make love to his assistant who was a male, to make love to other women who were part of his congregation...it was the devil! But how do you know it was the devil and not God? If you were not caught – and it is such an easy device...

Then all the criminals can say in the court, "I was inspired by the devil. I have not murdered, it was the devil who was forcing me to murder. I have not raped, it was the devil!" Then no criminal can be punished – "If you want to punish, punish the devil."

And that Bakker, after one year's penance, is back on the TV – again as God's representative!

Watching his whole strategy, I was reminded of a woman who was confessing to a Catholic priest....

She said, "I have been raped."

The priest said, "You have been raped continuously for six weeks. Every Sunday you come...how do you manage it?"

She said, "It is the same person. And it is not once in a night, sometimes twice he rapes me."

The priest said, "Do you understand the meaning of raping?"

She said, "I understand."

"The same person goes on raping you for six weeks? Sometimes even twice a night...and you just confess? And again the raping continues. Why do you confess?"

She said, "I enjoy confessing. It gives me such joy, almost exactly the same as when I am raped. Just the whole scene..."

And she used to describe it in absolute detail, minute detail.

Now can you conceive people's blindness? Bakker is back....

Mohammed, in the last part of his life changed those verses, and the reason was not the devil. The reason was a male chauvinistic idea. Then why had he written those three verses? The reason was his wife.

He married a very rich widow who was forty years old, and he was only twenty-six. The reason to marry that woman was simply her riches, her prestige, her power. She was a powerful woman, Khadija. She was the first Mohammedan.

Mohammed himself was epileptic. He used to have fits, and one day he came home trembling and feverish. Khadija asked, "What happened?" He was a shepherd. He used to take the goats and sheep to the mountains, and on the mountain it happened. Most probably it was again an epileptic fit, because there is no God to say anything to anybody.

He said, "I became almost unconscious. I was foaming – when I became conscious I saw the foam on my mouth, and God spoke to me. And since that moment I have been trembling and feeling deep fever."

So Khadija put as many blankets as possible on him, but he was still trembling. And she convinced him, "It was God! Don't be worried! And I am your first disciple."

Because of this woman, and because of her riches, Mohammed was able to spread Mohammedanism around Saudi Arabia. My understanding is, because of this woman he included those three verses saying that there are three female deities. Once Khadija was dead, there was no reason to keep those verses in the Koran. Now his male chauvinist mind – which has been there all over the world in *every* founder of *every* religion…

Jainism, which is one of the most refined religions in the world, declares that no woman can become enlightened. But one woman managed to become enlightened. And the whole reason that a woman cannot be celibate was because of her menstrual period. A man can pretend to be celibate, can manage, but how can a woman pretend that she is not having the menstrual period? And particularly in the religion of the Jainas, because you cannot become enlightened unless you become nude.

So there are five stages…slowly, slowly you drop your possessions, and the final stage is of the *muni* – the muni becomes naked. Now a naked woman – how is she going to deceive people when her period comes? This was the trouble.

People condemn me that I am concerned about trivia, and Mahavira and twenty-four tirthankaras of the Jainas were concerned about the woman's period! And because of the period – because you cannot hide it, and particularly when you are nude – the woman cannot become enlightened, she cannot be celibate. She cannot change her biology, nor does any man ever change his biology. It is beyond the mind's control. No man has ever been celibate...all pretenders, all hypocrites.

But one woman was very courageous, Mallibai – because women are courageous, particularly in a society like India where the woman has to hide herself in a sari... The sari is very beautiful in hiding the woman, her proportions, her curves of the body. The sari is a beautiful device. You only see the woman's face, you don't see anything else. And in such a country, in such a culture, the woman will be shy to be nude.

But Mallibai must have been a tremendously daring woman. I have immense respect for that woman who stood nude. And unwillingly they had to accept that she was enlightened. You cannot deny enlightenment, but they managed to once she was dead. They changed her name from Mallibai to Mallinath. Now Mallinath is a man's name. *Nath* changes everything. *Bai* means a woman, and Malli*bai* they changed into Malli*nath*.

And not only that... In Jaina temples you will find twenty-four statues of the tirthankaras, but you will not find any statue of a woman – they are all naked, so you can find out.

I used to harass my father every time I went with him to the temple, "Where is Mallibai in these twenty-four statues?"

And he used to say, "I don't know at all, and you continue to ask again and again. Whenever you come with me, the first thing you ask is about Mallibai. And how am I supposed to know? These twenty-four all are male, nobody is a female."

I said, "What happened to Mallibai?" They have changed even the statue. It is not of a woman, the statue is of a man. The name changed, the statue changed – because they have to save this male chauvinistic idea that only a man can become enlightened.

All the religions in some way or other, have condemned the woman. So Mohammed must have felt that when Khadija died, that it was time to change those three verses. Now, the blame goes to the devil.

The Koran is one of the most strange books, because it has not been written in a continuity – one verse today, one verse ten days after...because Mohammed was uneducated. He did not write it himself. He used to dictate whenever he found something worth dictating. So-called holy scriptures are written by self-styled prophets and messiahs – and they are called "holy"! I don't see anything holy in them.

So many Mohammedan friends have asked me, "You have spoken on many religions, why don't you speak on the Koran?"

I said, "Do you want me to be murdered?" I have something else to do meanwhile. Finally, when I think that it is time for me to leave the body, I will speak on the Koran, and I will manage to have one of my sannyasins kill me and get 2.6 million dollars for my work!

While my work is incomplete, I am not going to speak on such holy scriptures, because they are the most primitive kind of literature.

These so-called prophets are suffering from all kinds of mental sicknesses; they are epileptic, neurotic, psychotic and schizophrenic. They are not worth discussing at all. These priests all around the world are holding the whole of humanity in their clutches. They are vultures, not human beings.

This is your work: to spread the message of freedom, of individuality of a religiousness which is a quality, and not to be a member of any organized religion. It is purely an individual affair, just as love is. It is the greatest and highest and the purest love with existence.

You have fallen in love with a woman, this is a small matter. You have fallen in love with a man, this is a small matter. Once you fall in love with existence itself, with life itself, then it is the great matter. Zen masters call it The Great Matter.

But it is individual, it has nothing to do with any institution. In institutions, only mad people live. When people call marriage an institution, I agree. It is an institution, because in institutions only mad people live.

Religion has nothing to do with organization.

The moment you organize truth you kill it.

A bird on the wing is one thing. You can catch hold of the same bird and put it in a golden cage. Outwardly it is the same bird, but inwardly it has lost its freedom. It has lost its joy in the sun, in the rain, going beyond the clouds. It has lost its sky, its space; it is not the same bird. Just in appearance it is the same, but in truth it is a slave.

The bird on the wing was in total freedom, dancing over the clouds, going across the sun towards the unknown without any fear. But now, there is nowhere to go – although the cage is golden. All responsibility is taken by the owner. The bird will have his food, nourishment...everything, but it is selling your soul too cheaply.

Don't be encaged in any religion.

Be religious.

Create the vastness of sky which is already there. You just have to discover it within you and you will be free of all prisons, of all religions, and of all the holy Bibles, the holy Koran, the holy Gita... None of them is holy.

The only holy place is within you. And once you have known it, then you know that it is within everybody. Wherever there is life, all over there is sacredness, holiness.

You are not only being prevented from growing into your intelligence, you are being prevented from knowing the authentic divineness of existence, the authentic sacredness of life.

These priests are murderers – not literally, actually. They have murdered more people than the politicians. And they are still there; they are still openly declaring and supporting murder. And anybody who opposes it has also to be murdered. They know only one language – that of murder. They have not learned anything that can be called human; they are animals. But even animals are more cultured.

The first question:
God is a fiction of the mind, an invention of religious politicians. But my mind wants fictions, hopes, future. Is this natural?

No, not at all. You have been programmed, you don't know what nature is. All these hopes that you think your mind needs, are created.

The old economists used to say that wherever there is a demand there will be supply. Now things have completely changed. Manufacturers of all kinds of goods first start advertising, they have not yet manufactured the thing. They put more money into advertising than in producing the product, because that advertising creates a false need in people's minds that they need it. Once the need is there... It is false need, because they have never needed it.

Just this advertisement consistently, constantly, hammering on their heads from every television set, from every radio, from every corner of the street, from every magazine, from every newspaper – how long can you avoid? You are surrounded continuously by the same advertisement, and soon you start feeling that you need it, you cannot live without it. It is not even produced. When the manufacturer finds that people have started feeling the need, then he manufactures it. So now it is a created need which you take for granted as if it has been your natural need.

These priests, religious politicians, have been doing the same kind of advertising for thousands of years. They give you the idea, and they preach continuously. Their scriptures are continuously preaching all the old methods. And they are now using the new media also: television, radio, satellites...to propagate lies.

You think you need – your mind wants fictions.
No, these fictions are created.

Just don't tell a child there is a God, and he will never feel the desire to find God. It is so easy to understand. In the Soviet Union nobody is searching for God, because they have a totally different programming, the communist programming, atheist programming. From very childhood the child is told there is no God. But in the past, people were so stupid they used to worship a lie, a fiction.

One of my friends, Rahul Sanskritayana, a scholar of Sanskrit, Pali and Prakrit, was a Buddhist monk. But he also became interested in communism because of the simple similarity that Buddha has no God and Marx also has no God. So he started becoming interested in Marxism, and finally he became a communist. And the Soviet Union asked him to go to Moscow University to teach Sanskrit there. So he went to Moscow.

Out of India, in Moscow, things were different. Here it would have been impossible for him to remain a Buddhist monk and yet fall in love. In the Soviet Union there was no difficulty. He fell in love with a beautiful woman, Lola – she was also a professor in the same university, and she had two children.

But the Soviet government did not allow him to take the wife or children out of the Soviet Union. He could live there, but he wanted to come back to his own country. And he was also afraid. In a way the government was fulfilling his innermost desire – how could he go to India with a wife and two children? He would be condemned by everybody, particularly the Buddhists: "You are a monk!" So he was happy in a way, that the government itself did not allow it, so there was no question.

He came back. He told me, "When I first went to the Soviet Union, I asked a small boy, 'Do you believe in God?' He said, 'God? People used to believe in that in the dark ages. If you want to see the statue of God, you can go into the museum.'"

But this is also programming. It is not that these small boys know there is no God, or that even Karl Marx knew there was no God. Only a man of immense meditation can know whether God is or is not.

So you are programmed, and so deeply ingrained is the program that you think it is your nature. Your fictions, your hopes, your future...nothing is natural.

Nature knows nothing except this moment. Nature knows nothing about hopes and desires and wants. Nature simply enjoys whatever is available this moment, now and here.

You are asking:
Or is it a distortion, a reflection of a sick culture?

Yes, absolutely and categorically, yes. It is a distortion, a reflection of a sick culture.

And you are asking:

Is the state of grace that I seek hidden from me by nature for some purpose?
There is no purpose. Purpose again brings the whole lot of lies in. Existence simply is.

Just look at it from this angle. When you are sick you go to the doctor and you ask, "What is the cause of my sickness?" You ask for the diagnosis. But when you are feeling healthy, do you go to the doctor and ask, "Diagnose! What is the cause of my health? Why am I feeling so happy?" You don't go to the doctor, or to the psychiatrist, or to the psychoanalyst. And if you go, that means you are mad. If you ask, "Why am I feeling so happy…?"

No, happiness needs no cause. It is your simple nature, you are intrinsically happy. No cause, no purpose, no goal is needed. Life is in itself enough. It needs nothing else to complete it. It is complete! It is entire! It is already what it has to be. So there is no purpose in existence and no goal in existence.

Existence is a sheer dance.

Picasso was constantly bothered by people because his paintings seemed to be purposeless, meaningless. Once a critic was staying with him and he was painting. He watched and watched, and he said to Picasso, "Why are you wasting your time? This is nothing. There is no purpose in your painting."

He said, "This is strange. I am at least painting. And why are you sitting behind me? For three hours you have been wasting your time and you are telling me that I am wasting my time. I am enjoying immensely. There is no need for any purpose. Just painting, just playing with these colors is so great. Who cares about the purpose and the meaning and the goal?

"Why don't you go into the garden and ask the roses, 'What is the purpose of your being? Why are you dancing without purpose? Why are you looking so happy and smiling? Shut up! You don't have any purpose, and you are dancing in the wind and under the sun. What is the great idea? Why are you spreading your fragrance?'

"Why don't you go into the garden? And if a rose need not have a purpose, why should my paintings have a purpose? They are existential." And the man was perfectly right, just in a wrong place.

These people like Picasso needed the environment of Zen, but they were living in the West where everything has to have a purpose, otherwise you are insane. Why are you doing it? They can't understand that just doing it can be out of sheer joy. Playing with colors is a sheer joy in itself.

Trying to find meaning in it is just your programming: everything has to be meaningful.

I was a student in the university, and I was winning all kinds of debates, eloquence competitions, all over the country. I had filled the head of my department's office with all kinds of trophies and cups – gold and silver. And he started telling me, "If you go on winning in this way, I think I will have to move out of my office. There is no space left."

I said, "You don't have to move out, I will move all the trophies and all the cups."

He said, "No, that is credit to the department."

I said, "Then you have to decide whether you want to be in the office or not." And finally he had to move out of the office. He created another small office on the verandah where he used to sit, because his whole office became a showplace for any guest.

One day he asked me – because in my own university there was going to be a national university competition – "Why do you go on unnecessarily traveling long distances? What is your purpose?"

I said, "I don't have any purpose. I love it – that's my way of playing. That's my way of telling stories which have no purpose at all. Just the sheer joy, overflowing life. I am not old enough to think about purposes."

He said, "What?"

I said, "Yes, I am not old enough, and I will never be old enough to think about purpose and meaning. I rejoice in whatever I am doing. There is no purpose."

Do you think talking to you there is any purpose? I just enjoy it. You enjoy listening, I enjoy talking, it is complete. There is no need beyond it. If something happens within it, that is not my responsibility.

If you become enlightened, it is your problem.

So be careful!

I am just enjoying talking, you are enjoying listening. In between these two things anything is possible. You may become enlightened, but remember, never condemn me for your enlightenment. It is just your problem, not mine. I have my problem – you don't worry about it.

So I told my head of the department, "There is no purpose. I enjoy talking. I love a heart-to-heart talk."

And that day the competition was going to be held... There used to be two persons from each university – one opposing the subject and one supporting the subject. I was opposing the subject, but my partner became so nervous...it was his first time to come to the stage.

The student who used to come with me around the country had died in an accident, so I had to find a new partner, and that was his first time. I tried hard to prepare him...to repeat his speech many times, but finally when the time came he disappeared.

So the vice-chancellor asked me what to do. I said, "I can manage. First I will speak in support – because my partner is missing, and I don't want to lose that prize – and then I will oppose."

He said, "My God! You will do both the things?"

I said, "Just try. It will be a great enjoyment."

So I spoke for it, and I spoke against it, and I had both the prizes, first and second.

And as I was going out, the vice-chancellor took me into a corner and said, "It was a miracle. When you were speaking in favor of it, I was thinking what will you do? You are giving such a great argument in favor, I don't think you will be able to oppose it. But when you started opposing, I thought, My God! – your arguments are so clear. What happened to the other arguments...?"

He said, "But I want to ask you one thing, that's why I have pulled you out of the crowd. Do you have any convictions of your own?"

I said, "I just love talking. You have heard only two sides – there are many sides. And if you want some day I can speak from many points of view. These are only two polar opposites, but there are middle positions and there are at least seven positions on each subject."

He said "That would drive me mad. Just these two positions drive me completely out of my mind. I don't think I am going to sleep, because I am wondering what is right."

I said, "That is your problem. I enjoyed the whole game, and I have got both the prizes. And this is a far better arrangement. If you can convince other vice-chancellors that only one person is coming and he wiil represent both the sides, it will be far easier for me because I won't have to prepare the other person. It is better and easier. I don't have any belief, I don't have any prejudice. I am utterly open. And because I love, it is a game."

Your life should be a playfulness, not a purpose.

Your life should be a fun, not goal oriented.

It should not be business, it should be pure love. What is the purpose of love? If there is no purpose in love, why should there be purpose in meditation? Why should there be any purpose in nature and existence?

Purpose is always an end somewhere far away that you have to achieve. Purpose is an achievement of a distant goal, it is never herenow, and life is herenow. It is not going anywhere, it has no purpose.

And you don't understand the implication of the word 'purpose'. If once purpose is fulfilled, life will be dead. Then there will be no need for existence – the purpose is fulfilled, the game is finished. Because it is an ongoing game, eternity to eternity, it can't afford to have a goal, it can't afford to have a death, it can't afford to have a purpose.

Unless you understand how to live purposelessly, you have not understood the meaning, the significance of life.

Life has everything that it needs in itself; it is intrinsic, not outside. It is an unfoldment of more and more joy, of more and more blissfulness, of more and more ecstasy. But the unfoldment is in the present. As you go deeper and deeper, and higher and higher, you become more and more playful. And to be playful takes all seriousness away.

Purpose makes people serious, and I consider seriousness to be sickness of the soul. Laughter is health, but laughter has no purpose. It is so beautiful in itself, it need not have a purpose. It is not a means to any end. It is means and end both together.

And finally, you are asking:
Is my identification with the ego a necessary stage in a natural process?
No, it is again a created phenomenon by the priests, by the politicians, by your parents.

The child is born without any ego. Have you ever watched a small child who says – if his name is Johnny – "Johnny is feeling thirsty"? He never says, *"I am feeling thirsty," I* will come later on when programming has happened. In the beginning the child says, "Johnny is feeling sleepy."

One of the Hindu mystics, Ramateertha, never said "I" in his whole life. He would always say, "Rama is tired. Rama is hungry..."

He went to America. Here, the people who surrounded him, understood him, but in America it seemed a very strange type of language that he used. "Rama is feeling thirsty" – and people would look around wondering, "Who is Rama?" And they asked him, "Why don't you simply say 'I am feeling thirsty'?"

He said, "That I cannot say, because there is no 'I'. So I just use the name, which is a false thing, apparently false, because it has been given. It is a label put on me, but there is no 'I' in me. And my innermost space is neither thirsty nor hungry. It is the body, and the label of the body is Ramateertha. It is not my name. I am nameless and formless; name and form belong to the body. So I cannot use the word 'I', because there is no corresponding reality to it inside me."

And he was absolutely right.

The ego is created by ambition, by desire, by greed. Everybody is telling you: "Become somebody special. Have power, prestige, respectability, money, things that matter in the world." All these create slowly, slowly the idea of the ego, of superiority, of holier-than-thou, higher-than-thou. This ego creates your saints, this ego creates your so-called priests, your politicians, your presidents, prime ministers. This is all the projection of the ego.

But ego has no natural existence. It is a by-product of a certain programming that society manages to befool you with.

Once you see that the ego is false, handed over to you by others, the whole house of falsity simply disappears, like darkness when you bring light in.

Meditation will bring the light from your very center, a cool fire. And when your interior becomes luminous, you will not find any ego, any *I*. You will simply find the whole existence pouring into you.

The ego is also an imprisonment.

Being egoless you are again out of the golden cage.

My parents used to say to me, "The way you are going, you will end up being nobody." And somebody else would say, "You will end up in being good for nothing." I have ended up being nobody, good for nothing. But I am enjoying this good-for-nothingness, this nobodiness so much that each moment has become a splendor, a magic, a miracle.

Out of this nothingness arises my freedom, my wholeness. Out of this nothingness I meet with existence with an easy heart, relaxed, in a deep let-go. There is no ego, no somebody to prevent me. I don't have any borders, any limits. In this nothingness I have arrived at the very source of existence.

I would love you also to be good for nothing, a nobody. And then you will find a tremendous dignity – for no reason, but just because the whole existence is overflowing, and all around you flowers are blossoming, stars are dancing. For the first time when you are nobody, you feel your heartbeat and the universe's heartbeat are in deep synchronicity. That feeling is the greatest experience in existence, the most divine, the most godly.

Now the sutras:
Our Beloved Master,
Gosetsu, after becoming a monk under Ma Tzu, came to Sekitō and said, "If you settle this with one word, I will stay here. If not, I will leave."

His question certainly shows he is coming from Ma Tzu. Ma Tzu is the most strange master that ever happened. He must have heard this statement from Ma Tzu, or in the air of Ma Tzu where there were many people just becoming afire, coming to their real home.

He is asking Sekitō,

"If you settle this…"

Remember the word "this"; the whole emphasis is on "this."

"If you settle this with one word…"

He is saying, "By a single word if you can say what *this* is, I will stay *here*. If not, I will leave."

Sekitō, knowing that this man had promise…

His very question showed an intense longing to understand *this*. But he does not want to go into details, he does not want any unnecessary commentary. He wants simply a single word: "Settle it and I will stay here; otherwise I leave." A man fiery enough, bold enough, daring enough, challenging a man like Sekitō.

Sekitō, knowing that this man had promise…

He could see the promise in his eyes, in his very air, in his very approach.

…made a gesture.

A silent gesture. Even a single word is too much. That was the emphasis of Sekitō, "Why are you asking for even one word? One word leads to another and to another, and then the whole theology and the whole philosophy, and the whole religion goes on growing. Words and words…and you forget all about *this*.

"So I won't use even a single word – that is too much. You have already gone, you have already passed *this*. You have moved into language from existence. And that is the greatest distance in the world: the experience of this, and making a statement about it. That is the greatest distance possible. Even stars are not that far away. They may be millions of light-years away – that does not matter. The distance between *this* and the statement *about this* is the greatest distance between two points."

Sekitō avoided even a single word.

Always remember, one thing leads to another and to another, and then there is no end. You are lost in a jungle of words. So he would not say even a single word, he simply made a gesture. And his gesture was immensely profound, but it was utterly silent.

Gosetsu did not get it. He wanted a word. He was looking for the word, that's why he missed the gesture.

Whenever you are looking for something, you will miss the truth. Don't look for something! Just go empty handed, without any projection, without any prejudice, without any belief.

Perhaps he had come from Ma Tzu hearing his words, and he wanted Sekitō to say something greater, in a single word, condensed. But one word or one thousand words...it makes no difference.

Sekitō is utterly truthful, absolutely honest. Not uttering a single word, he simply made a gesture. And in his gesture there was thisness. In his gesture was suchness. In his gesture was the whole existence. In his presence and the gesture, everything was contained; nothing was left out. Nothing was said, but everything was indicated – a hint, a naked truth without clothes.

All words are clothes. The more words, the more clothes. Finally, you have layer upon layer of language, and the truth is lost in the jungle.

But Gosetsu missed it because he was waiting for a word. His focus was for a word, otherwise he would not have missed it. He was alert and waiting for the word, and the word did not come. Because of his narrowing mind upon a word, he missed the vastness of *this* that Sekitō was indicating by a gesture.

Never look for anything. That which is, will declare itself to you, you simply be silent and wait. Yes, waiting is the right approach to truth.

Wait, be a witness, be patient.

Keep your doors open for the guest, because one never knows when the guest comes and knocks on your doors.

Do you remember a small poem by Rabindranath Tagore, "The King of the Night"?

There used to be an ancient temple, very ancient. The temple was vast. It had thousands of statues and one thousand priests. The high priest one night dreamed that God was saying to him, "Tomorrow sometime I am coming to visit the temple. Clean it, prepare it. I am coming for the first time to your temple. You have waited long, now the time has come."

He woke up in the middle of the night. He called all the priests from their bedrooms. They were surprised: "What is the matter?" – because it had never happened before.

The arch-priest said to them, "I had a dream. Although it is a dream, who knows? It may be true, it may be just an indication that he is coming."

They laughed, they giggled. They said, "You are getting old, you are getting senile. A dream is a dream, and you disturbed our sleep."

The arch-priest said, "I am sorry, but I have to say to you not to take chances. There is nothing wrong in cleaning the temple and preparing the richest food, the best room for him to rest. Anyway this is going to give the temple a good spring-cleaning. It has not been cleaned for hundreds of years, so this is good chance. If he comes, good; if he does not come, there is no harm."

They could see the argument.

And he said, "If we don't do anything and he turns up, then don't blame me. I will not be responsible. I have told you."

They all felt that there was some grain of truth, an argument, very convincing in it. So they cleaned the whole temple the next day. It was a vast temple. To clean it – and it had not been cleaned for hundreds of years – was a tremendous job. They called many other people – one thousand priests and hundreds of other people from the nearby villages who used to worship. So they came, and all the statues were cleaned – fragrance, flowers, garlands, great sweets and delicious food was prepared. For the first time God was coming. But they all knew deep down, "It is just a dream, and we are unnecessarily being harassed, but what to do?"

And they waited and they waited and they waited. It was sunset and he had not turned up. And they were becoming angry because the priests could not eat unless God had taken the food. Every day they were offering food to the statues, and statues don't eat – that is the only good thing about statues. So they would offer the food, and they would take the food back. Now it had become sacred, God had given it as a gift. It became *prasad,* it became holy, sacred. Then they would eat it.

But today was different. God himself was coming, and if he found them eating before he had come, there was going to be trouble. But by the evening they became very angry with the arch-priest. They said, "Your dream has disturbed our night, has disturbed our day. We have been laboring the whole day and we are hungry, and we cannot eat, we cannot drink. And now it is sunset, the day is finished. So it is better that we now offer our food to our statues, take it back, eat it and go to sleep."

The arch-priest could not say anything more. He also felt, "They are right." But deep down his dream was so vivid and so colorful that only with reluctance did he allow them.

But he could see their argument: "How long do we have to wait? The day is over, we have waited enough."

So they ate. They were tired, so they went to sleep early....

And in the middle of the night the chariot of God came, making great noise...the chariot's wheels on a dusty road. Somebody heard the noise and half-asleep and half-awake he said, "Look! It seems he has come. I have heard the noise of a chariot's wheels."

Somebody shouted, "Shut up! Now don't bring that subject up again. Do you want to disturb our sleep again? It is not a chariot! It is just clouds thundering in the sky! Go to sleep!"

And then the chariot stopped in front of the temple, but the door was closed. Still, he went up the steps – there were many steps to the temple.

There are temples in India with one hundred steps, two hundred steps, three hundred steps…then you find the main door.

The King of the Night knocked on the door. And again, another priest heard the knock. He said, "Listen, somebody is knocking on the door. Perhaps he has come."

Again somebody shouted, "Will you not stop? Can't you allow us to rest? There is nobody knocking on the door! It is just the wind!" So they again went to sleep.

The King of the Night waited at the door. There was no sign of anybody coming to open the door, so he returned to his chariot.

In the morning, they saw that a chariot had come up to the door on the dusty road. They could see the marks of the wheels of the chariot, and they could see on the dust that had gathered on the steps, that somebody had walked up to the door. But now it was too late – nothing could be done. They missed it.

This is a small poem by Rabindranath Tagore, emphasizing one point: waiting. It is never enough. Waiting consciously, alert, witnessing whatsoever is happening but not asking a certain hypothesis to be fulfilled, because the mind has the capacity to create any hallucination you ask. You can see Christ, you can see Krishna, you can see anybody you want.

Mind has the capacity to dream, and it has the capacity to dream with open eyes – that is called hallucination. If you go on asking for something, it will appear as if it is real. Mind can give reality to all kinds of lies.

So you have to put aside all your prejudices, all your conceptions, all your projections, all your gods. You have to enter into your own being just watching, waiting, trusting existence that whenever a time is ripe and your spring comes, the grass will grow by itself.

Every tree trusts existence – the spring comes, the flowers blossom, the fruits arrive. Why can't you wait for the right time? Why should you make demands on nature? A demanding mind is not the mind of a seeker. A seeker simply waits and allows existence its own time, its own wisdom. Whenever you are ripe, whenever you are really ready, the doors will be opened for you. You don't have to knock.

Jesus says to you, "Knock and the door shall be opened." I say unto you, "Don't knock, wait! When the time is ripe, doors shall be opened unto you." Knocking is demanding, knocking is interfering. Knocking is not trust. Knocking is forcing existence to appear in a certain way according to your hypothesis, according to your belief system. No, no knocking! Just wait and watch.

Jesus says, "Ask, and it shall be answered." No, never ask, otherwise it shall never be answered. Just wait. In the right moment you will find the answer.

Jesus says, "Seek, and ye shall find it." I say unto you, "Don't seek, otherwise you will never find it," because seeking means you already know what you are seeking. Seeking means you already believe in a certain hypothesis. Seeking means you have already an idea about truth. This is dangerous. No seeking, just waiting...in utter silence, in tremendous trust. And as your silence deepens, you will see things are happening on their own accord. And as things start happening on their own accord, your trust deepens. This is almost spontaneous.

Just waiting, and Gosetsu would have understood the gesture of Sekitō. But he was asking, demanding. Just look at his question:

"If you settle this *with one word, I will stay here."*

As if Sekitō needs his staying there. He is making a bargain: "I will stay here if you explain this in one word" – now this is a demanding mind. "If not, I will leave." Whom is he threatening? But because of this he was full of bullshit and missed.

But even though he missed, Sekitō knew that beyond this bullshit there was someone very promising, a bodhisattva. Once this nonsense is dropped, that bodhisattva will surface as a buddha, as an awakened soul.

Sekitō, knowing that this man had promise, made a gesture, but Gosetsu did not get it. So Gosetsu took his leave and made for the gate, when Sekitō called to him, "Teacher!"

You have to understand the difference between master and teacher. The master is one who knows, the teacher is one who knows not but is knowledgeable. He has collected much information, but he has not gone through the transformation. So when Sekitō called to him, he used the word 'teacher', not 'master'.

He was full of knowledge; his question shows it. He has heard much, read much. He is a scholar, a knowledgeable person, learned; hence he called him teacher.

Gosetsu turned around, and Sekitō said, "From birth to old age, it is only the fellow there and nothing else – don't look anywhere further."

What is he saying? He is saying, "What are you asking for? It has been there within you from birth to death, from eternity to eternity. And just by turning back, you have yourself given the answer. Just look there, don't go anywhere else, turn back. Turn inwards – that is a complete turn back. Don't go further, just turn in, turn back, and you will find *this* – the suchness of existence, the *tathata*. It has been there always."

This turning around...

"From birth to old age, it is only the fellow there..."

Who has turned? Who has heard the word 'teacher'? And who has followed the word and turned around? This is it! The fellow there inside you...

"the fellow there and nothing else – don't look anywhere further."

At this, Gosetsu was greatly enlightened. He stepped on his stick to break it and stayed there.

People who go on the mountains take a stick as a support...steep mountains. So he has come with a stick to the mountain where Sekitō Stonehead was sitting on a rock.

You know that Ma Tzu said to another person who was going to Sekitō, "You are going. That's perfectly good, but do you remember Sekitō's path is very slippery?" He was sitting on a rock and the path was very slippery, so anybody who had to go there had to bring a stick with him.

This action of Gosetsu, of breaking the stick, shows that now he had found his master and there was no need to go anywhere. He was not going down that steep hill again. Finished! He had heard it, he had found it. This gesture on his part shows that now he is going to stay forever. All bridges were broken. With that stick breaking, all the bridges that lead backwards to the past were finished. He had found the man, he had fallen in love. He knew: "You are the master."

He became greatly enlightened by this simple act of Sekitō calling him – "Teacher!" – and his turning around and Sekitō saying to him: "This fellow has been there always and always. Don't go further."

A very immense statement, but it needs a very alert mind. First, he had asked the question, he was full of his question and wanted one word. There was wanting, desiring, and all kinds of things. Now, just as he was going out of the hut – he had dropped the idea of finding anything from Sekitō – suddenly he heard, "Teacher!" And he turned. He must have been utterly empty because there was no question. He had not asked anything. In that silence he heard that impeccable, that profound sentence: "This fellow who has turned around has been there always and always."

A single statement from a master sometimes triggers a chain reaction and leads a silent being into enlightenment. This is one of the most important gifts from Zen to humanity.

Once, Sekitō said to his assembled monks, "Even if language is used, it is irrelevant."

All language is irrelevant as far as truth is concerned.

Hearing this, another master, Yakusan, said,
"Even if language is not *used, it is irrelevant."*

Language certainly is irrelevant. You may not use the language, you may keep your mouth shut, but the language is going round and round in your head. So just not using language is not enough – that too, is irrelevant. Language or no language, both are irrelevant.

Sekitō said, "Here, even a needle cannot get through."
He is saying, "Here, even a needle cannot get through –
as far as truth is concerned, the path is so narrow, only a witnessing, silent witnessing can pass through. It is far more subtle than even a needle. Even a needle is too solid, too tangible, too material, it cannot enter into the immaterial space of your being."

Yakusan said, "Here, it is like planting a flower on a rock."
Both masters are enjoying pulling each other's leg. That can happen only in the world of Zen; otherwise, Ayatollah Khomeini…! These kinds of playful dialogues between masters are of immense beauty.

What Sekitō said was absolutely right, and what Yakusan said is also absolutely right – different expressions.

"Here it is like planting a flower on a rock."
You can't plant a flower on a rock. Putting language in the service of truth is just like planting a flower on a rock where it cannot grow. It will simply die. The moment you bring truth to language, it dies on the way.

But just not using the language is not enough either. You have to use silence. Not using the language is negative; using the language is the positive side – but both belong to language. Saying is positive; not saying is negative – but both are irrelevant. You have to indicate without using language, or without not using language. You have to create a device, a gesture – maybe just a look into the eyes of the disciple, or just as Sekitō called him, "Teacher!" and he turned around utterly empty. He caught him in the right moment.

When he first came he was too full of knowledge. Now he has dropped the idea of being with Sekitō, so he was caught suddenly. And whenever you are caught suddenly, your mind cannot function.

The mind needs time before it can figure out what is the matter. Just a small space of no-mind and no-time, and suddenly he realized Sekitō is saying, "This fellow who has turned around, this fellow is the answer. And this turning around is enough. Don't go further!"

Sekitō indicated his approval of what Yakusan said.

He did not say anything, but just indicated his approval. We don't know how he indicated. Maybe he just took Yakusan's hand in his hand and pressed it, or just looked into his eyes and showered his love, or just remained silent and closed his eyes, radiating the vibe of the man who knows his nothingness.

It is not said how he indicated, but there are millions of ways. According to each, a master uses a certain way to indicate. But he approved what Yakusan was saying. Both were making very significant statements.

Zen is not argumentative, it is what Martin Buber would have loved, it is a dialogue, a dialogue in which two persons are not forcing their ideas on the other, where two persons together are trying to find something existential. It is not a question of defeating the other or being victorious. A real dialogue is when two persons are discussing just to find the truth. And truth is nobody's monopoly – nobody is a winner, nobody is defeated. Truth is victorious, and both are surrendered to the truth. You have to remember in all these dialogues this different quality.

Socratic dialogues are argumentative, they are logical. Zen dialogues are

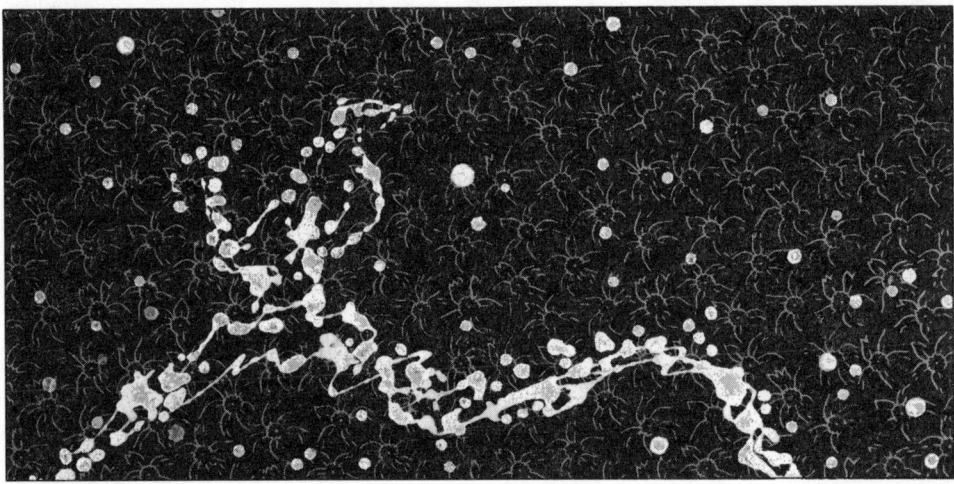

absolutely beyond logic, beyond mind. They are very mysterious, but far more profound than any Socratic dialogue. Even Martin Buber's understanding of dialogue is not the ultimate understanding. He continues the dialogue with these two words: *I* and *Thou*. But in the Zen dialogue there is no I, no Thou.

Two Zen masters, both are empty, and playing just like children playing on the seabeach – running around, finding colored stones and seashells.... Two Zen masters are just like children – shouting, shrieking, screaming, for no reason at all.

You know Avirbhava's shrieking.... That is Zen shrieking – for no reason at all. Because I don't do anything to her...! But I miss her when she is not there at the door. She is almost like a gong declaring: "The Master has come!" When she is not there, I miss her. Her screaming is just like a small child, so innocent, without any purpose. But she is total when she screams, it is not from her mind, it is coming from deeper spaces. So even sometimes when I have entered the hall, she goes on screaming. My car goes away and then she drops on the ground with immense joy.

The dialogue of Zen has a difference to Socratic dialogue, or to Martin Buber's idea of dialogue.

Martin Buber could not drop the idea of *I* and *Thou;* hence he remained in the mind, could not enter into the beyond. And the Zen sky is of the beyond.

Bonshō wrote:

The nightingale singing.
Thin snowflakes.

Do you see any connection? Do you see any logic?
"The nightingale singing" – that's one thing.
"Thin snowflakes" – that is completely another.

But in a meditative mind nothing is separate. All things are joined together. The nightingale singing and the thin snowflakes – both are part of one existence, they cannot be separated. Only mind separates them: this is one thing; that is another. And how are you *putting* them together? But they *are* together, and not only these two. Then the bamboos cracking, and the wind blowing through the pine trees, and the clouds coming with great lightning – everything is connected.

In these two small sentences he has said that everything is so connected with each other that you cannot create separations.

The nightingale singing
Thin snowflakes.

I have heard that scientists say that if – and someday it is going to happen – the sun loses all its energy... It is losing every moment; it is burning out. One day it will be simply a black hole, no light will be coming to the earth. It takes ten minutes for the light to come to you, so if the sun dies...and it is bound to die. Everything that is born needs one day to rest. Everything gets tired, everyone gets tired. Even suns are going to die, and new suns are being born.

It will take our sun four billion years, they say, to die. But in an eternity, four billion years are just like four seconds, or maybe not even that much. But they say if the sun dies, then for only ten minutes will you still be getting light. So for ten minutes only, life will exist after the sun dies. And then there will be no life without the sun, no warmth, no life.

But they have not looked at it from the other side, because they don't know that there is another side also. It is true that the sun gives us life, but it is one-sided. If on the earth life disappears, I say unto you the sun will die immediately. Not even ten minutes will be taken, because life is a continuous communication, it is a dialogue.

If we need the sun, the sun needs us! Without us do you think the sun will have a sunrise?

I am absolutely certain that without life on the earth, the sun will not rise again. For whom? For what? No flowers, no nightingales, no people, no birds.

On a dead earth even the sun will be ashamed to arise because everything is so deeply connected – from the smallest grass blade to the greatest sun in the sky.

Our sun is very mediocre, it is middle class. There are suns far bigger than it, but even the smallest grass blade on the earth is connected to the farthest star. They are all cousins, parts of the same existence.

But Martin Buber could not understand that between I and Thou there can be a discussion but not a dialogue. A dialogue needs no I, no Thou.

When I read his book, *I and Thou*, I immediately wrote a letter to him – he was alive – asking him to please try to understand, "No I, no Thou." And I said, "That is an absolute necessity for a dialogue. What you are talking about is not dialogue, it is only discussion."

I received a small note from him saying, "I will think it over." I replied immediately, "Thinking is not going to solve it. Thinking is the barrier. It is thinking that is making you propose that there is dialogue between I and Thou. I am speaking from a state of no-thinking. No I, no Thou, then there is a dialogue, and very playful dialogue."

He did not answer again, seeing the situation that whatever he would say would be part of thinking. He was a great thinker, no doubt, but even the greatest thinker has nothing to say about the truth. Only the space which is beyond thought brings you closer to life and existence. And when two persons are settled and at ease with existence, there is no I, no Thou, just a play. That play can be called dialogue. Only Zen masters know what dialogue is.

> Maneesha's question:
> *Our Beloved Master,*
> *Hubert Benoit suggests that even those people who are sufficiently intellectually evolved not to believe in a personal God, still retain the concept, although in different terms.*
> *He says, "They imagine their satori and themselves after their satori, and that is their personal God – a coercive idol, disquietening, implacable. They* must *realize themselves, they* must *liberate themselves. They are terrified at the thought of not being able to get there, and they are elated by any inner phenomenon which gives them hope."*
> *Beloved Master, would You agree that there is a danger of this happening to meditators?*

Maneesha, Hubert Benoit has written a very scholarly book on Zen, *The Supreme Doctrine*, but it is only an intellectual understanding. Although he went to Japan, and he lived in Zen monasteries and watched the meditators, and he thinks that he has known the inner story – that is wrong.

Just being in a Zen monastery does not mean you have become an insider. You are still a spectator – you are watching others meditating. *You* are not meditating, and unless *you* meditate there are bound to be such questions arising in you.

So Hubert Benoit has written a very beautiful book for intellectuals. He is a giant, and I don't think there is any other book from any Western philosopher or thinker, which conveys something about Zen in a better way than Hubert Benoit's *The Supreme Doctrine*. But still it is intellectual, highly polished, refined. His arguments are beautiful, but not based in experience; they are not existential.

That's why he could say that even people in their satori think they *are*. But if they think they are, then that is their personal God – again it asserts. They denied the God, but now they themselves become the God. But this is an outsider's viewpoint. He does not know what satori is.

In satori, or in samadhi – *satori* is the Japanese word for *samadhi* – one is not. So who is there to think of himself that he is God? Gautam Buddha uses the word *anatta*. In the Pali language, which was the language Buddha used, *atta* means self, and *anatta* means no-self. In samadhi, in satori, you come to a point when you suddenly remember you are not – just a pure space, throbbing with life, dancing with joy, but *you* are no more. You are dissolved just like ice melting and becoming the ocean.

He is concerned because he does not know the real experience of satori. He says, "They *must* realize…" There is no question of realization. There is nobody to realize, and there is no question of *must*. In the vocabulary of Zen there is no must.

I have read a book written by a famous American author, Napoleon Hill, *You* Must *Relax*. Now if there is a must, how can you relax?

Now Hubert Benoit says, "They *must* realize." There is no one to realize. Whom is he talking about? "They *must* realize themselves, they *must* liberate themselves." From whom? There is nobody. This is liberation: when you are not. It is not a question of liberating yourself, because if you liberate yourself, you will be there.

But it is the problem of all intellectuals. They can't look beyond the words, beyond logic and language. "You *must* realize," and "They *must* liberate" – but liberate? Neither is there one who is unliberated, nor is there one who is forcing them to remain unliberated. There is only liberation!

The meditator comes to see that he is liberated from himself. He is no more – that is his liberation. But looking from the outside, even a man of such a refined and cultured mind, Hubert Benoit, misses the point completely.

Once you are in deep meditation, you are not – this is liberation, and there is no other liberation.

It has been long enough to be serious. It is time for Sardar Gurudayal

Singh. Put on the lights! It is good you can be serious when it is dark, but when the light comes, laughter follows.

One afternoon in Doctor Feelgood's office, Buster Chubbs comes staggering in. He is the most haggard-looking patient Doctor Feelgood has seen in a long time.

"I cannot sleep, Doc," moans Buster, pulling on his thinning hair. "I have got dogs to the left of me, dogs to the right of me, and dogs running all around me! They bark all night – and I am telling you, they are driving me crackers!"

"Don't worry," says Feelgood, sympathetically. "There is a new sleeping pill on the market called Knock Out. I have been having a lot of success with it. Try it!"

Buster Chubbs calls in at the drugstore, buys a box of pills, and staggers home. One week later, he is back in Feelgood's office. He looks even worse than before.

"It is no good, Doc," groans Buster. "I have not slept all week. I am up all night chasing those *goddam* dogs. And even when I catch them, they refuse to swallow the pills!"

Young Duncan MacPherson tiptoes into the room where Hamish MacTavish is sitting by the fire, reading his newspaper.

"Mister MacTavish," says young Duncan, nervously. "I have come to ask for your kind permission. I would like to ask you if I can marry your daughter, Tillie."

"Well, well, lad!" says Hamish, looking up. "Before I say a word about the matter, my boy, have you seen my wife, Mrs. MacTavish?"

"Yes, sir," replies Duncan. "But I still prefer your daughter!"

The scene is outside Moscow in the heavy snows of midwinter. Colossus G. Magnus, the greatest Hollywood movie director of all time – known as "Big G." Magnus – is ready to complete his most daring epic, the multi-billion dollar movie: "Napoleon Eats Russia!"

Across the vast snowy plain, "Big G." Magnus has constructed four huge towers, each complete with camera, lighting and sound crews.

Gigantic snow machines are standing ready to whip up an instant blizzard of snow. The crews are ready, and the cast of five thousand soldiers, with horses, cannons, swords, and everything, are poised and ready to go.

The big snow fans slowly start to blow, and suddenly, director Magnus, sitting in tower number four, shouts out, "Action!"

An incredible flurry of battle follows with fury and authenticity. For forty minutes the Russian and French armies clash, recreating history amongst booming cannons, and screaming men and horses.

Finally, "Big G." Magnus shouts out through his microphone, "Cut!"

Immediately, all the actors, technicians, and crews burst into loud cheers and applause.

"Big G." smiles to himself with satisfaction, and reaches for his telephone. He dials up film tower number one.

"You got everything, Paddy?" asks the director.

"Mister Magnus," hiccups Paddy, "it is Thursday – the power failed! We did not get a single shot!"

...It seems Poona also belongs to Russia – every Thursday the power fails...!

"What?" screams Magnus, slamming down the phone and dialing tower number two.

"Seamus," shouts the director, "how was it?"

"Mister Magnus," replies Seamus, "please don't get mad, but my cameraman forgot to put film in the camera."

"Idiots! Turkeys!" shouts "Big G." "You are all fired!"

Frantically, Magnus dials up tower number three.

"What about you, Sean?" he cries, perspiring. "How did it go?"

"Ah! Mister Magnus," replies Sean. "Never was there such a scene! It will make film history! You are a genius...!"

"Cut the bullshit, Sean!" shouts "Big G." "Did you get it all on film?"

"On film?" asks Sean. "You wanted me to photograph it? I thought it was a rehearsal!"

"You moron!" roars Magnus. "You imbecile! You will never work for me again!" And he slams down the phone.

"Big G." Magnus mops his forehead with a handkerchief and then turns to his own cameraman, Stonehead Niskriya.

"Jesus Christ!" shouts Magnus. "Thank God you are here, Stonehead! I am sure everything here is okay!"

"Absolutely!" confirms Stonehead Niskriya. "First class – number one!"

"Enough film in the camera?" asks "Big G."

"Plenty, Mister Magnus," replies Stonehead.

"Sound okay?" asks Magnus.

"You bet!" replies Stonehead. "Perfect sound."

"Those new lights from Berlin working okay?" asks Magnus.
"Just great!" enthuses Niskriya.
"Thank God!" shouts Magnus.
"Ja!" says Niskriya. "I am ready to start when you are!"

Nivedano...

Nivedano...

Stop.
Close your eyes...
Be silent...
and feel your body to be completely frozen.
This is the right moment to look inwards.
Gather your energy, your total consciousness,
and rush towards the center of your being.
It is just below the navel –
two inches below the navel, inside.
The Japanese call it the hara.

It is the center of life.
You have to move faster,
with an urgency as if this is the last moment of your life.
Now or never.
Faster and faster...
Deeper and deeper...
As you are coming closer to the center,
a great silence descends over you,
just like falling rain, very soft rain.
You can feel the coolness of it.
A little closer to the center,
and a great peace surrounds you.
Your whole inner being becomes full of light,
a luminosity you have never known before,
a blissful moment, utterly ecstatic.
It is the right time to step into the very source of your life.
You will feel drunk with the divine.
You will find the original face.
Symbolically Gautam Buddha's face
has been accepted in the East as everybody's original face.
Just remember one thing:
the buddha has only one quality, that of a witness.
Witness that you are not the body...
Witness that you are not the mind...
Witness that you are only a witness and nothing else.
This will take you deeper and deeper into the source of your being.
It will open doors into eternity.

To make this witnessing more and more deep,
Nivedano...

Relax...
but remember you are only a witness.
You are not the body, not the mind, just a pure witness.

And immediately,
Gautama the Buddha Auditorium
starts becoming an ocean of consciousness.
Ten thousand buddhas disappear as separate beings
into one oceanic consciousness.

This moment you are the most blessed people on the earth.
Everybody is concerned with trivia,
nobody cares to look inwards.
Everybody's eyes are focused on objects
which are not going to help you,
which are not going to be with you.
Death will take everything away from you –
money, power, prestige.
Death will leave only one thing:
that is witnessing.
If you have it, there is no death.
If you don't have it, there is only death and nothing else.
There are three steps which can be remembered at this silent moment.
The first, the buddha follows you behind like a shadow.
The second, instead of buddha being your shadow,
you become the shadow of buddha.
And the third, you disappear even as a shadow,
only the buddha remains.
Only the witnessing pure consciousness remains –
no I no Thou, no God no soul, just a vast nothingness.
An immense universe opens all its doors to you,
it pours into you abundantly, splendors, miracles.
Your life starts becoming a magic, a grace, a beauty, a truth.

Gather all these experiences you are having now.
You have to bring them from the center to the surface,
to your ordinary day-to-day life.

And persuade the buddha to come along with you.
He is your dhamma, he is your nature, he is your tao.
He is bound to come.
He has been waiting and waiting,
but you never invited him.

189

You never even bothered about him.
It has been long,
a millennia he has been sitting there just like a seed.
Allow him space.
Invite him so he can surface just like a lotus
coming from the dirty mud and passing beyond the waters
and opening its petals to the sun and to the moon and to the stars.

Nivedano…

Come back…
but come as a buddha.
Come with grace, silence, peace.
Settle down just for a few moments
to remind yourself of the golden path you have traveled,
and the great silence, peace, ecstasy that you have experienced.
You are still drunk with the divine.
You can feel the buddha just behind you,
his warmth, his love, his presence.
He is only a presence, he is not a person.

I hope the first step will be followed by the second,
the second will be followed by the third,
and it will not be long before one day
you will find yourself no more and only existence is.
That will be the most glorious day of your life.
Not only will you celebrate,
the whole existence will celebrate with you.
Celebration is my manifesto.
Let it be your manifesto too.

Okay, Maneesha?
Yes, Beloved Master.

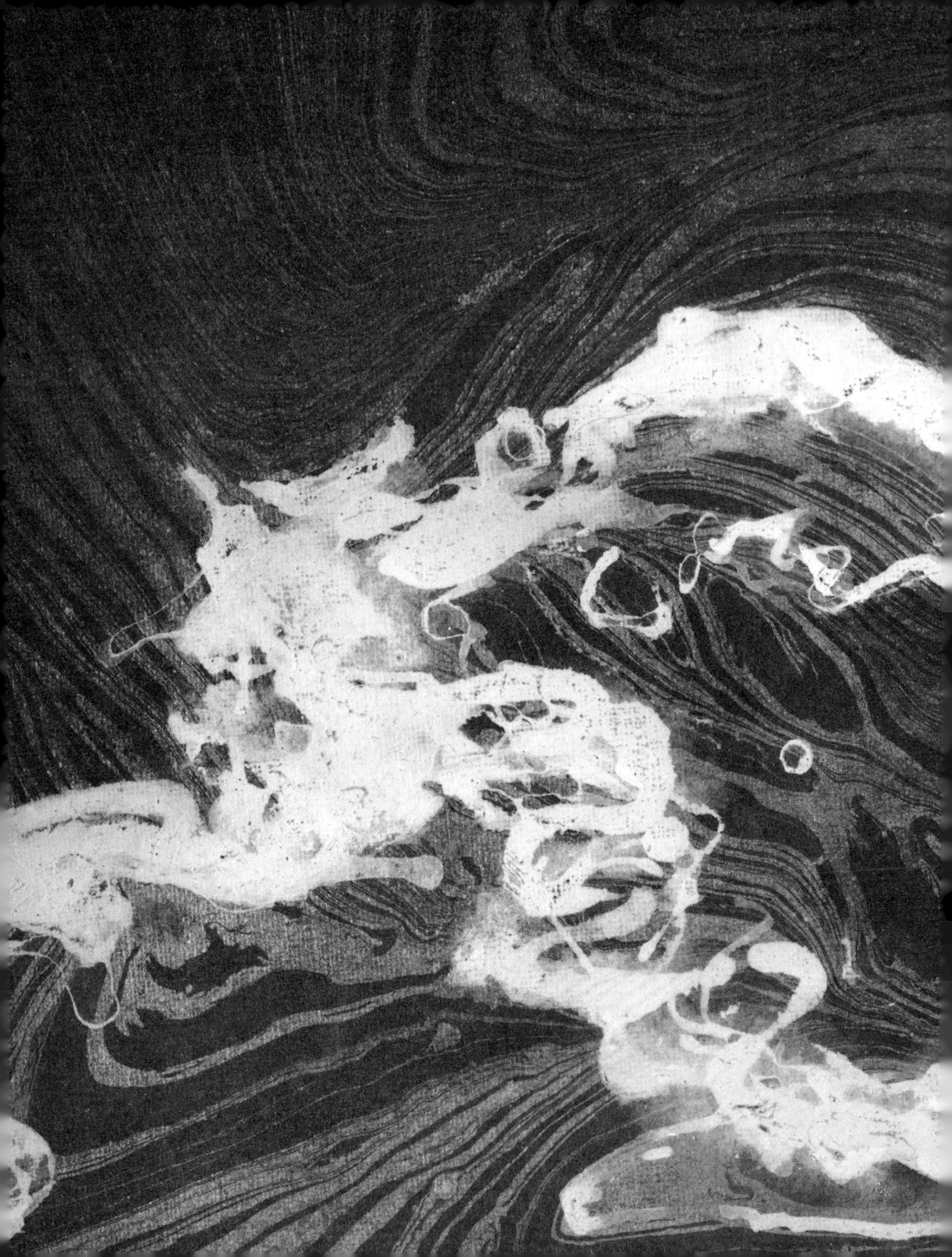

CHAPTER 6

Come to Your Own Festival

FEBRUARY 18, 1989

THE SUTRA

Our Beloved Master,

Shōdai, who was born in 738 in China and died in 820, was a disciple of Sekitō.
Shōdai stayed at Mount Nangaku under Sekitō for three years, then went to Mount Shuko where he saw Ma Tzu.
Ma Tzu asked, "What did you come here for?"
Shōdai said, "I came here for Buddha's Jamuna darshan."
Ma Tzu said, "Buddha has no Jamuna darshan. Jamuna darshan is the world of delusion. You are from Mount Nangaku, but it seems that you have not yet known that you need Sekitō. So you should go back."
Hearing that, Shōdai went to Sekitō. On meeting the master, Shōdai asked Sekitō, "What is buddha?"
Sekitō replied, "There is no buddha nature in you."
Shōdai asked, "What about all living beings?"
Sekitō replied, "They have buddha nature."
Shōdai asked, "Why don't I have it?"
Sekitō said, "Because you don't accept it."
At this, Shōdai decided to stay there.
Later, he lived in the Shōdai-ji temple and did not go outdoors for thirty years. Whenever a seeker came to him, he would say, "Go away – you don't have buddha nature."

Friends,

 famous psychoanalyst, Franz Strunz from Munich, has been studying child behavior in dreams, and he has found that Sigmund Freud's original idea was not right.

Sigmund Freud's original idea was that the child – every child, particularly in the civilized and cultured world – lives under repressive morality, repressive priesthood, repressive parents, and he cannot understand exactly why his natural and spontaneous behavior is unacceptable. He is not yet grown up in the mind. The mind will come slowly, but he has been born as a natural being. So he finds it absolutely difficult to understand why his natural behavior is condemned.

But because he has to be dependent on the parents, and he is utterly helpless, he has to accept the God that the parents believe in, and he has to accept all the commandments in which the parents believe. They drive the child to the church, or to whatever religious organization they belong. This is the beginning of programming the child.

Sigmund Freud's original thesis was that under these circumstances the child finds only freedom in his dreams. The parents are no longer there, the priest is no longer there, God is no longer there…no morality, no condemnation, no repression, no inhibition. In his dreams he lives a very natural and very pleasant life. That becomes a substitute for him. And I am absolutely in agreement with Sigmund Freud.

The child does not know yet what is dream and

what is real, it takes a little time. That is why you cannot remember if you go backwards. Up to the age of four you may be able to remember a few things; beyond that is a complete blank, but things were happening. From your birth, up to the age of four, things were happening but you don't have any memory of them because you did not have a mind yet.

The mind is a social product. It takes at least four years to program the child to be ready to accept anything that is told to him, because he knows if he denies it, he will suffer punishment – not only here but in hellfire.

But in his dreams, up to the age of four, he enjoys absolute freedom. Hence, Sigmund Freud said that children's dreams are very pleasant, very beautiful. In fact, the child can cope with reality only because of his dreams. The dreams are compensatory.

This man, Franz Strunz, has been surveying hundreds of children and their dreams, and his conclusion is that Sigmund Freud was wrong. So first I have to give you his statement.

Sigmund Freud's views on child dreams have been challenged by Munich psychologist, Franz Strunz.

Sigmund Freud claimed that children's dreams revealed the pleasure-oriented nature of nocturnal figments of an imagination, which was not hampered by the suppression and repression of the adult *emotional make-up, and which aimed at making secret wishes come true.*

Obviously, dreams are very private. Nobody can enter your dreams, and nobody can know what you are dreaming. The child has absolute freedom, but he is not free when he is awake – naturally he compensates. Whatever has been denied in his waking life, he fulfills those wishes in his dream. And because he cannot make the distinction that the dream is just a dream and the reality is a totally different matter, he is completely happy. He can tolerate this society and this repressive culture, and these unnatural demands made by religions, their God, their priests, just because he has a freedom at least when he is asleep.

This has been challenged by this Munich psychologist:

Strunz's research showed that children's nocturnal fantasies are mainly accompanied by stifling feelings of uneasiness and upset, and that all kinds of threat animals, thieves, robbers, murderers, catastrophies, death and frightening strangers greatly disturb sleeping children.

Most children, he said, are paralyzed with fear by the dangers they dream about.

I absolutely disagree with this Munich psychologist. In a hurry to criticize Sigmund Freud, he has forgotten that Sigmund Freud was surveying the dreams of totally different children. A great thing has happened in between that he has not taken note of: that is television.

It is television that has changed children's dreams – what God could not do, what the priest could not do, what the parents could not do. They used alphabetical language, logic, which the child was not yet capable of understanding. The child lives in a primitive way. Pictures he can understand; his language is pictorial. His dreams are very vivid, very colorful and very alive.

Television has created a great impact on children, on their behavior, on their dreams, because dreams and television look alike. Now the child cannot tell the difference between television and dreams. And on the television he sees all these things that this Munich psychologist is trying to use as a criticism of Sigmund Freud's fundamental hypothesis:

"*...stifling feelings of uneasiness and upset, and that all kinds of threat animals, thieves, robbers, murderers, catastrophies, death and frightening strangers greatly disturb sleeping children.*"

All this is the gift of television. It has nothing to do with Sigmund Freud's fundamental hypothesis; it is still right.

But this is how even your psychologists, world-famous people, behave unconsciously. He has completely forgotten that a new thing has happened between him and Sigmund Freud – and that is television. And it has changed not only the child's dreams, but his behavior too.

He sees all kinds of robberies, rapes, murders, thieves...all kinds of dangerous people on the television. Those are pictorial. The sermons of the priest were not pictorial, they were linguistic. His parents' teachings were linguistic, and he was not yet able to understand language and logic. But pictures he understands. So television has given all kinds of threatening, sensational, dangerous ideas to children's minds.

It is television that should have been noted by the psychologist. But rather than focusing on television, he has immediately gone to criticize Sigmund Freud.

I am taking it as an example to give you a sense that even your psychoanalysts, psychiatrists, psychologists, are as unconscious as anybody else. There is no difference.

Not only have the dreams changed, but even the behavior of children.

In America, just a few days ago, one child went into school with his father's gun and killed four children at random. And it was not that they were enemies or anything – just random.

He fired just because he had been watching continual killing, murder on the television...a great excitement. And it is not an exceptional case.

Young boys have been found trying to rape small girls. The idea is being given by the television. Children of the age of seven and eight are taking drugs. They have left hippies far behind. At least to be a hippie you used to be eighteen, nineteen, twenty...

Hippiedom exists only from twenty to thirty. After thirty the hippie disappears – in his place comes the yuppie. By the time he is thirty, he starts understanding that this way of life is not going to last long. Now his parents are refusing to support him, and the hippie has to change into a square world. He has to go back to the same society, clean shaved, well dressed, looking very professional and efficient. And yuppies have proved that they are capable of doing things. Now they have their homes, their cars, their wives, their children. And nobody can imagine that these people used to walk around the streets dirty, unclean.

Uncleanliness had become their philosophy. It was a reaction, because their parents were telling them, "Cleanliness is just next to God." And they have heard the news that God is dead. Now who is next to God? Cleanliness? The reaction was against the parents and their constant effort to repress their nature. They started moving to the one extreme, the other extreme. They started to have a philosophy of uncleanliness, dirtiness. But then they became dropouts, and society would not accept them; they became unfit.

But they could manage only up to the age of thirty. By that time their parents are fed up – they have been trying hard, but they were not listening at all. They were not going to the church, they were moving towards Kabul, Kulu Manali, Kathmandu, Goa...and ending up in Poona! This was their route. You know what route has brought you here – Poona was the dead end!

But the new children are taking drugs because they are watching all kinds of drug stories on television, and certainly they become interested. Children are very curious to explore anything that they see on television. Seven-year-old children are taking drugs, hard drugs, and it is becoming a widespread danger in America.

Their dreams are full of dangers, murders, suicide – that's what they are watching for almost seven-and-half hours on average per day! You cannot expect... If you are wasting one third of your life on television, then it is going to have a deep impact. Children understand the language of pictures, and television brings all these colorful sensational stories.

Their dreams have changed, their behavior has changed.

I would like this Munich psychologist to survey a place where television has not entered, and I am absolutely certain he will have to support Sigmund Freud's hypothesis. And if he really wants to go deeper into his search, he should go to the aboriginals, where not even television has entered. Even the priest has not reached, even God is unheard of. People are living naturally: no repressive, no inhibiting morality. If Franz Strunz goes to those places he will be surprised.

First, he should explore countries where television has not yet come, because these will be the children whom Sigmund Freud has studied.

I know children in India...almost ninety percent, or even more than ninety percent of India has no idea of television or movies. Small villages...there I have come across people who have not even seen a railway train. Electricity has not reached to many places, so there is no question. And television has just been introduced to India, so only big cities like Bombay, New Delhi, Calcutta and Madras may have television, but not the major part of the country. He can study the children there.

I have studied children for my own purposes, and I can give a guarantee that if television and movies have not reached, you will find Sigmund Freud's hypothesis absolutely correct. And if you go to the aboriginals...

Particularly one tribe of the aboriginals in Burma has been studied by psychologists and they could not believe it: that tribe had never been in any war. They don't fight with each other – not even in their dreams. They don't have so many dreams as you have. There are hundreds of people in that tribe who have never dreamed. When you talk about dreams, they just look at you – "What are you talking about? When we are asleep we are asleep. What do you mean by dream?" In their language there is no word for dream.

And if once in a while a child dreams, or a man dreams anything – for example, having a fight with some neighbor, or having a love affair with some woman – first thing, in the early morning, he has to confess the dream to his parents. And then all the elders of the village gather together to figure out who the person is that he has murdered in his dream, or was fighting with him in his dream, or who the woman is that he has fallen in love with in his dream. They figure it out. He gives the complete detailed description, very vivid and very real. So they can figure out who the person is – it is a small tribe.

Then the elders tell the person who has been dreaming, "You should take sweets and flowers and gifts to that woman, let her know that you have misbehaved with her in the dream, and you have come to be forgiven. Go with an apology to the woman or to the man with whom you have been violent. And unless they forgive you, don't return, sit there." And obviously, the person had nothing to do with it – you have not murdered him, you just dreamed – so obviously, he is willing to forgive you.

This has been their culture for thousands of years – that even the dream has to be taken into account. And the ultimate result is that people ordinarily don't dream. Only once in a while somebody does dream, and that happens only when he has repressed something natural. For example, he has been looking at a woman with lust, but could not express it in reality; hence the dream comes as a substitute for wish fulfillment.

That society knows a far better psychoanalysis than our so-called civilized world. They have been psychoanalyzing for thousands of years, and their method is far more effective. They have relieved people's sleep completely of dreams. They know authentic sleep, what Patanjali calls dreamless sleep.

He divides your states of mind into four: the so-called waking state, the dream state, deeper then is dreamless sleep, and deeper than that is samadhi, a real awakening. The first is called so-called waking; the last is called real awakening, which makes you a buddha.

But these aboriginal tribes don't have the dream state at all. From the waking state they simply move into dreamless sleep. And they are innocent, utterly graceful. Not a single war in their whole history, not a single murder in their whole history, not a single suicide in their whole history! They are just like flowers – innocent, natural.

And you call yourself civilized? And you call them uncivilized, primitive, pagans…?

So if this psychologist is really interested, first he should study people who don't know television, who don't know movies, and he will find the hypothesis of Sigmund Freud absolutely correct.

Then he should study those aboriginals who have lived so naturally, without any repressive church, without any Christianity, without any God, without any priest. Just like animals, just like birds, just like trees, part of this immense existence, naturally flowing, they don't have dreams at all. Once in a while somebody may have a dream, but only once in a while. And then the elders of the society gather together to decide what has to be done.

First, one has to figure out who really was the person he dreamed about. He gives the whole details, and then goes with an apology and with some gifts – sweets, fruits, flowers; they are poor people. He just offers these gifts and asks for their forgiveness. In his dream he has been nasty to them, angry to them, violent to them, lustful to them. Now it is absolutely obligatory that he should ask for their forgiveness: "Unless they forgive you, just sit down in front of their houses..."

This is a more authentic psychoanalysis – not lying on the couch of a psychiatrist or psychoanalyst and just talking about your dreams. It goes on and on, because every day you are repressing so much that it bubbles up in the dreams. No psychoanalysis has ever been complete. There is not a single man in the whole world whose psychoanalysis is complete.

It cannot be complete, because every day you are creating fresh material for new dreams. You go on getting analyzed, and you go on getting repressed by the priest in the name of God.

God and the priest together have conspired against human consciousness so deeply and so violently that they have disturbed your waking state, they have disturbed your dream state. And because these states are so disturbed, you cannot go beyond. This disturbance keeps you engaged and occupied.

People who are moving directly from the waking state to the dreamless sleep are very easily capable of slipping down to the fourth state. That's why the ancient Zen masters continuously say you have just to relax, you don't have to do anything.

It is not a question of doing, it is a question of non-doing. Just relax and rest, so that you can reach to the fourth stage where you are suddenly awake for the first time. Then you know that your so-called wakefulness was not authentic, it was a very small, thin layer, very fragmentary, not of much use.

You will be surprised to know that in these aboriginal societies, there are no buddhas. There is no need. Those people are naturally entering finally into the fourth stage. As they become more and more experienced, and become more and more peaceful, centered, they start moving into the fourth state without any effort, without any teaching, without any scripture.

If you understand me, a natural life will end up in enlightenment without any effort. You will suddenly find you are enlightened. That's why no recognition is given to the enlightened person. That is a natural phenomenon, just as every rosebush if watered well, if allowed to have some sunlight, if given good soil, will come to flowering. That is not a miracle.

Every man comes to flowering, he becomes a Gautam Buddha without any effort. And because every natural human being is bound to become an enlightened person, no recognition is taken of it. It is just as childhood is followed by youth, youth is followed by middle age, middle age is followed by old age and you know that old age is followed by death. It is just a natural sequence.

Buddhahood should be a natural sequence. It is not, because of your God and your priest and your scriptures; they are preventing you. Freedom from all these is absolutely necessary.

And strangely enough, every government knows that television is harming people immensely, ruining their physical health, ruining their mental sanity. Still, because all the great corporations which support the politicians for their elections own these televisions... The churches have their own television stations, radio stations, magazines, newspapers – in different names so you will not know it.

One of the British publishers, Sheldon, has published nine of my books. I had no idea that it was just a front, and behind it was the church. As the church authorities became aware that my books were being published, then I came to know. The man who was the manager of Sheldon Press must have been sympathetic to my thoughts, my approach to things. So without asking the church, he continued publishing. Nine books he published. And then he informed me, "The church has found that I have been publishing your books, so they have put an absolute ban on it. So please forgive me, I will not be able to publish any more. And they have ordered that these books should be given for recycling – whatever has been published – so they can be destroyed."

But the man must have been in great love with me. He did not give them to the recycling factory. He sold them to a secondhand bookstore, and he informed one of my sannyasins, "You can get them from the secondhand bookstore." So we got all the books at a throwaway price, but it was the Sheldon Press manager who managed it. Then we became aware that Sheldon was a front name. You would not think that it had anything to do with the church.

I have been informed from Germany that all the great newspapers are owned by the church, but you would not know. Television stations are owned by the church, radio stations are owned by the church. Satellites are owned by the church...and big corporations.

People have not looked into the big corporations. They are international like Coca-Cola. Only the Soviet Union was not aware of Coca-Cola, but now Comrade Gorbachev has brought Coca-Cola into the Soviet Union. Now the only international thing is Coca-Cola. Wherever you go you find billboards declaring, "Things go better with Coca-Cola."

There are ten rising corporations, and one survey says that in the coming ten years, there will only be these ten corporations in the whole world, because they are purchasing all the small corporations. The small corporations cannot compete. These ten corporations will have all the wealth of the world in different names so you will not even suspect a new kind of imperialism, and a very subtle kind that you will not be able to figure out who is behind it.

These corporations own almost all the television stations, and their interest is not in people's psychology or their disturbance. Their whole interest is that fifty percent of television time is devoted to advertisements – that is their income. But that income is possible only if millions of people are watching their programs, otherwise nobody is going to advertise.

To attract millions of people to the programs they have to make it as sensational as possible. It has to be a triangle story: two women and one man, or two men and one woman. And then murder, and suicide, and mental sickness, and insanity and all kinds of sensations have to be brought every day. It is the same story that goes on and on.

And they don't allow you to see the whole story. They give you a fragment, and then comes the advertisement. When you are getting hot, excited, then suddenly comes the advertisement. In that hot state, vulnerable, you immediately swallow the advertisement. You don't care whether it is healthy or whether you need it or not, it simply makes an imprint on your mind.

And again the story comes, so you don't even have time to think over what has got into your mind; they don't give you the chance to think. Again the story starts, and you forget all about the advertisement. A fragment again, and again the same advertisement is repeated. It goes on from six o'clock in the morning till twelve o'clock in the night. And people are just being imprinted by all kinds of nonsense and stupidity.

Television has become one of the great dangers to humanity. It could have been a great bliss, a great blessing. It could have been tremendously useful as education.

According to me, all television stations should belong to the universities, to the colleges, to the schools. And they should have programs which educate people. No advertisements – that is not education, that is *mis*education, that is exploitation. They should teach people history, geography... Small children who cannot get it through language, will be easily interested in learning history, in learning geography, in learning other kinds of subjects. Sciences, literature, fiction, poetry, painting...all kinds of arts can be brought to children of all grades.

So there must be television stations for small children, and then there should be some for the college graduates. And there should be television to the highest grade, postgraduate and research people. Professors have to be continuously made aware of all new kinds of discoveries, otherwise they are lagging behind, almost twenty years behind. They studied twenty years ago when they were in their postgraduate classes, but that knowledge has become out of date.

To update professors will be very easy with television. To bring students tremendous interest in all kinds of subjects, in whatever they are interested... If they are interested in music, they can be taught music, musical instruments. If they are interested in painting, they can be taught painting, sculpture. They can be taught meditation. All kinds of possibilities are there, once television is taken out of the hands of the exploiters, and out of the hands of the religious preachers. And then these children will prove Sigmund Freud's hypothesis absolutely.

This man has taken a revengeful attitude. It always happens. Because Sigmund Freud is the founder of psychology, every psychologist feels to take revenge, just as every child feels to take revenge with the parents.

This research simply shows a very deep hidden secret of this psychologist – that he wants to take revenge with the father figure, Sigmund Freud. Otherwise, this was so simple to understand that technology has brought so many things to the children which were not available in Sigmund Freud's time. The new children were not available for him to study, nor was he aware of the aboriginal children. He was aware only of Christian and Jewish children – both repressive religions.

Christianity is a child of Judaism. So is Mohammedanism. All three religions born outside India are branches of Judaism, repressive. The God is angry, the God is jealous, the God is going to punish you with eternal hellfire. But these words do not get into the minds of the children. They start after four years of age, but television can be watched before four years of age.

Small children are watching television because they know the language of pictures and color. Their world consists of pictures. That is why in children's books first you have to print a big picture. If you want to teach them what a mango is you have to put a big picture of a mango. Saliva comes first; then comes the word 'mango'. Looking at the picture, the child starts feeling to eat it, and the picture becomes associated by and by with the word 'mango'. As the child grows, the mango picture becomes smaller and smaller and smaller. In the university, pictures completely disappear from the books; words become very small, longer, complicated, and sentences become complex. Now the child has moved from pictorial language to an alphabetical language – to words from pictures.

Now words don't have color, and words don't have that kind of impact which a child can understand.

So what this psychologist has to understand – I am going to send him the whole discourse – is that his hypothesis is absolutely wrong and biased, and it is just a revenge against Sigmund Freud. Otherwise, a conscious researcher would have looked at what changes have happened between the time of Sigmund Freud and our time.

Are the children the same that you are surveying? They are not the same children. Then you cannot condemn Sigmund Freud's hypothesis because he was studying a different kind of children. Those children are disappearing from the West completely, so this hypothesis will be accepted. That's why I have taken it for your consideration that this hypothesis is wrong. This hypothesis is bound to be accepted, because you can study the children and that study will support it. But the reason is television, not the children! Remove the television and you will find children exactly as Sigmund Freud found them. But he also missed the aboriginal children who don't have any dreams at all.

He could not have conceived that there are people who don't have any dreams, because the Christian-Judaic religion is so repressive. People who have been brought up in that culture cannot conceive that there are still aboriginal people around the world, hidden in deep forests, who are absolutely natural beings. Those people have never heard that there is anything to be repressed.

Just in the middle of India there is a state, Bastar. It used to be an independent state under British rule, and the king of Bastar was my friend. And he became my friend by a strange coincidence....

We both were traveling in the same train compartment, and we both looked alike. He had a beard exactly the same size as I had at that time, and he used to wear the same kind of long robe with a lunghi wrapped around. So we were sitting in the same compartment looking at each other and thinking, "This is strange." And he was also looking at me and watching, thinking, "What is the matter?"

Finally, he said to me, "We both look so alike. From where are you coming?" I told him. He said, "Strange...and where are you going?"

So we were going to the same place, Gwalior. And we were going to be the guests at the same palace of the Gwalior maharani, the queen of Gwalior. We were both going to participate in an annual conference she used to call a World Conference of All Religions.

He was going to represent the aboriginal idea. They are pagans, they don't have any organized religion or dogma; they don't have any holy scripture, they don't have any priest. And because he was an educated person, he was going to represent pagans.

I was invited by some misunderstanding. The maharani must have read some of my books and thought that I was a religious person. On the first day of the meeting, she became so worried, because at least fifty thousand people were there in the palace grounds.

Gwalior's palace is a very big palace, and has acres and acres of greenery around it, and small bungalows, and it is all in a walled garden. Almost half of the city belongs to the palace. And just behind the palace is a huge mountain where they run a school for all the princes of the country and even outside the country. That school belongs to the palace. It was created just for Gwalior's sons and daughters in the beginning. Then it became a royal school for all the royal states of India.

It is a beautiful palace, and it has a huge ground where fifty thousand people can sit every year. But when I spoke, she was completely shattered. She could not sleep. At twelve o'clock in the night she knocked on my door. I had left her at ten o'clock after the meeting. I could not think who would be knocking on my door, so I opened the door, and it was the queen herself.

She said, "I cannot sleep. You have shattered my whole mind. And now I cannot allow you to speak tomorrow." The conference was going to continue for seven days; I spoke only one time. And she said, "My son wants to see you, but I have prohibited him." She said, "Whatever you said feels to be true, but it goes against all our beliefs, all our religious feelings."

I said, "Do you think about truth, or do you think about lies and consolations?"

She said, "I can understand, but my young son who is going to be the head of the state is too young, and he will be impressed by you immediately." She requested me, "Just for my sake – even if he comes, don't allow him in."

So I said, "If I am not going to speak, then I don't have to stay here. You have asked me for seven lectures, and just one lecture and you are finished. Let me do my job. Those fifty thousand people will ask for me."

She said, "I know it, because you were the only one they seemed to be interested in, and there was absolute silence. I have never seen such silence in the crowd. The priests go on speaking, who cares? They are telling the same thing again and again, year after year, the same dogmas. For the first time," the queen said to me, "I understood what it means to have pindrop silence. So they will be asking, but it is difficult, because all the other participants are absolutely against you."

Hindus and Mohammedans and Christians – they were all there, so they approached the maharani after the lecture, "If this man remains here for seven days, then we are leaving. We cannot sit on the same stage together, because he is destroying every religion."

I said, "They are so many, they can defend. I am alone" – there were almost twelve people on the stage with me – "They have enough time...there are twelve, they can defend."

The maharani said, "I know they cannot. They don't have the guts, they don't have the argument, they don't have any idea how to defend. And you have destroyed their smallest things, which I could not have conceived *can* be destroyed!"

Just before me, one of the shankaracharyas was speaking, and he told a small story which I love to tell myself, but when anybody else tells it, that is a different matter.

It is an ancient story he was telling....

The story is that ten blind men were crossing a flooded stream. Being frightened, they were holding each other's hands, and somehow they managed. It was not deep, but the current was forceful. They reached to the other side, and somebody amongst them said, "We should count, because we don't know if the river has taken somebody away, or we are all together still."

So they started counting. Everybody counted, and it was always ending with nine because he was leaving himself out. He would count the others: one, two, three, four, five, six, seven, eight, nine – one man was missing! They all tried, but it always stopped on the ninth!

One man, sitting by the side of the road, working in his field, was watching all this nonsense that was going on. And all the ten blind men had started crying and weeping, because one of them, one friend of theirs had been taken by the current.

So finally, the man came up and he said, "What is the matter?"

They said, "We were ten, and one person has gone with the river. Now we are only nine."

The man immediately looked – they were ten. So he said, "I have been watching. Now I will count. Stand up! I will go on slapping. First I will slap the first person one slap, and I will say one! Then I will slap the second person twice, and I will say two, and the third person three times, and I will say three...and this way I will count."

They said, "Any way...just bring our tenth man."

So he counted – and they were ten. And they were rejoicing, although they had been beaten well.

It is an ancient story. And the shankaracharya was telling it to show that this is the way we are: forgetting ourselves and looking around the whole world; trying to find peace, trying to find bliss, trying to find God, and not looking inwards, not counting ourselves.

After him I was to speak, and for the first time I had to criticize this story, which I have told you. But my context was totally different!

So I said to the shankaracharya, "Your story is absolutely stupid, because you have first to explain how they came to know they were ten. Before they started moving into the river, how did they manage to count? And if they knew how to count, how did they forget it just by crossing the river?"

Now he was at a loss.

I said, "There are only two possibilities: one is that somebody else has counted them just as somebody else counted them afterwards."

He said, "Perhaps."

I said, "That's the trouble with borrowed knowledge. Because somebody else has counted them, that created the trouble. It was not their own understanding that they were ten. It was somebody else's understanding that they were ten, and they were carrying borrowed knowledge. That borrowed knowledge is not going to help. When they themselves counted, the borrowed knowledge did not help at all. Again they needed somebody else to count them, again the borrowed knowledge."

"I am against borrowed knowledge because it is not going to help you. It is going to create more misery, more anguish, more anxiety. What happened to those blind people?" And I asked the shankaracharya, "Whatever you know, is it your knowledge or just borrowed? And be honest, because I have ways to check out whether it is your knowledge or borrowed."

He said, "I don't know myself; I am a scholar. I know the Vedas, I know the Upanishads, but I don't know myself."

I said, "Then you are a blind man. Sooner or later, passing any current you will be in difficulty. You will always remain dependent on others, you will never be free. And without freedom there is no spirituality."

For the first time I suddenly found the criticism, I had never thought about it.

But the queen said to me, "This is dangerous. You finished that shankaracharya, and everybody was laughing and enjoying. Now that shankaracharya is very angry. He is sitting in my palace."

I was staying in the guest house. Everybody had a guest house. They had at least twenty guest houses in the thick garden…huge and ancient trees. The shankaracharya was sitting in the main palace where the queen and the king lived. And he said, "I am not going to leave unless you make the arrangement. Either we all will leave – twelve persons…"

I said, "Don't be worried, I will speak for three hours continuously. Those twelve persons are not needed. I will manage the fifty thousand people. In fact, tomorrow you will have difficulty because more people will be coming. These fifty thousand people are going to tell at least one hundred thousand people. So don't be worried, there is going to be a double gathering. You have to make arrangements. Let these twelve people go, I will manage the seven days."

She said, "But I cannot do that. I am an orthodox Hindu."

I said, "That does not matter. I will finish all orthodoxy in seven days."

She said "That I can understand. You will finish, but I cannot tell all those religious leaders to go away. They are twelve, and you are alone."

I said, "That does not matter. I am enough for those twelve. If they don't want to sit on the same stage, make another stage for them, and I will just sit alone on my stage. I will take care of each of the twelve."

She said, "You are going to create trouble, and I want no trouble."

I said, "Then if you want to keep those people, you don't understand. You will be in trouble."

At that moment the Bastar maharajah also came in. He was staying in the next room in the guest house with me. And he said to me, "You have done a great job, and if you have to leave, I am coming with you."

That's how we became friends. And he invited me to his state. So from Gwalior I went directly to Bastar. It is far away from Gwalior. And he introduced me to the people of Bastar. They are aboriginals, and they live almost naked. They put only a small piece of cloth around them when they come to the main capital, Jagdalpur – otherwise, in the forest, in the mountains they live naked.

You can ask a woman, even by touching her breast, "What is this?" – and she will not feel embarrassed, she will not feel offended. She will say, "This is just to give milk to my child," with no idea that "you are being offensive, you are touching my breast." She is not going to scream, and she is not going to any police station; in fact, there is no police station there.

The people are so innocent, that rarely does it happen that somebody kills someone. It has happened perhaps twice in this maharajah's lifetime. Then the person who has killed comes to the capital himself, because only the capital has the police station and the court. He goes to the police station and informs them: "I have killed a man and I need to be punished." Otherwise no one would ever have known that he had killed anybody. Nobody goes into those deep forests. They live in caves; nobody goes there. And they have such beautiful caves.

And they are such beautiful people. You will not find anybody fat, you will not find anybody thin – they all look alike. They live long, and they live very naturally. Even about sex they are very natural, perhaps the only natural people left in India.

And exactly what they do, has to be done all over the world if you want people not to be perverted. Behind all kinds of mental sicknesses is sexual perversion. In Bastar I found for the first time, people totally natural.

After a girl and a boy come of age – that is thirteen and fourteen... They have in their villages, in the middle of the village, a small hall just made of bamboos, as their huts are made. The moment a girl starts having periods, she has to stay in the central hall. By the time a boy is fourteen, sexually potent, he has to live... All the girls and the boys who have become sexually mature, they start living together, sleeping together, with one condition – and that is a beautiful condition – that no boy should sleep with a girl for more than three days. So you have to become acquainted with every girl of the village, and every girl has to become acquainted with every boy of the village.

Before you decide to marry someone, you must know every woman of the village, so there is no question arising afterwards that you start feeling lustful for some woman. You have lived with all the women of your age, and it is your choice after the experiment with all the women.

And there is no jealousy at all, because from the very beginning everybody is living with every girl. Every boy has the chance to be acquainted with every girl of the village, and every girl has the chance to be acquainted with every boy of the village.

So there is no question of any jealousy, there is no competitive spirit at all. It is just an experiment, an opportunity for every child to know sex with different people, and then find out who suits you, and with whom you were the most happy, with whom you settle harmoniously, with whom you felt your heart. Perhaps this is the only scientific way to find a soul mate.

But these people are called uncivilized, and missionaries are doing a great job of civilizing them: opening schools, hospitals. They don't need hospitals. They are such healthy people, and these missionaries bring all kinds of diseases to them. They have never heard about gonorrhea, they have never heard about all kinds of perverted diseases. The missionaries bring the diseases, and then the hospital.

The missionaries bring the idea to them that you are poor. They have never thought about it – they are all equal, equally poor. There is no question of comparison, and they are living perfectly well, and healthy, on one meal a day. They are more healthy than anybody else in the world.

Just recently, scientists have been experimenting on rats, and they were puzzled. They kept two categories of rats, the same kind. To one category they were giving as much food as they wanted – American rats. And to the other category, the Bastar rats, they were giving food only one time. And they were surprised. The rats who were given whatever they wanted, lived to be only half of the age of the rats who were fed only one time. They were double the age – twice the American fellows!

So Bastar people live longer, although they don't know how long they have lived, because they cannot count. They live up to one hundred years very easily, one hundred and twenty very easily. If you search deeper in the forests, perhaps you can find a person who has lived one hundred and fifty years. They don't know it – you have to figure it out. And they don't look that old either.

Even the oldest person goes on working. Life is hard, but it is beautiful. Every night – particularly when it is fullmoon nights – they dance to abandon. The whole day they have been working hard, and in the night they dance. All the women, all the men together...no question that you have to dance with your wife. People go on changing partners. It is a social phenomenon, it is not a question of possessiveness that you should dance with your own wife. And if she is dancing with somebody else, then you are looking jealous, you are looking murderous.

I have watched their dances. They look so beautiful. There is no question of any lust, because they are fulfilled, sexually fulfilled, physically fulfilled.

They don't have dreams. I have asked many. I have asked the maharajah. He said, "They don't have dreams, but I have because I am an educated person. They destroyed me. I was born in these hills, and I would have loved to remain just as uneducated, as uncultured as these people. Their joy is infectious, their laughter is infectious. But they don't have any dreams."

There is no need for dreams. A dream is a need created by a repressive morality, by a repressive God, by a repressive priesthood. These are the people who have created dreams. And then another priesthood has come into being, the psychoanalyst. They exploit your dreaming. One priesthood has created the dreams, another priesthood...and both were Jews.

Jesus was a Jew, and Sigmund Freud was a Jew. One Jew has created Christianity – the most repressive religion in the world, and the other Jew has created psychoanalysis to analyze your dreams. And both are having great fun. Both are the most highly paid people...psychoanalysts and the missionaries, and the priests and the bishops, and the cardinals and the pope....

Psychoanalysis will remain incomplete unless it comes to understand the people who don't have dreams. Then you will have to change the whole idea. It is not that by analyzing people's dreams you are going to give them mental health. The question is how to help them move from dreamless sleep to relax into the fourth stage called *turiya, samadhi, satori,* where one becomes utterly awakened, the state of a Gautam Buddha.

And a good news before I take the sutras....

A famous New York sculptress, Martine Vaugel has just now taken sannyas from the New York Center of Neo-Sannyas International. She is a world-famous sculptress. She must have been listening to my tapes, and must have been hearing Sardar Gurudayal Singh's name every day. So, without seeing him – she has not yet come to Poona, and she has not seen Sardar Gurudayal Singh...but this is the sensitivity of an artist, a creativity. She has made a statue of Sardar Gurudayal Singh, and she has sent me a picture of the statue to see whether she is right. And I was amazed. She is absolutely right. The picture looks almost like Sardar Gurudayal Singh.

LAUGHTER

SARDAR GURUDAYAL SINGH

(The Master holds up the photograph of Sardar Gurudayal Singh for all to see. In response, everyone cheers and claps.)

Sardar Gurudayal Singh...take your picture!
(The Master, enjoying the situation immensely, holds out the photograph for Sardar to take.)

The first question:
So-called "modern Christians" particularly young Protestants, talk about God as if he is not a person – like "God is everywhere, in every being, in every tree, in nature" – not a person hidden in the clouds.
Do they get the point or is it just out of cunningness, because they see that the old-man God has no grounds at all and no future?

It is out of absolute cunningness, because they go on saying that God is not a person. Then why do they go to the church? Then why do they continue to pray to God as a person? If God is not a person, prayer should be stopped, going to the church should be stopped. If God is not a person, then Jesus cannot be his begotten son. Then you have to drop the idea that Jesus is related to God especially.

If God is really everywhere, then he is no more in Jesus Christ than in you. Then why should you worship? Then what is the function of the priest if there is no God as a person? The priest has to disappear.

That's why I say these people are simply repeating the approach of Zen – which has become known to the West now – that there is no God. But they cannot say it exactly, "There is no God." It hurts their programmed minds. So they are finding excuses in such a way that it appears God is, but it is not a person.

But they don't understand the implications. They say, "God is everywhere." If God is everywhere, then no place can be called sacred. If God is everywhere, in every being, then you cannot be violent to the animals, you cannot hunt animals, you cannot kill animals for your food. You are killing God. If God is in every being, then everybody has to be vegetarian. Nobody can be non-vegetarian; otherwise you are killing God and eating God.

In every tree in nature...and you are cutting trees, you are destroying the ecology of nature.

Just when India became independent, forty years ago, there were nearabout one hundred and fifty million hectares of trees in the country. Now there are only sixty million hectares. Over half of the trees in India have been cut. And the Christians are saying now that God is everywhere, even in trees...? Hindus have been saying it for centuries that God is everywhere. That is the meaning of 'omnipresent'. And if God is everywhere, then why do you go to the church, why do you go to the temple, why do you go to the mosque? And why do you listen to the sermons? Why do you carry a holy Bible or a holy Koran?

I don't think a non-personal God can write the Vedas and the Bible and the Koran – or a non-personal God can send messengers and prophets and messiahs. Then if you are honest all your holy scriptures have to be burned. And all your churches have to be demolished, if you are honest. And all your priesthood has to be told: "You have exploited enough; now start working. Unless you work you will not have anything to eat."

If you don't do that then it is mere cunningness, because you cannot prove the personal God anymore. You are trying to create an impersonal God, but your whole religion continues to be the same. It does not change.

It is such a great change from a personal God to an impersonal God that your whole religion will go through a revolution – no church, no priest, no holy scripture. Then the whole existence becomes the holy scripture.

And if God is everywhere there is no need to pray. The closest is your own being, so first find God in your own being.

But still these Christians are not interested in meditation. These Christians are still praying, to an impersonal God.

Prayer is absolutely absurd. And if these Christians do understand the implications, then Christianity disappears and the pagan appears again. That was the only problem. Christianity killed millions of pagans who believed in the whole of nature, in the whole of existence as divine; who worshipped trees, who worshipped the moon, who worshipped the sun, who worshipped rivers, mountains, anything – because everything was sacred. Christianity destroyed them, and converted those pagans into Christians – from an impersonal God to a personal God, from natural people into repressive maniacs!

And now if you again disperse the personal God into the whole of existence, you will have to disperse the whole of Christianity. You will have to disperse all the religions, and the whole earth will be full of pagans, Zorbas.

That is my effort – to create the Zorba as a solid foundation for a buddha.

Zorba is the earth.

Buddha is the sky.

And when these two meet there is communion. When these two meet, there is synchronicity. When these two meet there is revolution. You are no longer the same, nor is the world anymore the same. Everything changes in a totally new perspective. New doors open – and a new human being, and a new, fresh existence without any priests to poison your nature.

No, these people, the so-called new Christian theologians are just deceiving themselves and other Christians, because their whole structure remains the same. Just God…because they cannot support by logic or evidence, and they can see the point of Zen, at least intellectually. Not to feel inferior, they are talking about the impersonal God.

That's what Eckhart was doing, that was what Saint Bernard was doing – trying to make God impersonal. But they don't understand that it means destroying your whole structure of religion. If they truly understand the phenomenon they will destroy all Bibles, all churches, popes, the Vatican... all should be finished, there is no need. God is everywhere – there is no need for any priest to stand between you and God. He is surrounding you, he is in the air, and he is in your blood and in your bones. He is in your very marrow and he is in your inner space – as he is everywhere.

But to know that he is everywhere is not a logical conclusion. To know he is everywhere has to be an existential experience. First you have to go into yourself. Unless you know it in yourself, you cannot say it is in the trees and it is in every animal and it is in every living being. You are a living being – first enter into yourself.

These Christians are not talking about meditation at all. So all the talk is simply to deceive themselves and others, as if they have risen to the same height of Zen. Just by talking you cannot do that. You have to give evidence, proof, by your every gesture, by your every action, by your every word.

But I watch, I have been aware of these new Christian theologians, and their behavior is the same as any Christian. That behavior proves that their understanding is just to camouflage people's minds, to create confusion. They are protecting the old God with a new name – "impersonal God" – because their whole religion remains the same.

How can it remain the same if God is impersonal? That is the equivalent to there being no God, only godliness, a quality pervading the whole cosmos.

There is a beautiful story....

Al-Hillaj Mansoor, who became finally a great enlightened being, was murdered by the Mohammedans. He was a poor man and he wanted to go to Kaaba because it is the duty of every Mohammedan, at least one time in your life, that you should go for *haj*, for a holy pilgrimage to Kaaba. If you don't go at least one time you are not a Mohammedan. So even the poorest Mohammedans sell their houses, their land, and go at least one time to Kaaba.

Mansoor was very poor. His father and mother died when he was very young, so he was almost an orphan, a beggar. The neighbors helped him up to his youth and then he started – because there was no education for him.... People were going...there is a special month every year when Mohammedans from all over the world go to Kaaba. Many people from the village were going, and he started telling them, "I would like to come." But they said, "You don't have any money." So he collected money from every house. But by the time he had collected money, the other pilgrims had already left.

So alone, he started his journey. Just outside the village, underneath a tree was sitting a man who was going to become his master – Junnaid. And he said to the young man, "Where are you going?"

Al-Hillaj said, "I am going to Kaaba. All the pilgrims from my village have already left."

Junnaid said, "Come here!" The voice of Junnaid was such…his eyes were such that al-Hillaj could not say no. He said, "Give me the money! There is no need to go anywhere. I am the Kaaba and I have come to your village just for you. You can make seven rounds of me, just as the other pilgrims will be making seven rounds of Kaaba. That is a stone – I am a living human being."

Al-Hillaj was so magnetically drawn to the man that he gave all his money to him, and made seven rounds.

And Junnaid said, "Now you can go to your village. And I will be leaving tomorrow morning, so if you want to come with me, you can come."

He went to the village. The villagers asked, "What happened? You had gone to Kaaba" – it used to take three months walking to Kaaba, and three months to come back – "and you are back just within half an hour! Where is the money?"

Al-Hillaj said, "What to do? I met Kaaba just outside the village. He was sitting under a tree."

They said, "You idiot! You have given the money to *that* Kaaba?"

He said, "He asked, and he told me to make seven rounds around him. So I made seven rounds and I am feeling so fulfilled, and so dignified that Kaaba himself has come."

They said, "You come with us. We want to see who this man is who has cheated you. You are a simpleton! How can Kaaba come here, and for you?"

He said, "You can come. Tomorrow morning I am leaving with Kaaba."

They said, "You come with us. First let us see who this fellow is – he is a man?"

Al-Hillaj said, "Of course. And a very magical man. I think it is Kaaba personified."

They said, "You keep quiet, you just follow us."

The whole village gathered, and they could see. The man had a tremendous light around him – it was night now – and they could feel as they started coming closer to him, that he was in deep silence with closed eyes. The light was radiating, and al-Hillaj was not wrong, there was an immense attraction, the man had charisma.

They all went around him and Junnaid opened his eyes and said, "First put the money! I have traveled to your village and you are doing your *haj* without paying the money. Bring the money first!"

Al-Hillaj said, "Now you know that he is not an ordinary Kaaba, he speaks too!"

And the whole village, whatsoever they could bring, brought and gave to him.

Junnaid allowed them to make a round, and the day after, he left with al-Hillaj. The whole village had come to send them off. They thought, "This al-Hillaj, although he was an orphan, proved to be more blessed than we are. He has found a master."

Only the enlightened man can say such a thing, that there is no God, because he knows God is a quality, it is the fragrance; you cannot catch hold of it, but it is everywhere. Wherever life is, wherever laughter is, wherever love is, that quality pervades, penetrates your heart. And in meditation it goes to the deepest part of your being. Only then can you say there is no God. That does not mean you are atheist, that simply means you are denying a personal God, a creator God, and you are accepting existence itself as divine. But then there is no church and then there is no priest, and then there is no holy scripture.

If these neo-theologians are really sincere, honest human beings, they should start destroying the holy scriptures – at least the Christian ones, since they are Christians. And they should start demolishing the Vatican, taking away the power from the priests, and abolishing the monasteries.

But they are not doing anything of the kind, so it is all bullshit – just bullshit and nothing else.

The sutra:
Our Beloved Master,
Shōdai, who was born in 738 in China and died in 820, was a disciple of Sekitō. Shōdai stayed at Mount Nangaku under Sekitō for three years, then went to Mount Shuko where he saw Ma Tzu.
Ma Tzu asked, "What did you come here for?"

You can see the difference between so-called religious people and the Zen masters. Ma Tzu knew that he was coming from Sekitō. Rather than feeling happy that he had got a disciple from Sekitō and his number of disciples had at least increased by one, Ma Tzu said, "What did you come here for? Sekitō was enough for you."

This is the beauty of Zen – an immense reverence for everyone who is enlightened. There is no competition at all. Never heard of in the world of Zen is the word 'competition'...no effort to convert anybody. Ma Tzu simply asked him, "Why have you come here? For what? Everything was available where you are coming from."

Shōdai said, "I came here for Buddha's birth celebrations, Jamuna darshan." Buddha's birthday was coming. And Buddha's birthday has a very special coincidence. He was born on the same fullmoon night as he became enlightened, and in the same month, on the same fullmoon night, as he died eighty-two years afterwards – the same month, the same fullmoon night. A strange man – birth, enlightenment, death, all happened on the same fullmoon night, in the same month of the year. So his birthday is also his enlightenment day. It is also his death celebration. So in a single day all three experiences happened. That's why for Zen the full moon has become something special – because everything that happened to Buddha happened on the fullmoon night.

So in every Zen monastery on the fullmoon night people just sit under their trees and watch the full moon. The full moon has become symbolically connected with Gautam Buddha. And just watching and witnessing the full moon, they enter into deep meditation.

The fullmoon night has a specialness that is now being recognized by science itself. They have to approach it from the wrong side, because scientists are living on the wrong side of the earth, in the West. They became aware that more murders happen on the fullmoon night, more suicides happen on the fullmoon night, more people go insane on the fullmoon night...strange. This fullmoon night certainly affects people and their psychology. It affects the ocean – that is a known fact. On the fullmoon night waves become very tidal – as if the ocean is trying to reach to the moon. Man consists of eighty percent ocean water, so something in him also starts feeling a subtle vibration. Scientists say that the first living being was the fish. Man is the other end of progress – in the beginning was the fish. So we have a very deep connection. Our real forefathers lived in the ocean – they were fish.

So don't eat fish! You are eating your own forefathers, and that is nasty! And I see people carrying tinned fish – forefathers tinned! And people love eating fish....

If life was born in the ocean then life is bound to be affected when the ocean is affected. There is a deep connection, underlying currents. But Western psychologists became aware from the wrong side: suicide, murder, madness. The East became aware that more people have become enlightened on a fullmoon night; in fact, almost all except one, Mahavira.

He became enlightened on the no-moon night, *amawas*. The fullmoon night is called *purnima* – the moon has become perfect, *purna*. And the no-moon night is when there is no moon at all, absolute darkness. Except Mahavira, nobody has become enlightened on amawas, no-moon night. Mahavira's name was not Mahavira – *mahavira* means a great warrior. His name was Vardhaman. But because he became enlightened on amawas, the no-moon night, he proved that he could go against the current. It was natural for everybody to become enlightened on the fullmoon night, but this fellow Mahavira tried to go against the normal order of things, and still he managed to become enlightened.

In India, people have completely forgotten why every year on a particular amawas, no-moon night, they celebrate Diwali, a festival of lights. You must have seen people putting all kinds of candles, lamps, lights in their houses. This is the night when Mahavira became enlightened. And this festival is in remembrance of Mahavira but nobody even thinks of Mahavira.

Those firecrackers are in celebration of Mahavira. He certainly did something unique which never happened before and never happened afterwards. So it is perfectly right to call him Mahavira, a great warrior. A very strong man...otherwise it is almost impossible for anyone to become enlightened on the no-moon night.

In Zen, on the fullmoon night of every month, they watch the moon the whole night. And as they go on witnessing the moon, a deep tranquility and silence descends over them, particularly on the night when Gautam Buddha was born, became enlightened, and died. So this is a special, very special night for the people belonging to the small stream of Zen.

Shōdai said, "I have come here for Buddha's birthdate celebrations." Ma Tzu was a very famous master; Sekitō was not that famous. Slowly, slowly he became famous after his death, but Ma Tzu was famous while he was alive – very famous, because of his strange behavior. Shōdai must have thought that on the celebrations of this moon, it would be good to go to Ma Tzu – something might transpire. So he said, "I have come here to celebrate the birth of Gautam the Buddha."

Ma Tzu said, "Buddha has no birth, no death – Buddha is eternal. Life has no beginning, no end, it is eternal. The very word 'birth' belongs to the world of delusion, because that which is authentic in you is never born. It has been coming from one house to another house, from one body to another body, but it is eternal in itself. So no birth, no death happens to it. It happens only to the outside of the house, which becomes tattered so it has to be renewed, or else you have to move into a new house."

Ma Tzu said, "Buddha has no birth, no death. The very idea of birth and death is delusion."

"...You are from Mount Nangaku, but it seems that you have not yet known that you need Sekitō."

"He is your master. I don't think it is the right time for you, or that there is any need to change your master. You have not allowed your master to transform you yet."

"...So you should go back."

"You cannot stay here."

Hearing that, Shōdai went to Sekitō.

On meeting the master, Shōdai asked Sekitō, "What is buddha?"

All the way coming back he must have been thinking, "Ma Tzu said there is no birth of the buddha and no death of the buddha. Then what is the buddha?"

The buddha is equivalent to awakened life.

Sekitō replied, "There is no buddha nature in you."

Shōdai asked, "What about all living beings?"

Sekitō replied, "They have buddha nature."

Sekitō was strange in his own way. Ma Tzu had very strange behavior; he went to the extreme. But Sekitō was not just a normal enlightened master either; he had his own uniqueness. He said, "All living beings have buddha nature, but Shōdai, you don't have it!" This is a very strange statement. Why does this poor Shōdai not have the buddha nature? When all living beings, even animals, even trees have buddha nature – only Shōdai has not!

Shōdai asked, "Why don't I have it?"

Sekitō said, "Because you don't accept it."

The only question is of recognition, of accepting, of remembering. Even if you have immense treasures but you are unaware of them, what is the point whether you have them or not?

An ancient story says that one master and his disciple were moving from one village to another village. But they started late because people were trying to persuade them to stay a little longer in their village. Starting late, the master was continuously looking into his bag. That he had never done before. And the disciple was behind – he was also thinking, "What is the matter? Why does he go on looking into the bag, and then close it?"

And again and again he said, "We should go faster, we have to reach the other village before sunset."

The disciple simply could not believe it, because there had been many nights when they stayed in the wildest parts of the forest where there were all kinds of dangers...and the master had never bothered. They had slept soundly under the trees, knowing perfectly well there was danger all around. But what had happened today? He wanted to reach to the other village before sunset. There was danger – what kind of danger?

Then they stopped at a well, and the master had to wash his face and do his evening prayer before the sun set, so he was in a hurry. He gave the bag to the disciple and told him, "Keep it carefully." That too was strange. He had given the bag to him many times, but he had never said, "Keep it carefully." Of course he *had* always kept it carefully.

So when the master started drawing the water from the well, the disciple looked in the bag. And then he knew what the problem was: he was carrying a golden brick, a complete brick of pure gold. He knew now what the danger was. So while the master was praying – and he was praying quickly, and fast – the disciple threw that golden brick at the side of the well into the forest and took a stone of the same weight and put it in the bag.

The master quickly finished his prayer and immediately took the bag…felt the weight. The sun was setting and it was getting dark. Feeling the weight, and touching the bag, he was perfectly satisfied. They started moving and the master said, "We have to run. We have to reach the village anyway, we cannot stay in the forest in the night. It is dangerous."

After two miles of running, both were tired, huffing, puffing…. Finally, the master said, "It seems we are on the wrong track because there seems to be no village ahead. Far away we can see – not even a single light. And the danger is there…"

The disciple said, "Don't be worried, I have thrown the danger near that well."

He said, "What!!" He looked, he took out the stone, and he said, "You threw that brick of gold? I told you to keep it carefully!"

And the disciple said, "I *have* kept it carefully! For two miles you have also been keeping the stone carefully. Not knowing that it was a stone, you were worried. Now can we stay overnight?"

He said, "Now there is no problem! You really threw away the whole danger."

They slept very well in the night….

If you don't know, you can carry a stone as if it is gold. And you can carry gold as if it is nothing if you don't know.

You are carrying a tremendous treasure within you – the buddhahood, the enlightenment. But unless you realize it, whether it is there or not does not matter. It is the same.

That's why Sekitō said, "You don't have it. All other living beings may have it, but you don't have it. That much is certain. All living beings are not here, so I don't know, but about you I know – you don't have it."

He said, "But why? Why make me an exception then? Every living being has it...!"

Sekitō said, "Because you don't accept it."

"You don't explore it, you don't recognize it. You don't remember a forgotten language."

At this, Shōdai decided to stay with Sekitō.

Ma Tzu was right. This was the right man for him.

First, he must have felt a little disappointed in Ma Tzu, a little humiliated that he had been sent back. But now he recognized: "Ma Tzu was right. Sekitō has the secret in his hands, and he is my master. Ma Tzu has a different discipline and he will have to begin from ABC, and Sekitō has been working for years over me."

So now everything was clear why he had been sent back. "Go to the same master who has been working on you, and he has been working perfectly rightly. His method is his; my method is different."

But methods don't matter, they are pure devices to bring you a certain awareness, a certain realization, a certain deepening of your consciousness. This statement: "Because you don't accept it, you don't have it. Just realize it and you have it. You have already had it for centuries, but you have never looked at it..." At this, there must have been a lightning flash in Shōdai's mind, in his consciousness. He decided to stay with Sekitō.

Later, he lived in the Shōdai-ji temple...

He created a temple, and he lived in the temple, which used to be called Shōdai-ji temple.

...and did not go outdoors for thirty years.

This is simply symbolic and factual, both. He did not go outside the temple for thirty years. After this statement of Sekitō – "You have it, but because you don't accept it you don't have it" – for thirty years he did not go outside the temple.

Nor did he go out of himself for thirty years, he went on in and in and in. Those thirty years he was not even counting. The only thing that mattered was that he had to remember the hidden secret of buddhahood. He had to give birth to his own buddhahood – and he had gone to Ma Tzu for the birth of Buddha's celebration.

How can you celebrate Gautam Buddha's birth if your buddha is still unborn? You can't understand what buddha means, you can't understand what this festival is for, because you have not come to your own festival.

First you have to celebrate yourself.

Only then can you celebrate all the buddhas, awakened or asleep, can you celebrate the whole existence.

...And did not go outdoors for thirty years.

Neither out of the hut nor out of himself – he went on in and in, went on digging.

Whenever a seeker came to him, seeing the temple, and knowing that Shōdai was inside meditating for thirty years... People used to bring some rice, some food, some water, inside the temple. But he never asked anybody in and he never went out.

In the East that has been a very virtuous act if somebody is meditating so deeply that he has no time for food, no time to beg, no time to go out. People have a tremendous reverence for meditators. They may have been poor and they may have cut their own food into two pieces – one they would eat, the other piece they would go and offer to Shōdai.

In the East, meditation has not been thought of as a personal matter. It is not that you are doing something selfish for your own self, it is something that you are doing for the whole existence. If you become blossomed, you will be a proof to everybody that they can also blossom. You will become an argument for the inner world. You will become an incentive for others also to explore – it is possible; it is not impossible. It is not only that Gautam Buddha can become enlightened, Shōdai also can. He has been refused by Sekitō – "You don't have it!" This hit him hard.

But this was the device of Sekitō. He needed that much of a hit. So he retired into a temple, meditated for thirty years, became enlightened.

But whenever anybody would come to him, *he would say, "Go away – you don't have a buddha nature."*

The same device that had been used on him by his master, he went on using his whole life. And he helped many people, because the moment he would say, "You don't have buddha nature," immediately they would ask, "What about other living beings?" And he would say, "Of course, they have it."

Naturally, the same dialogue happened again and again, and the person would say, "You are being absurd. If everybody has it, why have I not?" And he would say, "Because you don't accept." Just remember – it is a forgotten nature. Just go in.

Shōdai was not very inventive – that's what I call a "normal" Zen master. He simply had one small statement. Even that small statement helped many, but could not help a really great number of people, because those people who were coming to him were not in the same state in which he was when he asked Sekitō. He had been meditating with Sekitō for years. He was just on the verge...the last hit....

But the people who were coming were absolutely beginners, so with many nothing transpired. Once in a while, if a man had come from some other master...perhaps the master was dead, or perhaps he had become tired – how long had he to wait? And he became anxious: "My master is becoming old and I am not yet enlightened..." People like these who had been meditating and were just on the verge – this man Shōdai succeeded by hitting them. He knew only one hit – a poor Zen master.

There are poor Zen masters and rich Zen masters and super-rich Zen masters. You are caught up with a super Zen master! I hit you without hitting you. I hit you in so many ways, from every direction possible, and my hits are not cruel and primitive. They are very contemporary – in fact very few contemporary people are going to understand me. Perhaps a century or two centuries afterwards, my hits will shake people into awakening. But right now you are caught up, and you cannot go anywhere because you will not find me anywhere around the world. You will find just poor masters. Those super-rich masters have disappeared from the world.

We are living in a poorer world spiritually than before. Materially we are living in a richer world, but spiritually it is a very poor world. When Ma Tzu was there and Sekitō was there and Rinzai was there and Nangaku was there, Yakusan was there...there were so many masters just in Japan – or in China...! When Gautam Buddha was here in India there were eight masters just in the small province of Bihar, and they transpired hundreds of people into enlightenment.

But you are blessed. You have found a super-rich Zen master. Don't miss this opportunity, because the world has been becoming thinner and thinner as far as spirituality is concerned.

You have to create a great rebellion around the earth.

You have to upset all the organized religions.

Only then will people be liberated from their mind programs. And to liberate anybody from his mental programming, conditioning, is one of the greatest virtues. You are helping that man towards freedom. But you can help only if you are free. If you are not free, there is no possibility to help. A blind man cannot help another blind man. First you have to open your eyes and recognize *your* buddhahood, and then it is very easy to trigger the same experience in others.

There are many who are ready, on the verge, but there is nobody to push them. Everybody needs a push, and everybody needs a certain proof that buddhahood is a reality.

You will be surprised to know that when the Christian missionaries first came to India – and they were the first to translate the Buddhist scriptures into English – they did not think that a man like Buddha had ever been there. It seemed to them almost an impossibility; they had never heard about enlightenment. They had heard about prophets coming from God, they had heard about messiahs, messengers, they had heard about the only begotten son Jesus. They *believed* in them, but they had never heard about enlightenment.

Was Moses enlightened? Was Jesus enlightened? They had no answer. They had never heard about the phenomenon at all. So Buddha was a strange phenomenon. The early missionaries simply canceled the idea that he was a historical person. It took almost one hundred years of research for Christian missionaries to accept that Buddha was a real human being, not a fiction. This shows that they had been believing in fictions!

So they thought, deep down...nobody can believe in Jesus and his miracles. Howsoever great an effort you make to believe, the doubt will remain underneath and will surface whenever your belief will be shaken by something – and it will be shaken by anything, because a belief has no evidence, no proof.

Every Christian, every Jew, every Mohammedan, every Hindu, is living under such beliefs which they themselves know cannot be true. But out of fear they are accepting it.

But fear cannot transform you. There is only one way to be transformed, and that is to find your buddhahood. That will give you the proof that other buddhas have actually happened.

If you can become a buddha, you are the argument, you are the proof. And unless you know buddhahood you cannot come to a trust that such a miracle is possible. And it is the greatest miracle. Walking on water is just stupid; it is not a miracle.

It happened once....

A man came to Ramakrishna and he had trained himself in a certain yoga method. There are yoga methods by which you can throw all the air out of the body so you become a vacuum inside. You cannot remain in that vacuum for more than ten minutes, but ten minutes is enough to show that you can walk on water. If you are a vacuum you can walk on the water.

But it takes almost eighteen to twenty years to learn that method of creating the vacuum. Once you have created the vacuum...I have seen one man only. If you can create a vacuum you can do strange things. I have seen this man in my childhood, and my memory is absolutely clean about that man. I can see him still, because he was doing such a strange thing. From his prick he would drink water! And that is possible only if you can create a vacuum inside. Then the vacuum pulls the water, pumps the water in. But I have come across only one man. I have tried hard again to find somebody...

I asked him, "How long did it take for you?"

He said, "It is a very difficult job. It took at least twenty years for me to create the vacuum. And only for ten minutes...!"

A man came to Ramakrishna and he said, "I have heard much about you, but can you walk on water?"

Ramakrishna said, "That's nothing. You can?"

He said, "Of course."

Ramakrishna said, "I prefer riding on a cloud. Do you know the art?"

He said, "No, I have never heard."

Ramakrishna said, "How long did it take for you to learn the knack?"

The man said, "Eighteen years continuously I have been..."

Ramakrishna said, "You are an idiot. Because when I want to go on the Ganges" – and they both were sitting by the side of the Ganges under a beautiful tree where Ramakrishna used to sit and just watch the Ganges flowing. It is a beautiful place where Ramakrishna lived – outside Calcutta, a very silent, peaceful place. Just one temple existed at that time in which he lived, just on the bank of Ganges.

So Ramakrishna said, "Whenever I want to go there, you see that ferryboat? – it takes only two paisa. And that too, that boatman does not take from me. He says, 'Not from you...I earn enough, I can take you without it.' So when I can go to the other side without even giving two paisa, why should I waste eighteen years of my life in learning to walk on the water? And do you think it is something of spirituality? All the fishes are doing that, and there are so many water animals...so what is the point? How do you think it is connected with your spiritual growth? You wasted your eighteen years in sheer stupidity. And I don't ride on the clouds either. I was just trying to show you that even riding on the clouds will not be of any value."

The real value is: are you acquainted with your buddha?

It is the only thing that matters.

When Christians, the missionaries, came to know about Buddha and his scriptures they were very much amazed, because these sutras of Buddha have such beauty that the Bible simply fades away, looks very childish.

One great missionary in Japan had gone to see a Zen master, and he believed he could convert him. His idea was that if he could convert this Zen master, to whom even the emperor of Japan comes – and he had a large following – just converting this one man, he could convert the whole of Japan. The emperor would be converted, thousands of his disciples would be converted. So rather than working on ordinary people, it was better to work on this man. And certainly there are beautiful statements in the Bible, particularly the Sermon on the Mount, so he took the Bible.

He was greeted by the Zen master, and he said, "I have brought you my holy scripture. I would like to read it to you and I would like to know your opinion."

So he started reading the Sermon on the Mount. He had gone two or three lines when the Zen master said, "Stop. Whoever wrote it, in his next life he may become enlightened."

He did not even listen to the whole sermon. He said, "Just stop. Whoever wrote it, in his next life will become enlightened. But right now these sutras are coming from an unenlightened person."

Shocked, the missionary could not understand – "Jesus Christ is unenlightened?"

But the idea of enlightenment has never happened in the West. The very idea is missing. So it was very difficult for them to understand that there have been a totally different kind of people. They have always believed in God, his son, which is not possible without God. His prophets which come from God, his messengers, they come from God – everything comes from God. That hypothesis is fundamental. If you deny that, then the whole of Judaism, Christianity, Mohammedanism, all three religions flop down. They simply disappear with one hypothesis which is absolutely unproved.

Here they came to understand a totally different process. A buddha does not come from above, he comes from below and he rises upwards. You see the difference: he becomes godly as he goes on upwards. And all the Christian or Jewish or Mohammedan prophets and messiahs come from up to down.

Buddha is an evolution. It is an intrinsic potentiality that starts going upwards like a tree, and when the spring comes it blossoms. They have never thought that man becomes godly; they have always thought only God can come down. Hindus believe in incarnation – God comes as Krishna, God comes as Rama...

And it is absolutely clear that God has been coming so many times – and the world is such a mess! What has God done to the world? God comes in Krishna as a perfect incarnation – and what has that perfect incarnation done? Nobody asks the question: Why has he come in the first place? And if he has come then what has he done?

Krishna has promised, and Hindus are still believing that he will be coming. His promise is: "When there will be danger, when humanity will be in pain and anguish and anxiety, when there will be atheism spreading in the world, when saints will be tortured...whenever there will be such a crisis in religion, I will come." But I have been asking so-called Hindu saints, "The last time he came, what did he do? And why are you waiting for him? The last time he proved nothing. Even if he comes he is not going to do anything. And how many times has he come?"

Hindus believe that he has already come twenty-three times; the twenty-fourth time he has to come. But twenty-three times he has been a failure. That is enough proof: the twenty-fourth time he is not going to be a success.

And what have the prophets of the Jews done? And what have the prophets like Jesus or Mohammed done to Christianity or to Mohammedanism? They have created an ugly human psychology, neurotic. They have not been helping the evolution of consciousness.

So Buddha is completely a different category. He is not coming from any hypothesis downwards. He is not special. He is just an ordinary human being like you and me, but he starts growing his potentiality upwards. He touches the very stars, he grows roots into the earth, goes to the deepest possibility. He stands vertical, leaves the horizontal plane of consciousness which belongs to the animals. He is really a rebel, an authentic rebel.

Naturally, every word that has come from him has tremendous meaning, because he is not accepting any lies, any consolations. And he is not

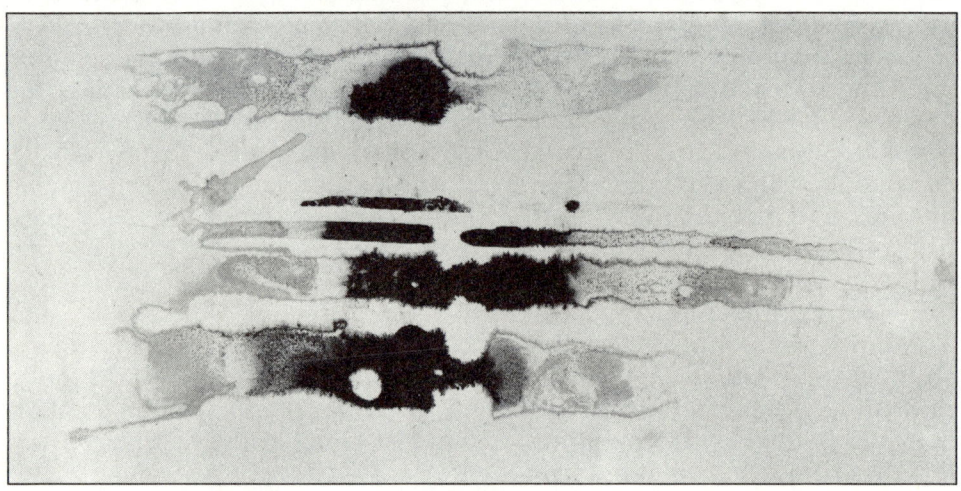

giving any lies to people or any consolations. He is simply saying what his experience is, and that it can be your experience also.

Buddha created a totally different world, and following him, masters upon masters...but certainly they remain a very thin stream. Buddha belongs to the very intelligent people. It is not for the mediocre, it is not for the retarded, it is not for the masses.

But if the intelligent people of the world rise into buddhahood, they will help the whole of humanity at least to see what is possible for a human being, what is hidden in us. And if thousands of people can bring it to blossoming, why cannot we?

Every buddha becomes a proof, an argument to the whole of humanity. He raises the level of existence spiritually, and each buddha goes on raising the level of humanity without your knowing. You are more close now after twenty-five centuries than you were when Buddha was alive.

Most of you must have been around him. Most of you must have been around other buddhas, because you are not new to the world. You have been here always, but you never managed up to now to go as intensely as possible. Hence my insistence: Don't miss this opportunity.

You have to decide – you have to be very decisive: "I have to bring my potential to its ultimate flowering. I have to become a celebration, a festival. I have to contribute to the beauty and truth and the divineness of existence."

Bashō wrote:

Early spring
a nameless hill knee deep
in the gauze of morning stillness.

These are all statements of meditators, and Bashō is a great master and simultaneously one of the greatest haiku poets.

"Early spring" – just visualize. "Early spring" – it has just come fresh.

The trees have been waiting for it, the earth has been waiting for it. Those who have some aesthetic sense – the painters, the poets, the musicians, the dancers, the sculptors – they have been waiting for it. It has come. Early spring – such a joy comes following with it, such freshness all around. Such fragrance of flowers.

"A nameless hill knee deep in the gauze of morning stillness." Even the hill is feeling the spring breeze, "knee deep in the gauze of morning stillness." Not only am I kneeling down in my gratitude for existence, for this fresh spring, but once more, the mountain is also knee deep – is as grateful as I am.

Early spring
a nameless hill knee deep
in the gauze of morning stillness.

Those small hours before the sunrise, when the night is just going and the sun has not arrived on the horizon, are the most peaceful. And meditators have found that that is the best time to meditate – particularly in the East, when those moments are the coolest in the day.

Perhaps it may not be true about the West; it may be too cold. Perhaps for the West the best time will be midnight. It is good for the East also, but the early morning when just the flowers are opening to welcome the sun, and the birds are fluttering their wings getting ready to sing their songs and dance into the air...

And that stillness... Night is gone, almost gone, and the morning is not born yet. That in-between moment has been given a special name in the East, *sandhya*. *Sandhya* means the interval between day and night. So it comes two times – in the morning and in the evening, when the sun has set and the night has not come. So these two times are called *sandhya*, intervals.

In these intervals you can meditate more deeply than at any other time. It is just an existential experience of thousands of meditators.

Bashō is expressing his own experience in this haiku.

Maneesha's question:
Our Beloved Master,
Paul Tillich, the Protestant theologian, asserted that "God will remain somehow remote and 'out there,' unless there is a complete turnabout in which all references to the high and the beyond are translated into terms of depth. This infinite and inexhaustible depth and ground of all beings is God. That depth is what the word 'God' means. He who knows about depth knows about God."

Would You like to comment?

Maneesha, Paul Tillich and all neo-theologians are trying their hardest somehow to save God, and there is no way to save him, he is already dead!

Now he is giving another idea: take God from there beyond the clouds and put him deep down. But what is the difference? Deep down where? – in America? Because from this place, if you go on digging you will suddenly see, My God! all Americans are walking upside down. Are they doing *shirshasan,* headstand? Because from here you will reach exactly into America – the shortest way. People are unnecessarily flying…just dig a hole! And from both the sides it can be started – from America towards India, and from India towards America. And the meeting will happen just in between.

But as far as America is concerned, India will be the depth. As far as India is concerned, America will be the depth. Where are you going to put God? In the depth? They are just trying absurdities to save the name God, because the danger is that God is becoming more and more an impossible hypothesis to prove.

So change his place. Take him out from the clouds, take him from there in the beyond, and put him there in the depth.

But you cannot save him. He is dead there in the beyond, and he will be dead in his grave in the depth. You are only digging a grave. Paul Tillich is just a gravedigger and nothing else.

And you can see clearly what he is saying, "God will remain somehow remote and 'out there,' unless there is a complete turnabout…" But still the distance will be the same.

First he was beyond in the clouds; now he will be deep inside the earth. In fact, it was easy to go to the clouds, going inside the earth will be more difficult. And you don't know what is inside the earth, volcanoes… It is all hot and melted. The deeper you go, you will come to a point when everything is melted. Fire, still alive, that comes through the volcanoes. You can see it. You are putting God there? I like the place. That will be his funeral pyre.

"This infinite and inexhaustible depth and ground of all beings *is* God." But he will cling to the word 'God'. There is no change, just the place has been changed. God is the same – he has moved the house. "That depth is what the word 'God' means." First he was the height, now he is the depth, but he *is.*

"He who knows about depth knows about God" – great!

Those who have known the depth or the height are the people who have declared there is no God. There is only a quality, a fragrance, which you cannot catch hold of, but you can feel overwhelmed by it. But it is not God, it is the very flavor of existence itself. It is the very life.

Why create an unnecessary hypothesis? Be a little scientific. In science it is an accepted fact that no unnecessary hypothesis should be accepted. Do with as few hypotheses as possible, because every hypothesis creates new problems and solves nothing – and particularly unproved hypotheses which for centuries man has been trying to prove and has failed.

All theologians have failed! No theologian has been able to give any proof for God. They are trying to do, Maneesha, something impossible.

God is dead, and it is good and great that God is dead, because it brings freedom and dignity to life, to existence. It destroys our spiritual slavery, it gives us a great pride that we are existence and nobody is above us.

One of the Baul mystics, Chandidas, has made a beautiful statement:
Saabaar upar manus satya, taahaar upar nahi.
He is a Bengali mystic; the statement is in Bengali.
Saabaar upar manus satya – above all is the truth of man.
Taahaar upar nahi – and beyond that there is nothing.

This is what I call the dignity of man, of life, of existence. Why unnecessarily drag humanity into slavery? Paul Tillich, and all those who are trying to save God, the neo-theologians of Christianity, are going to fail, because all that they can do is give new words, new meanings, new references, new addresses. But when you reach, you will find nothing. Neither is he beyond there, nor is he in the depth somewhere hiding.

God does not exist and has never been in existence.
Life exists.
Celebrate life.
Rejoice life.
Let life be your freedom, your pride, your dance, your celebration.

This is the right time for Sardar Gurudayal Singh. Put on the light!

Old Miss Crumbum, the Jehovah's Witness, is going round from door to door collecting money to send missionaries abroad. She knocks on the door of Hamish MacTavish, the Scotsman, and when Hamish opens the door she starts her speech.

"Praise the Lord, good sir!" intones Miss Crumbum. "We are planning to send twenty Witnesses of Jehovah to the African countries. Please give generously for our missionary service overseas!"

"Absolutely not!" replies Hamish. "I totally disapprove of those foreign missions."

"But, good sir," cries Miss Crumbum, "the scriptures command us to feed the hungry!"

"Well, that's fine," says Hamish, "but surely we can feed them on something cheaper than missionaries?"

The new priest in the village, young Father Fever, is coming to visit the Sidebottom household. So little Sally's mother gives her daughter some instructions.

"If the new priest asks you your name," says Mrs. Sidebottom, "say Sally-Jane. And if he asks you how old you are, say you are seven years old. And if he asks who made you, say, 'God made me!' Can you remember all that?"

"I think so," says Sally.

A few minutes later, young Father Fever arrives, puts down his hat and his Bible, and walks up to little Sally. He pats her on the head and says, "I am Father Fever, your new priest. And what is your name, little girl?"

"Sally-Jane," replies Sally.

"And how old are you, Sally-Jane?" asks the priest.

"Seven years old," replies Sally.

"Well, that is nice," says Fever. "And do you know who made you, Sally-Jane?"

Little Sally hesitates for a moment, and then says, "Shit! Mom did tell me, but I have forgotten the guy's name!"

Late one evening on the little Greek island of Crete, old Mrs. Lilypopolis is weeping into her black handkerchief, mourning the recent death of her old friend Mrs. Acreepolis.

"Ohhh!" wails old Mrs. Lilypopolis to Bishop Kretin who is holding her hand, "God is so unjust! He is knocking off us old ladies one by one. I must say, Bishop Kretin, that my faith in the Blessed Bleeding Virgin is beginning to wobble."

"Don't worry my child," comforts Bishop Kretin, impatiently. "You are only ninety-seven years old, you have lots of life in you still. Just pray to God Almighty and everything will be fine."

But over the next few days, old Mrs. Lilypopolis gets freaked out. She starts looking around for something else to strengthen her faith. One night she is wandering around the streets of the village and finds herself in Madam Goggle's fortune telling parlor.

"I have been a Blessed Bleeding Virgin Christian all my life," says old Mrs. Lilypopolis, "and you are a spiritualist and a pagan – but I have come to you because I have lost faith in Bishop Kretin. I come to you in the hope of receiving the answer to one question."

Madam Goggle nods her head and closes her eyes, lapsing into a deep trance.

"Go ahead," she says in a spiritual voice, "tell me your question."

"I want to know," says old lady Lilypopolis, "when I die, will I go to heaven – I mean my Christian heaven – to be reunited with my friends, Mrs. Souvlaki, Mrs. Theocrapolis and Mrs. Acreepolis, in the glory of eternal paradise?"

After some time in a deep trance, Madam Goggle opens her eyes and speaks, "I have asked the sacred ones if you will go to heaven," moans Madam Goggle. "And their answer is...their answer is..."

And the old fortune teller rubs her thumb and forefinger together under the old Greek woman's nose.

"Oh, yes!" cries old Mrs. Lilypopolis, fumbling in her purse and bringing out a handful of money. She puts it on the table and then Madam Goggle continues.

"Well, there is some good news and some bad news. First the good news.... Yes, Mrs. Lilypopolis, because you have been such a good person you will be transported by the heavenly angels to paradise – to the Golden Throne in the skies. And there you will remain throughout eternity with all the other blessed virgins, sitting on God's knee."

"Oh!" cries old Mrs. Lilypopolis, "Oh, I am completely overwhelmed!"

"Wait!" continues Madam Goggle. "And the bad news is..."

"But, Madam Goggle!" interrupts the old lady. "After such wonderful *good* news, what news could possibly be *bad?*"

"Well," says Madam Goggle, "you will be going there *tonight!*"

Nivedano...

Nivedano...

Be silent...
Close your eyes...
and feel your body to be completely frozen.
This is the right moment to enter in your inner world.
You have to reach just below your navel,
two inches exactly below, inside.
Gather your energy and total consciousness,
and rush with a deep urgency
as if this is going to be your last moment on the earth.
Only those who have such urgency and intensity
ever reach to their center of life.
Faster and faster...
Deeper and deeper...
As you are coming closer to your center,
a great silence descends over you just like soft rain falling.
You can feel the coolness.
A little closer,
and you find an explosion of light.
Your inner world becomes luminous.
A little deeper,
and flowers of blissfulness, flowers of ecstasy

suddenly start showering on you.
Existence is rejoicing in your inner journey.
This is the only spiritual pilgrimage.
Just one step more
and you are standing at the very center of your being.
This is the state of a Gautam Buddha,
the space of all the buddhas.
At this moment you are no more, only the buddha is.
And the buddha has only one quality:
witnessing.
Witness that you are not the body.
Witness that you are not the mind.
And witness that you are only the witness.
This pure witnessing
opens all the closed doors of existence and life,
of song and dance,
of the ultimate celebration of becoming one with the cosmos.

To make this witnessing deeper,
Nivedano…

Relax…
but continue to witness.
That is your very eternity – no beginning, no end…
infinite, inexhaustible, sacred.
This is your original face.
We in the East have symbolized Gautam Buddha's face
as everybody's original face –
that is only a symbol.
Recognize it!
And rejoice in its recognition.
At this moment you are the most blessed people on the earth.
Everybody is concerned with the trivia,
you are trying to explore the very center of life and existence.

Other than this,
there is no religiousness.
Other than this,
there is no spirituality.
And this experience is absolutely individual,
it has nothing to do with the collective,
with the society,
with an organized religion.
And from this opening,
you can see there is no God,
there is only godliness surrounding you –
all around limitless.
The height is infinite.
The depth is infinite,
but you don't find any God anywhere.
On the contrary,
you start melting and disappearing.
Gautama the Buddha Auditorium has become an ocean of consciousness.
Ten thousand buddhas have joined together into one consciousness.
This is your truth,
and this is the beauty of the truth,
and this is the divineness of the truth.
One who knows this center and this opening into existence,
knows all.
Collect as many flowers as you can of serenity,
of tranquility, of silence, of peace, of ecstasy,
of a divine drunkenness.
You have to bring all these juices of life
from the center to the surface of your day-to-day life.
You have to start living like a buddha,
with the same grace,
with the same beauty,
with the same truth,
with the same authenticity,
with the same originality.
This opening and the experience of it
will bring you a dignity which is not ego,
a pride which is not ego,
but simply a joy,

simply a remembrance that you are existential, not accidental.
Hence, the possibility of celebration.
The accidental person lives in anguish,
in anxiety, in angst.
The existential person lives in celebration,
in love, in grace, in gratitude.
Do not forget to persuade the buddha to come with you.
These are the three steps of enlightenment.
The first step,
buddha comes behind you as a shadow.
But the shadow is luminous, it has tremendous warmth,
and it surrounds you with a new fragrance,
fragrance of the beyond.
The next step, the second step,
you become the shadow, buddha comes in front of you.
Your shadow goes on becoming thinner and thinner
as buddha becomes more and more solid and existential.
A moment comes and the third step happens on its own accord:
your shadow has disappeared, you are no more;
only the buddha is, only life is, only the existence is.
Hence the celebration.

Nivedano…

Come back…
but come with all the glory and the splendor of a buddha,
with all the grace and silence and peace.
Sit down just for a few seconds
to remind yourself of the golden path that you have followed,
and the depth you have reached within yourself,
and all the experiences.
And feel the presence of buddha behind you.
The day is not far away
when the first step will turn into the second step,

and the second step will turn into the third step.
You will be no more.
And when you are no more
there is dance, there is song, there is joy,
there is celebration of life.
I celebrate myself,
and I teach you nothing else but celebration.
Religiousness has fallen into wrong hands,
and they have made the whole world sad and miserable.
I want the world to be filled with laughter, with joy, with festivity.
The whole life,
moment to moment has to be lived as a celebration.
That is the only religious life.
You have every potential and every opportunity.
Just a little relaxed effortless melting into the ocean that surrounds you –
and the dance begins.
And the dance never ends.

Okay, Maneesha?
Yes, Beloved Master.

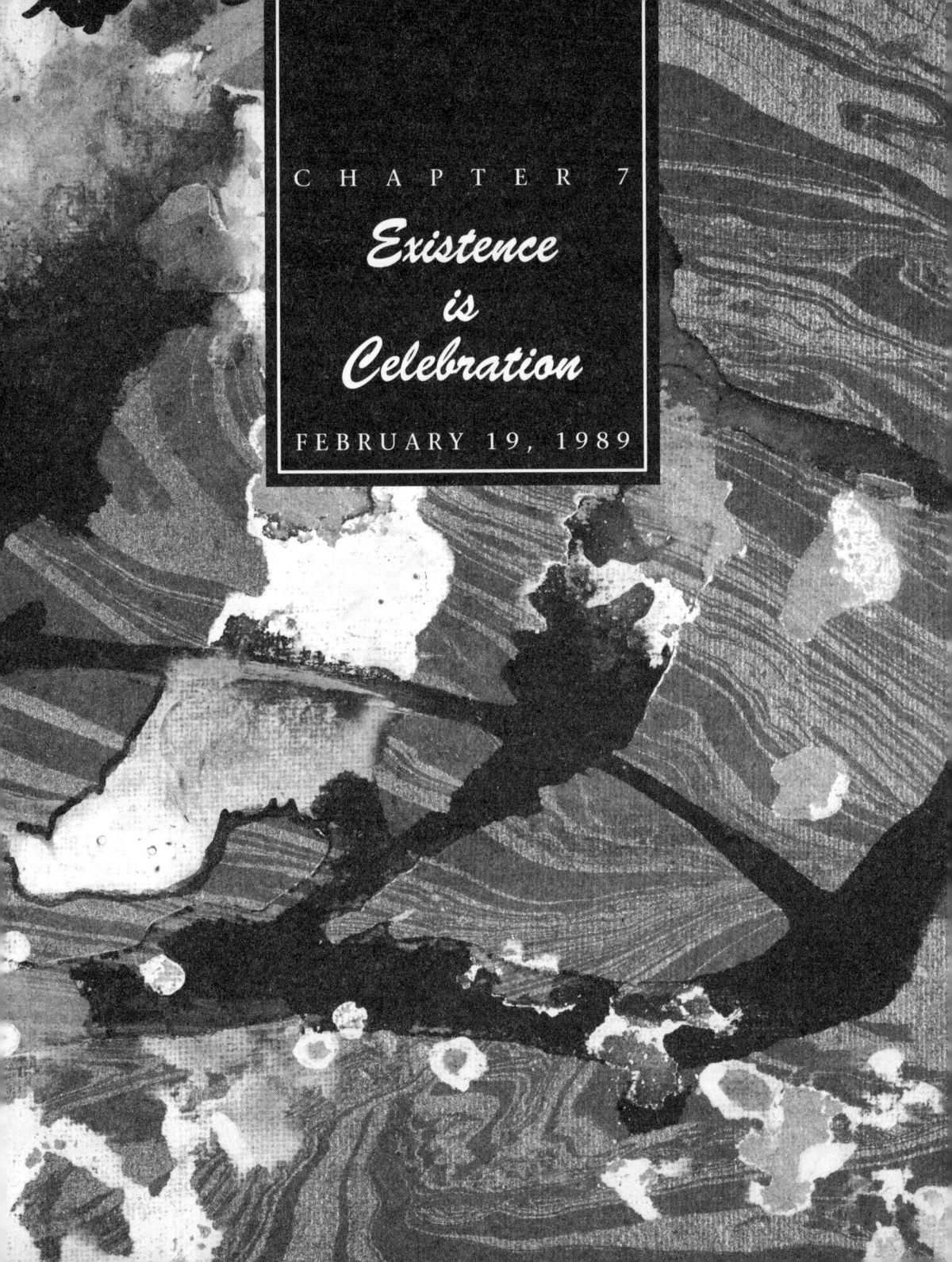

THE SUTRA

Our Beloved Master,

One day, Sekitō announced to everybody that the next day they would weed the grass in front of the Buddha Hall. The following day, all the monks gathered with sickles in their hands, but only Tanka came with a tray filled with water. Before coming there he had washed his hair, but it was not yet shaven. Now he kneeled down in front of Sekitō, and seeing him, Sekitō laughed, and shaved Tanka's head. As the master usually did, Sekitō gave Tanka some specific commandments, but as he did so, Tanka walked away covering his ears with his hands. Tanka then left for Kōsei to see Ma Tzu. Arriving at the monastery, he went into the hall and, climbing on the statue of Manjushri, sat there. The other monks were astonished and told Ma Tzu, who came in, looked at him and said, "My son is Tennen."
Tanka came down, made a bow and said, "Thank you for giving me a dharma name."
Ma Tzu then asked, "Where do you come from?"
Tanka said, "I come from Sekitō."
Ma Tzu said, "The path on the stonehead is slippery. Did you fall over?"
Tanka replied, "If I had fallen over, I wouldn't have come here."

Friends,

First the questions.
The first question:
It seems that never has any God-oriented religion been more anachronistic than it is today; yet curiously, Christianity at least seems to be blooming. Born-again Christians, Jesus freaks, and fundamentalist Christians are rife.
Are we seeing the phenomenon You have described when something is about to die? You have compared it to a candle going out, having a last, final spurt of energy before it splutters into extinction.

It is exactly what has happened. Not only is Christianity going out of existence, all religions as such are already out of date. They are living a posthumous life.

Whatever they have been teaching to humanity has been found criminal. Their God is a fiction, a lie. They all have been telling people to be truthful, and they are teaching lies about heaven and hell and God. They have made the whole of humanity hypocrite.

The misery that you see all over the earth is created by your religions. Once you make a man feel guilty he cannot enjoy life, he cannot rejoice in existence. You have cut his roots, the very roots that nourish your joy, your blissfulness.

All the religions have been against humanity. They are bound to go into extinction. The sooner they disappear from the earth the better. Man needs to sing with the birds, to dance with the trees. Man needs to rise to the heights of a Gautam Buddha.

The religions have not been helping any evolution of consciousness; on the contrary they are the greatest obstacles. Religion has become a business in the hands of the priests. And certainly an authentic religiousness has nothing to do with business. It has something to do with your blossoming, it has something to do with your initiation into eternity, into truth, into beauty, into good.

Religiousness has no way to make humanity spiritually slave, but that's what religions have done. Everybody is enslaved, oppressed, exploited. Everybody is being poisoned by the religions, forced to be unnatural. And the moment you force somebody to be unnatural you are committing the greatest crime against existence.

All the religions, God-oriented or not God-oriented, have been teaching man to renounce life. They are anti-life, they are against everything that can make you a whole person. Not only physically, not only psychologically, but spiritually too. They have been cutting you into pieces, and they have been trying for centuries, insistently, to enforce the idea of renouncement. This is not a right approach to existence.

The moment you start renouncing, you start shrinking. Rather than growing, rather than becoming vaster and infinite, you start shrinking into yourself. You lose all interest in existence, in love, because you are told to torture yourself.

Renunciation from the world is another name for self-torture. And a man who is torturing himself – how can you expect him to dance? How can you expect him to be ecstatic? He is committing a slow suicide. God-oriented religions, and not God-oriented religions – both are going to disappear.

Religion is an individual matter; it has nothing to do with collectivity. It is not a social phenomenon, it is very private, absolutely private, your innermost affair. Even love is not that much private, because at least two persons are involved in it. In meditation, nobody is involved – only you are. It is absolutely individualistic.

I teach you to be individuals.

Never belong to any organization, never belong to any holy scriptures, churches, temples. Never belong to any monastery. This whole existence is available for you – rejoice in it, celebrate in it.

No religion teaches celebration; they teach celibacy! I am absolutely against celibacy and all for celebration. I am making every effort to bring a new approach towards life which the past humanity has missed – a new freedom, a new sky to open your wings. All religions have been cutting your wings, putting you into cages and making you believe that this is all that life is. There was a reason for them to do this. Unless you take away people's individuality and destroy their wings and their freedom and cut their roots of nourishment, you cannot enslave them. It is impossible to create armies and wars; it is impossible to make millions of people suffer in poverty – they would have revolted long ago. But religions are keeping them subdued by the fear of God, by the fear of punishment in hell, and by the greed that if you follow their commandments you will be rewarded immensely.

I have told you about this man Salman Rushdie. The way Ayatollah Khomeini and the other religious leaders of Iran have behaved…ordinarily people think that this is very strange from a religious man. I want to tell you this is not – this is what religions have been doing for centuries.

Mohammed himself carried a sword his whole life, killing people, and he has given the name *Islam* to his religion, which means peace! And on his sword was written in letters of gold, "Peace is my message" – on the sword!

Ayatollah Khomeini is exactly behaving as religions have always done. It is absolutely irreligious behavior. But Ayatollah Khomeini is not the only one responsible for it, he is simply a representative of the whole past history of religions: killing, murder, crusades…fights over strange things.

Christians, Mohammedans and Jews, all three religions have been fighting over a strange idea which can be shared very easily, that Jerusalem is the holy city. So what is wrong? All three religions can enjoy going to Jerusalem. But they have been fighting. Jews have been claiming, "It is *our* holy city." And Christians of course were saying, "It is *our* holy city because Jesus was crucified here." And Jews are saying it is their holy city because the ancient Jewish temple used to exist in Jerusalem and there is still the great wall where Jews weep, cry – that is their prayer, in front of an ancient wall. You will find hundreds of Jews every day standing in front of the wall or kneeling down in front of the wall. It is *their* holy city.

And then came the Mohammedans and with a strange fiction they have made it their holy city. The fiction is that Mohammed went to heaven sitting on his horse, and just on way to heaven he stopped for a rest in Jerusalem. Now, I cannot conceive how Jerusalem comes on the way to heaven. It does not exist somewhere in the clouds….

So the rock on which he had rested for a few minutes before ascending to heaven is the holy rock. And because the holy rock is in Jerusalem, Mohammedans have been claiming, "It is our holy city." And all three religions have been fighting and killing for hundreds and thousands of years. I cannot understand why they all cannot share the holy city – they all can go and worship. But the very claim that it is "ours" is absolutely non-religious.

A religious person has no possessiveness. These are not religious people, they belong only to pseudo-religious organizations. And they are doing everything wrong in the name of God. That gives a sanctity to their immoral acts.

Ayatollah Khomeini's death sentence on four persons was absolutely immoral, absolutely unspiritual. And then another ayatollah came and declared that he would give 2.6 million dollars to the person who brings the head of Salman Rushdie to Iran.

I was hoping Salman Rushdie would prove to be a man of integrity – he did not. He has started falling from integrity, from individuality. Today he has requested Ayatollah Khomeini – "I can feel that I have hurt so many people's religious feelings..." Yesterday, Ayatollah Khomeini said that if Rushdie asks for forgiveness and is ready to receive a penance, then he can save his life. Otherwise there is no way.

This statement is not accurately speaking an apology, but just a recognition that he had unconsciously hurt the feelings of thousands of Mohammedans, and that he would be more careful in the future. But he was not aware that Ayatollah Khomeini is not a sane man. He rejected the statement, and said again on the radio, "Rushdie has not apologized and whatever he has said, we reject it."

Now Salman Rushdie has started falling. Soon he will have to apologize, and after apologizing, Ayatollah Khomeini will ask him to do penance – "Come to Kaaba and fast for one month..." Salman Rushdie has taken a wrong move. This is how people out of fear have been kept imprisoned.

I was hoping that a man of the intelligence of Salman Rushdie would prefer death to apologizing. He has not committed any sin, and he has not done anything wrong. I was hoping that he would put Ayatollah Khomeini in a corner. He should ask him, "On what grounds are you saying that I have committed anything against Islam? Tell me exactly what is the reason that you are asking for an apology or giving me a sentence to death." And that would have exposed Ayatollah Khomeini because none of these ayatollahs have given a reason.

Rushdie simply stated a historical fact, that a few of the verses which Mohammed wrote in an earlier version of the Koran he dropped later on saying that he had been inspired by the devil to write these verses. Now, this is a historical fact, it is not Salman Rushdie's imagination. Why should he ask forgiveness?

He should have said, "Give me the reasons," and he would have put these fanatics into a corner, because they cannot say what really is the problem. I want you to understand it because that will give you an insight into the murderous instinct of all the religions. This does not make any sense because it is a well-established fact, accepted by Mohammedan scholars for centuries, that a few verses have been dropped. And the statement of Mohammed is well known to those who have ever studied the Koran and the history of Islam. If anybody is at fault it is Mohammed, not Rushdie.

So they cannot really say these are the verses that are creating trouble, because then immediately the question arises that they are historical facts. So nobody has said what the problem is. The problem is that if Mohammed can be influenced by the devil, and he withdraws a few verses as the devil's inspired verses, that makes a crack in the whole fanatic idea that the Koran is infallible, that Mohammed is God's only *paigambar*, only authentic prophet. "One God, one prophet Mohammed, and one holy book the Koran" – these are the three basic principles of Mohammedanism. Accepting the fact that Mohammed could be influenced by the devil and could not recognize it for many years makes the whole Koran dubious, makes the prophet Mohammed fallible. These are the reasons hidden behind, implied, and they cannot say why they are so angry.

They are angry because if the whole world knows that Mohammed could be deceived by the devil, then he is not a perfect prophet of God. What about the other verses in the Koran? Who knows which verses are inspired by the devil, which verses are inspired by God? Just to avoid this implication becoming clear to everybody, these people are getting mad.

For the same reason, Galileo was called by the pope. He had written that it is not the sun that goes around the earth but on the contrary, it is the earth that goes around the sun. But the Bible states the commonsense view. Just as we see the sun rising in the morning and going around from the east to the west, setting, so it appears that the sun is going around the earth. This is a commonsense view. But the question that Galileo had asked the pope was, "Why are you are so much afraid of a truth? I have been experimenting; this is my whole life's work. And even if I withdraw the sentence that you are wanting me to withdraw, neither is the earth going to change its course nor the sun, because they don't read my books. The earth will go on circling the sun. But why are you afraid?"

Galileo had asked, and he had cornered the pope: "You either prove that I am wrong on scientific grounds...because it is not a religious matter at all. What has religion to do with whether the sun goes around the earth or the earth goes around the sun? It has nothing to do with any spirituality, it is a scientific area. If anybody can prove anything scientifically against me, then of course I will withdraw. But why are you afraid?"

Cornered in this way, the pope had to accept that the real problem was: "We are not concerned whether the earth goes around, or the sun. Our concern is that even if one sentence in the Bible is found to be wrong, the whole credibility of the Bible goes. Then it is not a work of God. God is infallible, God cannot commit such a mistake. He made the earth, he made the sun, and he does not know who goes around.

"The point is that one sentence proved wrong will create doubt about the whole authenticity of the Bible, so we cannot allow you to create this doubt in people's minds."

Galileo was very old, almost on his deathbed. He had been dragged from his deathbed to the court of the pope. He said, "I don't want to get into any unnecessary trouble. I am already dying. So I will cancel the sentence." And he must have been a man of a great sense of humor. He canceled the sentence. But in a footnote he wrote, "Although I am canceling this sentence, the fact is that the earth goes around the sun. They are not going to listen to me, and they don't follow any religion and they are not Christians."

Certainly the earth is not Christian, nor is the sun Christian. And certainly whoever wrote the Bible is not omniscient, is not infallible.

Hundreds of facts have been found in these three hundred years after Galileo which go against the Bible, which go against the Koran, which go against the Vedas...which go against every religious scripture in the world. And that proves that these books have not been written by God, or written by the only begotten son of God, Jesus Christ, or by prophets like Mohammed or Moses who represent God. And they are the messengers.... Certainly these messages are their imagination.

All these holy scriptures are full of common sense, not of any scientific inquiry, nor of any spiritual inquiry.

It is so strange to read the holy scriptures. They look such rubbish that even newspapers seem to be more important. And if God is writing, or his special messengers are writing these scriptures, they cannot be counted sane.

My whole understanding is that all these prophets and messiahs and avataras and tirthankaras – the founders of all the religions – are basically megalomaniacs, great egoists. This is the greatest ego in the world, that you are related with God in a manner nobody else is related.

That's why Jesus excludes the idea that there is another son, another brother to him, or another sister. God has only one begotten son and that is Jesus Christ. Why does Mohammed close the doors – "I am the last prophet of God; now there will be no more prophets coming. So the holy Koran is the final message from God; no correction can be made in it." But he himself corrected it, and he himself accepted that he was inspired by the devil.

Religions have been repressing truths, and now it is time that the truth should be declared, freedom should be declared, individuality should be declared. Man has lived under slavery long enough. The night has been too long; a new dawn is needed. A new man is needed, a new humanity is needed, and that humanity necessarily needs all these so-called religions to disappear from the earth.

They are having their last breaths, so your question is exactly right. The same is the case with a candle going out – having a last final spurt of energy before it splutters into extinction.

This happens to man also. Physicians have been observing it for centuries that before death the person becomes perfectly healthy; all his diseases disappear. And they could not understand – "What is happening? He is going to die; the logical thing would be that his diseases become more dangerous because they are going to kill him. But at the last moment all diseases disappear."

It is the last spurt of energy. Before going into darkness, the candle flares up. And many times, physicians have been deceived by this flaring up of energy; they think they have cured the person. And by the time they have reached home, the phone rings to say that the man is dead. And they were thinking they had cured him, because everything becomes normal before death. The man is making his last effort – of course unconsciously – to remain alive. He is for the first time being total, so the whole energy is gathered. That gathering of the energy gives a false appearance of health as if he is cured.

All these religions are gathering their whole energy – the last flare-up of life before they disappear forever with their God, with their priests, with their monks, with their churches, with their holy scriptures. That day will be the greatest day in the history of man. Man will become free.

Hence I say that the days for celebration are coming closer. Get ready!

Celibacy is no longer scientific; we have to fill up the gap with celebration. Renunciation is no longer logical, rational; we have to fill the gap with rejoicing. That is the reason so-called religious people are against me, because they can see what I am saying destroys their lies and their fictions and their consolations. This destruction they call "having their religious feelings hurt."

Just today one man has asked the government of India, "Just as you have banned Salman Rushdie's book, why don't you ban Osho's books which are far more dangerous?" It is true, they are far more dangerous. Rushdie has not done anything, and is unnecessarily being harassed. If you harass me that will be absolutely right, because I am stating things against every religion.

But to ask the government to ban my books is to accept defeat. Why can't you argue with me? Why can't you bring a dialogue into existence? If you think your religious ideology is right, I am ready for any challenge to discuss it. Why are you afraid? In a cultured society, in a democratic nation it is against the constitution to take away anybody's freedom of speech. I am ready to confront anybody – Hindu, Mohammedan, Christian, Jaina, Buddhist. Whoever they are, I am ready to confront them, but because they don't have any way to answer my questions they immediately take the course of asking the government.

The Indian government is secular, it has no way to defend any religion or anybody's religious feelings. And it is barbarious to ask the government; it simply shows you are primitive and you don't know how to behave in a civilized way.

If Ayatollah Khomeini was a civilized, sane man, he would have asked Rushdie, "Are you ready for an argument?" To declare a death sentence… and Mohammedan criminals, professional murderers have already entered Britain from different Mohammedan countries. Even Pakistan has sent people. I was shocked because the woman who is now the president of Pakistan, her father, Bhutto, was sentenced to death for no reason at all. He was the most prominent person in Pakistan, the most influential person. And because of him, the man who was in power – he was a military general, it was a military dictatorship – was afraid to call elections, so he was tolerating and making excuses and postponing. But how long can you postpone? People were asking again and again, "Why are elections not happening?" And the reason was that Bhutto was alive. He used to be the president of the country, and this was a takeover by the army, by force. Bhutto had to be killed before the elections.

So they brought all kinds of imaginary crimes that he had not committed. He was a well educated man, and he was not a fanatic. They killed him. No appeal was granted to him; he could not appeal to the president for mercy. It was against Pakistan's constitution, against Pakistan's law, but General Zia, who was in power, was not a man of any influence with the public. He had come into power by force and violence because he was the commander-in-chief of all the forces – the navy, the air force, and the army.

It was just luck that a few days ago, General Zia, with his seventy-four most intimate people from all the armies, had an accident, an airplane accident, and all seventy-five people died.

This woman is General Zia's enemy and has been fighting from Britain, trying to get into Pakistan. And General Zia was not allowing her, because people would have sympathy for her because her father had been killed illegally, unconstitutionally. But when Zia was dead she immediately rushed to Pakistan and she has been elected. Now she is the president – a young woman, well educated, but she is doing the same stupidity as Zia did. Zia killed her father without any reason or rhyme, simply because he was the most impressive person in the country and Zia could not stand against him and win the elections. That was the reason.

Now, I was thinking that this woman would behave – and she has been educated in Britain, just as her father was educated in Britain – in a different way. First, she is a woman, and has more heart than any man. Secondly, her father has been killed. She should reconsider the very desire for killing people. And now she has sent a death squad to Britain, professional murderers, to kill Rushdie and the other three persons who are involved in the publication of the book.

It seems people don't learn at all. That's why history goes on repeating. The repetition of history simply shows that people don't learn at all. Otherwise, there is no reason for history to repeat – if you learn, you only commit a mistake once, not twice. That's what learning means: commit as many mistakes as you want, but only commit one mistake once. Committing mistakes is not bad – that is the only way of learning; you have to commit mistakes. If you don't commit mistakes you cannot find the way from this darkness that surrounds the earth. But don't commit the same mistake, otherwise you will be in a vicious circle.

Committing the same mistake again simply shows you are unconscious, you are not behaving consciously. Now, this woman, Bhutto's daughter, is doing the same as Zia was doing. And the man, Rushdie, has not done anything wrong.

But he seems to be a coward. And because of these cowards these insane people have been in power.

I am ready for any argument with anybody, because I know their whole religious belief is absolutely unfounded. They cannot prove God, they cannot prove heaven, they cannot prove hell. They cannot prove that God created the world, because there is no witness. How have you found it? Who told you? Obviously there cannot have been any witness when God created the world. If there was a witness, the world was already there. It is intrinsically rational to accept that there cannot be any witness – because there was no world. From where will the witness come? So God cannot have a witness; then how have these people come to know? From whom?

Their whole idea is based on the lie of God. And I always strike at the very foundation, I don't bother about the branches and the leaves. I cut the very roots. And they cannot defend, because they don't have any foundation to their temple.

I once went to see a temple which is a very rare temple, near Indore. There is a very small village where the temple is; it is a Jaina temple. Jainas have the mythology that the temple has fallen from heaven. It does not look very heavenly....

And it fell because the gods – Jainism does not believe in God, it believes in gods – and the devils were fighting about who should own the temple. The fight was going on just above the clouds, and they became so much engaged in fighting that they lost control of the temple and it fell near the village.

The only reason they could manage to create this mythology was that the temple has no foundation. You can put a thin wire underneath and you can go around the whole temple. The wire goes through to the other side. Then two persons can take the wire and go around the whole temple – it is a round temple, it has no foundation at all.

So this has given the idea that it must have fallen, because how can you make a temple without a foundation?

It can be made, there is not much problem in it. It is a small temple, and just some architect's imagination to make something absolutely new...he had raised this temple without any foundation.

But when I went to see the temple – a few friends had accompanied me from Indore, and they were all amazed. They said, "Perhaps the mythology is true."

I said, "You are idiots! No temple has any foundation. No church has any foundation. No belief system has any foundation. This temple is proof!"

Humanity requires a totally different approach. We should discuss. Why is there so much fear about discussing? The fear is valid – they know they cannot win. All their religions are slipping out of their hands; they cannot win, they are fighting a losing battle. If they are men of intelligence it is better that they come out of the temples and the churches and the monasteries and declare their independence.

My whole effort is to give you freedom from all chains, from all prisons, so that you can celebrate life.

Friedrich Nietzsche's statement, "God is dead; hence man is free"...but free for what? That he has no idea. That's why he went insane. God was dead – that was the consolation. Now the consolation is gone and there is a vacuum. If you leave the vacuum, the whole of humanity is going to be mad.

Great intellectuals in the West have committed suicide or gone mad. In fact it has become almost a criterion: if you don't go mad or you don't commit suicide you are not much of an intellectual! The greatest intellectuals have gone mad, have suffered suicide, because they could not find how to live without God. Without heaven and hell, how to live? They suddenly saw their future was complete darkness, death. To live for death...? Without God they lost all reason for living.

And my whole effort is that before your God is taken away – and it is going to be taken away, because it has no foundation in truth – you should learn the art of living. You should learn the art of celebration so you never suffer the vacuum which creates insanity and all kinds of neurosis, psychosis.

Even the founder of psychoanalysis, Sigmund Freud, because he did not believe in God... He said God is a father fixation – and his analysis is correct, intellectually correct. That's why you call God "the Father" and that's why you call even the Catholic priest "father" – who has no wife, no children! What kind of father...? At least God has only one begotten son, something to brag about. But these Catholic priests – unless they have illegitimate children – cannot claim to be called fathers. It is very strange – what kind of father...?

Sigmund Freud is right that the child grows up with the idea that the father is his security. He is so powerful to the small child, seems to be all-powerful, he can do anything. But as he grows he finds that the father is not all-powerful. His security starts disappearing, he starts feeling insecure, unsafe.

Sigmund Freud's analysis was that this fear of losing security and safety has been the cause of creating a Father God far away in the sky, who never dies, who is always there to protect you; he is compassionate... Jesus says, "God is love." He will be very loving and very compassionate, so you need not be worried about anything. All that you have to do is to believe in God.

But once this God is found to be dead, as Nietzsche found – that we are carrying a corpse, God is dead... He was not aware that he himself was going to get into trouble, because his own make-up was of a father-fixation psychology. Now he found the father – even the ultimate father – is dead. These temporary fathers go on dying; it is okay. "Daddy" has been always dead, nothing much in it. But the eternal God...to find him dead is such a shock that although Friedrich Nietzsche wrote it, after writing it immediately he went mad.

The moment he concluded *Thus Spake Zarathustra,* where he states this sentence that "God is dead and man is free," he started behaving strangely. And finally, his friends, and particularly his sister who was taking care of him, had to put him into a madhouse.

He could not find the alternative. "God is dead and man is free" – but free for what? That he does not say at all in the whole book. And just to be free is not enough. Free *from* something is not enough, you have to be free *for* something. So there are two sides of freedom – from and for. You can be free from God, but if you don't have any freedom *for* you will go mad. That consolation has been very ancient and very deep rooted; it will kill you. You cannot live in insecurity, you need an immediate alternative – freedom *for*.

Freedom for celebration, freedom for meditation, freedom for rejoicing, freedom for dancing – because God is dead. Now there is nobody above you and you are ultimately free from any spiritual slavery. Now you can dance without any guilt. You can love without any guilt. You can live as abundantly as possible. There is nobody to dominate you, and there is nobody to send commandments to you, and there is nobody to frighten you with hellfire, and there is nobody to provoke your greed for heavenly pleasures.

Sigmund Freud analyzed from a different angle, psychoanalysis. But he found himself in the same trouble as Nietzsche. He never went mad, but almost touched the boundaries. Because God was no longer there, death became the only thing that you are moving towards. He became so much afraid of death – God was a security, he would be there to welcome you after death. Now there is no one, now once you enter this tunnel of death there is no way out. He became so much afraid that even the word 'death' was prohibited. He had hundreds of disciples, he created the whole movement of psychoanalysis. It was prohibited in his presence ever to mention the word 'death', because it was so frightening that the moment somebody mentioned death he would fall into a fit and start foaming from the mouth.

And this is your great psychoanalyst. But he was suffering from the same problem. God was the security. He psychoanalyzed people and found that there is no God, it is just an invention of a sick mind. Logically right...but what about himself?

You will be surprised to know that Sigmund Freud founded psychoanalysis but he himself was never psychoanalyzed, because he refused. He was asked again and again by his disciples, who had become well-known psychoanalysts. They said, "It will be good if you yourself get psychoanalyzed. Now we are ready, you have prepared us so we know the whole technique. And we would like to look into *your* dreams. It will be an immense treasure to find out the dreams of the man who found dream analysis."

He refused. And the reason he refused was he was afraid because he was boiling with the same repressed desires as you are boiling. It would be a great threat to his whole movement if people came to know his dreams. They would be as sexual, as criminal, as anybody's – maybe more. Why was he afraid? He knew his dreams.

And that shows that the man was not well psychologically, although he was the founder of psychoanalysis.

And this goes on and on. Psychoanalysts themselves are the most highly vulnerable group of people to become insane. And they go on psychoanalyzing each other. But that does not bring sanity, that brings only normal insanity.

The whole of humanity is normally insane – a few people become abnormally insane; they go beyond the border of common sense. But the difference between your insane and the so-called sane is only of degrees. Perhaps you are ninety-nine degrees and the other person has gone to one hundred and one – past that line. And all that psychoanalysis is to bring him back to the ninety-nine degree insanity. One hundred and one degrees is dangerous.

The whole of psychoanalysis and all kinds of other schools that have developed – analytical psychology, or psychosynthesis, Assagioli, Carl Gustav Jung, Adler, and then there is a long line of people who are inventing their own therapies – they are as sick people as anybody. Your priests are as ignorant as anybody, your psychoanalysts are more in danger than you are – because they know there is no God. Your philosophers, your giants of intellect are in more danger than the retarded people. The retarded people don't worry at all; they don't know that God is dead. They have not heard it yet.

But sooner or later they are going to hear it. How long can it remain a secret? The priests have been keeping it a secret too long, and now they are themselves becoming aware that there is no God as they used to believe. So they are inventing new gods – a last flare-up of energy before the candle goes out and it becomes dark.

My effort is not an ordinary religious sermonizing. My effort is, before this candle goes out you should have your inner light ready, so you don't fall into darkness, that you don't go mad. I want you consciously to drop God, consciously to drop all lies and fictions in the name of religion, and start the other side. First, freedom *from,* and then the other side, freedom *for* – freedom for celebration, freedom for rejoicing.

Now there is no longer any point in renouncing. Nobody is going to reward you; don't unnecessarily torture yourself. The whole sky is open for the first time; just open your wings and enjoy this freedom.

Very few people are capable of enjoying this freedom, because they don't know how to dance. They have become crippled. They don't know how to sing, they don't know how to love. People say to each other, "I love you" – but just ask them, "What do you mean?" They will shrug their shoulders and they will say, "I don't know…"

But what *is* love? Their love is just a fiction. You cannot love anybody unless you know yourself. *You* are not there – who is going to love? You cannot love anybody unless love starts like a flood and starts overflowing you.

First you must have love, then you can share it.

But do you have love? It is a by-product of meditation. Only people who have meditated deeply know what love is, and then there is no question of "falling" in love. Then comes the rising in love, you go higher and higher; your love becomes your religion, your love becomes your very existence.

I teach you love, not renunciation.

I teach you celebration, not celibacy.

I teach you to be natural, to be existential.

Then you will find yourself being very creative in some dimension or other, and you will not be suffering from a vacuum.

Celebration has to fill up your vacuum, otherwise the whole of humanity is going to suffer badly. These religions are dead. Sooner or later everybody is going to recognize the fact and then there will be an immense vacuum which God used to fill. It was a lie, but it was a great consolation that there was somebody who was caring for you, who was your security. Even in death you need not be worried – beyond death is paradise.

But now there is no paradise, no God. Nobody is waiting for you beyond death. You will be going alone.

You have to learn how to be alone.

You have to learn how to rejoice to be alone. You have to learn how to dance – alone; there is no need for spectators. And there is no need even for partners. You can dance alone the way a rose dances in the wind, in the air, in the sun, in the rain. Do you think the rose is waiting for spectators or for partners?

Meditation gives you the deep insight into your aloneness. And remember the difference: aloneness is not loneliness. If you don't learn aloneness, you will feel yourself very lonely. God no more, all consolation gone, no paradise after death...suddenly you feel accidental, not wanted by existence, not needed by any God. You don't have any purpose, you don't have any meaning. Suddenly your whole personality which was supported by lies, falls down.

This is what brings neurosis, breakdown.

Unless you learn meditation you cannot change your breakdown into a breakthrough. The whole alchemy of meditation is to change breakdown into breakthrough, to teach you freedom *for*.

Freedom *from* is simply clearing the ground, creating a dancing hall, removing all gods and temples who are cluttering the whole space.

You cannot dance in a church, where everywhere you see all around Jesus crucified with a long face – and you can celebrate this situation?

A small boy was for the first time found doing homework. His parents were surprised, because he never did it.

They asked, "What is the matter? We have been telling you to do homework and you never listen – what happened?"

He said, "The new school..."

They had changed him from the old school because they had changed their neighborhood, so he had to go into a new school. The new school was a convent school, and the little boy said to his parents, "In this school they have one Jew named Jesus, crucified everywhere – and I am the only other Jew in the whole school! So I have to do homework and everything they say. Immediately I do it, because I don't want to be crucified!"

He is being very sensible and very rational. He is only the second Jew... His number is just number two – one has been already crucified. Maybe he was not doing his homework or something....

You cannot dance when Jesus is crucified. When all your gods are watching you, you cannot love. It is loving in a crowd of gods, who will be all pointing their Saint Finger towards you: "You are committing a crime!"

You have to throw away all these gods. They are all man-made, so there is no need to be worried; they are our creation. We have invented beautiful lies to console ourselves, so we are absolutely capable of throwing them away; nobody can prevent you.

But you have to learn, side by side. As you are clearing the ground, start singing a tune. Start moving your legs; get out of the crippledness of centuries. It is not only Jesus who is crucified – all those who believe in Jesus are living a crucified life, crippled. Of course Jesus cannot dance!

That would have been a real miracle, if he had danced on the cross. He could not even laugh – that would have been a real miracle. But he is so sad that perhaps he is having second thoughts…

And he shouted at God, with anger, "Have you forsaken me?" Because he was waiting for six hours, and not a single white cloud. The whole sky was blue, as far he could see. There was no sign of God coming.

At least he could have sent some saints – if he was not coming then servants would do. But somebody should have been there! Six hours he has been on the cross, waiting and waiting, and looking all around, and finally finding, "It seems that I have lived in a false consolation." He died in sadness.

That sadness pervades every church, and that sadness has become ingrained all over the world, not only amongst the Christians. Christianity is the biggest religion in the world; half of the earth is Christian – but other religions have been immensely influenced, without their knowing, by Christianity.

For example, a man like Mahatma Gandhi. I have looked very carefully and I have found that ninety percent he was a Christian, nine percent he was a Jaina, one percent he was a Hindu – and he was born a Hindu. What happened? In his life, three times he was just on the verge of being converted into Christianity. His wife just made such a fuss that he stopped. He said, "Okay, wait…" It was the wife who prevented him from becoming Christian. Many wives are doing great jobs! She would start beating her chest and crying, "We are Hindu, and what are you doing?" And she would make such a scene that neighbors would gather and they would say, "This is not good. She is right – why are you becoming a Christian?"

But he was influenced, and it is happening all over. You can see how Christianity is influencing – because they serve the poor, every religion starts serving the poor. Otherwise they will not look so religious as the Christians. The Christians are taking care of the orphans, so Hindus have to open orphanages, otherwise their religion will look a little unconcerned about suffering people. So they open hospitals, which they have never done in the past. They have been in existence thousands of years before Christ and they have never made hospitals, they have never served the poor. They have told the poor, "You are suffering from your evil acts of the past life, so there is nothing to be done. You just finish it! Get cleared out."

But Christianity has been a tremendous influence. It has poisoned almost the whole of humanity, made them sad and miserable.

So once you start feeling a vacuum, your sanity is at risk. Before the vacuum comes, I want you to learn how to fill it with beautiful songs and flowers and ecstasy, and a divine drunkenness and a festivity.

The only art of life is to transform it into a celebration.

The second question I have already answered. It is:
Is it because of God that society created madhouses?

Of course! Without God there is no need for madhouses. The pagans who don't have any God never go mad. Animals never go mad – I mean animals in wildlife. Animals in a zoo of course go mad, because they are living amongst insane human beings. In a zoo they start being influenced by human beings; only in a zoo do they start behaving unnaturally. Only in a zoo has it been found that animals turn into homosexuals because they can't find a female animal.

A zoo has to be studied very carefully. Your monasteries are zoos where you cannot find a woman; your nunneries are zoos where you cannot find a man. Then women turn into lesbians, and men turn into homosexuals.

All perversions you can see in a zoo. In a zoo, animals go mad – but only in a zoo. It seems that human insanity is infectious. But in wildlife, in the forest, no animal has been ever found insane – utterly intelligent, utterly sensitive, alert, completely alert. Because they don't have any god, they don't need any madhouses.

God creates guilt. Guilt creates unnatural behavior. Unnatural behavior leads you into madhouses. It is a very cunning device. Priests and psychoanalysts are in a deep conspiracy without perhaps knowing it. The priest creates the mad, and the psychoanalysts try to cure them. And back they go to the church!

People are moving between the church and the couch of the psychoanalyst, and they don't understand the secret conspiracy.

The third question:
Could it be that the word 'God' in ancient times, before the priests, was used by people to explain the unexplainable, the divine existence, the nature of being, the buddha?

Before the priest there was no God – not even the word. God and priests come simultaneously. In fact the priest will be needed to come in first; then he brings God in. God cannot exist without priests.

There was no God before the priests. People were just pagans; they loved life, they rejoiced in life. They had no idea of heaven or hell. This earth was enough, this life was too much; they lived moment to moment. In fact they had no idea of calendar and time, because they had no watches and no calendars. They had no idea when the year ends and when the year begins. They had no idea how many days are in a week, how many days are in a month, how many months there are in a year. All these things came very late.

If you had gone to the real, the original people on the earth they were the happiest people ever. They simply lived – without fear, without greed. They loved nature. Everything was mysterious, miraculous. A sunrise again, and they danced; a full moon again, and the whole night they danced to abandon. They had no God and they had no madhouses; they had no priests and no psychoanalysts. They had not heard about the buddha, yet they were all buddhas. But very natural buddhas, not philosophizing about it, so they never used words like "inexpressible, unexplainable, the divine existence, the nature of being, the buddha…" All this nonsense comes afterwards!

When the priests came they took power in their hands and declared, "We represent God…" It took a little longer time for the priests to invent God and slowly slowly refine it. And they are still refining and trying to deceive humanity even into the future. That was what Paul Tillich was doing – trying to improve the image of God. If God has failed as someone far away there, beyond, perhaps we should change his place.

That shows that it is our idea that he is there: "We should change our idea. That idea has failed; it worked long enough. Now put God into the depths. Not faraway there, but faraway *there*." But it is far away always, because they cannot put it close by. Close by you will see this is not God.

So it has to be far away – either way, this side or that side. But far away has to be there between you and him, an unbridgeable distance so you never can come to see him and take a close-up photograph.

No photograph exists because nobody has ever been close to God to take a photograph.

Priests have been trying to improve the image so it appeals again to the newer generations, but now they cannot manage it. Once it is declared God is dead, you may go on giving him artificial breathing, but everybody knows he is on artificial breathing. Just switch off and the fellow is gone.

A little biographical note before the sutras…
As a young man, Tanka Tennen first studied Confucianism.
Confucius seems to be a giant in creating confusion! He has confused the whole of China for centuries.

He has no God, but he substitutes God with morality, and he makes so much of moral preachings that people have to live in a tight space, almost imprisoned. And he became a great influence over China.

He was a great intellectual, no doubt, but he never looked beyond intellect. So whatever he says is just rationalization, creating more convenient societies. Etiquette, morality, behavior, all are based on creating a better society. It is because of Confucius that China easily became communist, although Confucius lived twenty-five centuries ago, a contemporary of Gautam Buddha and Lao Tzu and Socrates.

China's conversion to communism is strange, because it was a poor country, it did not have a capitalist class to exploit. It was still feudal with landlords; it was an agricultural society. It has not come to technology yet.

Marx failed in all his prophecies. He is the greatest failure as a prophet. He never said that Russia would become communist, or China would become communist, no. He could not conceive, because these countries were not even capitalist; communism can only come, according to him, after capitalism has developed to its climax and society is completely divided between the proletariat, the have-nots, and the bourgeois, the haves – a clear-cut distinction. Naturally the haves will be in the minority and the have-nots will have a tremendous majority.

In his Communist Manifesto the last line is: "Proletariat of the whole world unite. You have nothing to lose except your chains." When you have nothing to lose, revolution is possible. But if you have something to lose you cannot become part of a revolution; there is danger, you may not get anything. And what you have got may get lost – that may also be taken away.

China and Russia both were never conceived. Not even for a single moment did it come to Karl Marx's mind that they would become the first communists – vast countries, both together almost half of the world.

China became communist because of Confucius, because Confucius was absolutely materialist. No God, no heaven, no hell; you come from nothingness and you go to nothingness. There is no life before birth, and there is no life after death. So all that you have got are these seventy, eighty, ninety, perhaps one hundred years. Make the most of it. So his whole teaching is a materialist morality. Because you are not alone, you are living in a society, you have to take care that you don't trespass other people.

His whole idea is ethical, not religious. He managed to lay the foundation of the Chinese mind, and Karl Marx immediately got a completely ready-made foundation: materialist, atheist, believing only in this life, no eternal being, no eternal life. That was the reason China easily became communist. Confucius had done almost half the work.

But he was a well-known teacher, so people used to go to that great scholar. Even the emperors used to send their sons to learn how to be utterly moral. That would give you the ego – he created ego. He believed in strengthening your ego, polishing your ego; giving it a prestige, an image that would be respectable in society. But he had nothing of religiousness in him.

So when this young man, Tanka Tennen, first studied Confucianism… he had gone there in search of something essential, not outward behavior. One day he was on his way to the city – frustrated with Confucius; all that he was saying was about social behavior. He was the first behavioral psychologist.

One day he was on his way to the city when he came across a man of Zen, who asked where he was going.

Tanka replied, "I am going for the government service examination."

That was the most respected, prestigious profession, and being a student of Confucius he would be accepted for any high post. The very recommendation, that he had been with Confucius, was grounds enough that he was the right man.

The Zen man said, "Master Ma Tzu is working in Kōsei county. That is the place for choosing buddhas – you must go there."

"Rather than going into government service, at least give it a try. Ma Tzu is very close by, where buddhas are blossoming. You can go to the government service any time – but Ma Tzu may not be available. Such a great master is so close by, just working in Kōsei county. You must go there."

Suddenly, the hidden desire that had led him to Confucius – and Confucius had completely changed his search for truth. He used to say, "There is only behavior – good behavior, bad behavior – there is no truth to be found. Don't waste your time." So he overpowered the young man, convinced him that the best thing is, "You are intelligent, you go into government service. And with my recommendation you will be immediately accepted."

Suddenly a hidden seed surfaced. Because of this man of Zen... A man of Zen simply means a man who has become a buddha but who is not a master. He knows the truth but he has no way of conveying it. He is a mystic in his own right but he is not a master; he is not articulate enough to manage the inexpressible in some device to be conveyed to you. He does not know how to transmit the lamp. So he...that type of mystic is simply called, in Zen, "a man of Zen." He is as experienced as any buddha, but because he is not a master, he knows the truth but he has not the way to lead others to it. But his personality will be luminous, his eyes will have a different quality, his gestures will have a different grace.

So when this man of Zen met the young man and told Tanka, "Master Ma Tzu is working in Kōsei county; that is the place for choosing buddhas – you must go there," without any hesitation, without thinking again that he was going to become a government officer and suddenly he has moved on a different path altogether, Tanka went to Kōsei. He did not even answer the man, "I am going."

Such a deep search must have been hidden, and forced deeply into the unconscious by Confucius. It suddenly surfaced. Seeing this man was enough, that the path is towards Ma Tzu. If this man, who is not a master, has an aura of mystery around him, an energy, a charisma, then what about Ma Tzu? Without saying anything to him, Tanka went to Kōsei right away.

> When he saw Ma Tzu, the master pulled Tanka's head towards him and looked at him – into his eyes – face to face, for a long time. Then Ma Tzu said, "Sekitō of Mount Nangaku will be your master."

He was looking into this young man's eyes – what kind of potential? Who will be the right master for him? Should I accept him? Will it be quicker with me or with Sekitō?

And you can see the non-competitive world of Zen. He saw in the young man's eyes that Sekitō would be a far more suitable master for him than he would. So he told him, "Sekitō of Mount Nangaku will be your master."

Seeing Ma Tzu, he could see the difference between a man of Zen and a master of Zen. A man of Zen is a small flame; a master of Zen is the whole forest afire.

And when Ma Tzu looked into his eyes, he was also looking into the eyes of Ma Tzu. He could see the compassion, the great love. It is out of compassion and love that he tells him, "Go to Sekitō. That will be quicker; here it will take a little longer time. Why waste time?" And he was so much impressed by Ma Tzu that he immediately followed his advice.

> *So Tanka went to Mount Nangaku. When he saw Sekitō, Sekitō said to Tanka, "Go and work in the rice-polishing room."*

It almost always happens in Zen monasteries when a new initiate comes in, the master, even when he enters the room – the way he walks, the way he sits – the master is witnessing what will be right for him in the beginning. He has to be trained according to his potential. No Zen master ever imposes himself on anybody. So Sekitō said to him, looking at him, he felt that he needed to learn first, waiting. He said, "Go and work in the rice-polishing room."

> *Tanka made a bow and left for the dormitory.*
> *He worked in the kitchen for three years.*

He never went again to ask Sekitō, "How long do I have to polish rice?"

A Zen master creates such a tremendous trust.

It is not belief – belief is in theories, theologies.

Trust is a personal intimacy, a feeling that "he understands me; that's enough. Now whenever the time is ripe he will call me."

People have waited not only three years but thirty years, polishing rice.

Once it happened...

The man was polishing rice for thirty years, and the master had told him, "Unless I call you, you should not come. And you are not to attend the scholarly discussions in the monastery, you are not to read the scriptures. You simply polish rice from the morning till late in the night. There are ten thousand monks, and you have to take care of the rice."

So for thirty years the man completely forgot thinking – because what is the need of thinking when you are just polishing rice every day for thirty years? Almost half of his life had gone into polishing rice. And it is such a simple process you don't need any mind, you don't need any thinking. And he had been prohibited from going to the discourses, going to the sermons, going to the discussions of the monks, told not to read scriptures. He had been prevented completely from anything that could create a mind. He had been given a simple task that was going to uncreate the mind. Whatever mind he had got would be uncreated.

And these people were of great strength, integrity. Just to wait for thirty years, without any complaint, without even seeing the master again...and because the master had said, "This is the only thing you have to do." He was not even talking to any other monk. People had completely forgotten about him.

He lived in a small hut by the side of the kitchen. In the morning he would enter the kitchen; late in the night he would fall back into the hut, go to sleep. This was a simple process. In thirty years' time there was no mind.

And an incident happened. The master was getting old, and seeing that his death was coming close, he informed the ten thousand monks – excluding the one who was just polishing the rice – "If anybody wants to be my successor he should come in the night and write on my door just the essence, the very essence of Zen."

There were great scholars, and the whole monastery knew who was the most scholarly person; perhaps he would be chosen. That scholarly person, when the master had gone to sleep, stole very silently so that nobody would find who had written it. He was even afraid; he knew the master. You could not deceive him, that was certain. And he himself knew that he knew nothing of Zen as far as experience was concerned, although he could make a scholarly statement. But that old fellow was not going to be deceived by scholarship.

And he made a beautiful statement; he wrote it on the door, very silently so that the master did not wake up: "Zen is nothing but getting out of the mind, and the beyond opens its doors." But he did not sign it, afraid, and very cautious – "If he finds it right, I will stand up and say I have written it. If he finds it wrong, I will simply sit silently." That old fellow used to beat the disciples.

In the morning, when the master opened the door and saw the sentence, he said, "Who is the idiot who has written this?"

And there was no answer from the ten thousand monks.

So the master washed it off, and said, "Don't destroy my door! Unless you *know*... I can die without a successor, but I will not have any scholar to be my successor."

Of course the statement was perfectly good, you could not improve on it: "Zen is going beyond the mind." It could not be condensed more clearly and accurately.

But masters have their own ways of finding....

Two monks simply passed by the rice-polisher. People did not even know his name, they simply called him the rice polisher. They did not consider him even a monk; he had never told anybody that he had been initiated, and nobody ever bothered about him, what his name was. He never came to the discourses, he never came to meditations, he never came to scholarly discussions. And the whole campus was agog with all kinds of philosophical discussions; when scriptures are read, sutras from Gautam Buddha were read, he never came. What kind of man…? Just doing one thing…people had completely forgotten how many years he had been doing it.

Two men was just passing by, discussing, "The sentence was perfectly right, but this old fellow is very strange… How did he manage to find that it is a scholarly statement but not existential, not experiential?"

For the first time the rice-polisher monk laughed. In thirty years that was the first expression. Those two monks looked at him, and they said, "Why have you laughed? And we have never seen you laughing…"

He said, "I laughed because whoever wrote that must be an idiot!"

They said, "Exactly – these were the words of the master! Can you write something better?"

He said, "I don't know how to write. I have forgotten. In thirty years the little bit I knew how to write, I have forgotten. And anyway who wants to be the successor?"

They were shocked, "This man is strange. Thirty years completely silent, and suddenly exploding…"

In the middle of the night the master came to the rice-polisher and he said, "Can you improve upon it?"

The rice-polisher monk said, "There is no mind; how are you going to go beyond it? And there is no beyond – all is here and now. One has to go nowhere, not even beyond mind. Mind is a fiction, and the people have created another fiction of going beyond the mind. But forgive me. I don't want to be your successor. I am so happy. You are such a great man, you gave me such a meditative job…"

The master said, "You will have to accept my successorship because there is nobody else whom I can trust. They are all filled up with scholarship and all kinds of knowledge. You are the right person, and I have been waiting these thirty years that perhaps you will be the successor. This waiting proved to me absolutely that you must have experienced something that is keeping you centered, without any worry, no tension. You have not even uttered a single word to anybody; you just do your job and go to sleep. But one thing: these scholars and these ambitious people will create trouble for you. So I have brought my robe and my staff and my cap" – these are the things that the successor gets from the master. "So take this robe, this staff, and this cap." He put it on the rice-polisher monk's head, and told him to escape from the monastery as quickly as possible.

"Just go deeper into the mountains. Those who need will reach you. But beware! If anybody finds it out from this monastery they are going to kill you. They will not accept a rice-polisher monk as their master."

So the poor fellow took the robe, the staff, and escaped. But while he was escaping from the gate, the gatekeeper saw him with the robe and with the hat and the staff of the master. So he immediately informed all the ambitious monks who were trying, working out how to improve, "Now stop! The man has been chosen."

They said, "Who is the man?"

They said, "Do you remember a man who came thirty years ago and never spoke for thirty years? The rice-polisher! I saw him just going out of the gate with the master's staff and cap on his head, and the robe he was carrying in his hand and running!"

So, many ambitious people took their swords and rushed towards the way the guard had told them. And they soon found that poor rice-polisher, surrounded him with their swords, and told him, "Give the robe. You don't know a single word about Zen."

The poor man laughed. He said, "Do you think there is a word that one has to know before he knows Zen?"

They were shocked. It was true, but still their ambition...and they could not accept him. But he said, "There is no problem. Keep your swords in their sheath, there is no need to be worried. This is the cap" – he threw the cap on the ground. "And this is the robe, and this is the staff. If you can take it, take it."

But although they were ambitious, they had a certain sensibility, living with the master so long. How could they take it? If the master had given it to him, then it would be absolutely wrong. And they knew that they knew not, and this fellow seemed to know. It did not matter that he was a rice-polisher.

So they touched his feet and said, "We were wrong. We were just ambitious. You please come back."

He said, "But I don't want to be the successor. I had refused, but the old man was so insistent. You please take all these things. Whoever wants to be the successor, he can. I am going to the mountains."

They said, "No, you have to come back."

He became the successor.

Zen is a very strange path. No scholarship is needed, no knowledge is needed. What is needed is an immense silence, and waiting, watching.... Whenever the time is ripe, existence pours all its mysteries into you.

So for thirty years he worked in the kitchen.

Now the sutra:
Our Beloved Master,
One day, Sekitō announced to everybody that the next day they would weed the grass in front of the Buddha Hall. The following day, all the monks gathered with sickles in their hands, but only Tanka came with a tray filled with water. Before coming there he had washed his hair, but it was not yet shaven. Now he kneeled down in front of Sekitō, and seeing him, Sekitō laughed, and shaved Tanka's head. As the master usually did, Sekitō gave Tanka some specific commandments, but as he did so, Tanka walked away covering his ears with his hands.

...giving the gesture that "I don't need any knowledge, I know it. Don't fill my ears with nonsense. Don't fill my ears with words. I have come to experience the wordless." That gesture shows that Tanka had arrived.

Tanka then left for Kōsei to see Ma Tzu. Arriving at the monastery...
Because it was Ma Tzu who had sent him to Sekitō, now he had completed the job. He got his head shaved after he had completed the job. Ordinarily, when one becomes a monk his head is shaved. But because he was told immediately to go to the kitchen and work there... In those three years just waiting and watching and being aware, he realized his very nature. That very nature is the buddha, so now was the right time to be initiated. Before it, it would have been a formal initiation. Now it was going to be authentic initiation. And that's why, when he bowed down in front of the master, Sekitō laughed – "This fellow is really clever! He has not even shaved his head for these three years. He was waiting for the moment when he would be really worthy of initiation."

He shaved his head, and as every master does after shaving the head – that is the initiation process – he gave him a few commandments. But as he did so, gave the commandments...

Tanka walked away, covering his ears with his hands.
...showing absolutely to Sekitō, "You don't have to teach me anything. You have put me in the device and I have come to the space where no teaching is needed."

Tanka then left Kōsei to see Ma Tzu.

Because he was his original master who had looked into his eyes, and directed him to the right place where he could become quickly a buddha, he needed to show his gratitude, to show what he had attained and get his recognition.

Arriving at the monastery he went into the hall and, climbing on the statue of Manjushri, sat there.

Manjushri is one of Gautam Buddha's very important enlightened disciples. He chose the statue of Manjushri – there must have been other statues, of Sariputra, of Mahakashyapa, of Maudgalyan, other disciples who had become enlightened when Gautam Buddha was alive. So they are the original forces. Manjushri he had chosen for a particular reason, because...I have to tell you a little bit about Manjushri.

Manjushri was always sitting under a tree, the same tree. He never asked a question to Gautam Buddha, never read any scriptures. Every day he would come whenever Gautam Buddha was talking, in the morning, in the evening. He would sit under the tree with his eyes closed. And everybody was wondering why he did not ask anything.

One day, suddenly in the morning as Buddha came...Manjushri was sitting under his tree. Suddenly, flowers from the tree started falling over Manjushri. The tree must have been blossoming with hundreds of flowers, and they were showering like rain. And Buddha told the whole ten thousand disciples to look at what was happening. All looked – they could not believe their eyes. Why were all the flowers suddenly falling on Manjushri's head, his body, his lap? He was almost covered with flowers.

Gautam Buddha declared: "Manjushri has become enlightened. Even the tree is giving him recognition. Existence is celebrating."

And Manjushri had arrived without asking a question, without getting an answer – just waiting silently. Nature was celebrating. One of nature's ambitions was fulfilled: one man again had become a buddha, had reached to the ultimate consciousness.

Tanka certainly chose the statue of Manjushri and sat upon it:

The other monks were astonished and told Ma Tzu, who came in, looked at him and said, "My son is Tennen."

In Chinese, *tennen* means natural. That was the very quality of Manjushri. He had become attuned with nature. Just sitting with that tree, he had become almost one with it. So when he became enlightened the tree could not resist the temptation to shower all the flowers – not a single flower was left on the tree. All the flowers had showered.

So Manjushri's enlightenment is called natural, spontaneous enlightenment, with no method, with no device. Tennen means natural, and when Ma Tzu saw him sitting on the statue of Manjushri...and every disciple of Ma Tzu was stunned, they could not believe how this man was behaving. But Ma Tzu could see: the man had changed. It was no longer the same man whose eyes he had looked into. He simply said, "My son is Tennen."

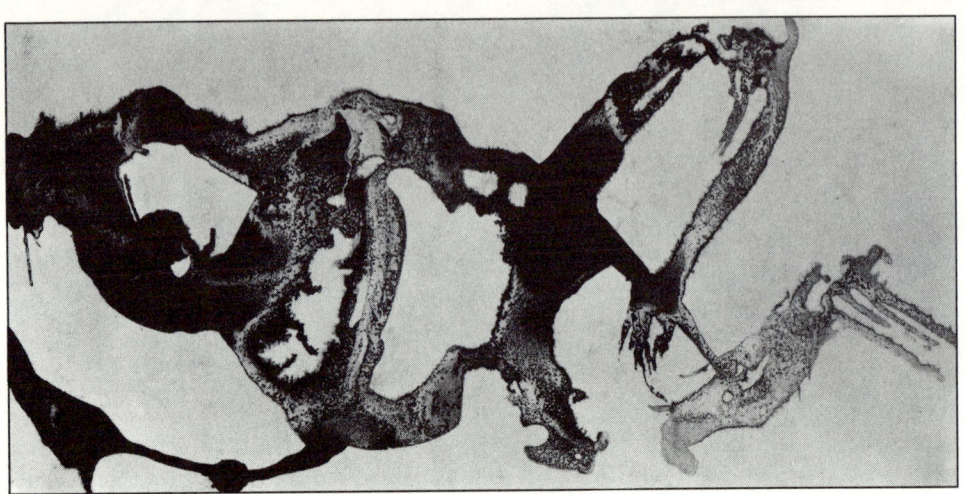

My son is just natural, a natural buddha.
    Tanka came down, made a bow and said, "Thank you for giving me a dharma name."
He accepted that word 'tennen' as his dharma name, his sannyas name. Since that time he started calling himself Tanka Tennen. Tanka, the natural one.
    Ma Tzu then asked, "Where do you come from?"
    Tanka said, "I come from Sekitō."
    Ma Tzu said, "The path on the stonehead is slippery. Did you fall over?"
    Tanka replied, "If I had fallen over, I would not have come here."
I would have waited. I have not fallen over, I have risen above.
    That's why he was sitting on the head of Manjushri, declaring, "I am another Manjushri and I have not fallen over; otherwise I would not be here. I would not have come to show my face to you again without becoming a buddha."
    This man, Tanka Tennen, became a master in his own right. But his whole teaching was just to be natural.
    That's my whole teaching: just to be natural. Nature is dhamma, nature

is Tao, nature is Zen. And the moment you are natural, flowers will shower over you. The moment you will be natural, not only will you celebrate and dance, the whole existence around you will dance and celebrate.

Hakuin wrote:

> *Your singing-and-dancing*
> *is none other than*
> *the voice of dharma.*

Your celebration, your singing-and-dancing, is none other than your very nature. And this nature has been crippled by your so-called religions – your God, your priests, your theologians.

Zen is a rebellion against all religion. It is all for religiousness but not for religion. Religiousness is a totally different phenomenon from religion. Religion is a doctrine, a creed, a cult, an organization. Religiousness is simply a quality that naturally blossoms in you. You have just to go deep down into yourself to find the seed of the buddha that exists at the very center of your being.

All our meditations are concerned only with one thing: how to take you to the seed where the buddha is hidden, just as flowers are hidden in a seed. And once you have reached to the center, the seed starts growing.

Then, becoming a buddha is not a faraway phenomenon. You have started becoming a buddha, you have started on the path which brings the transformation. Right now you are all bodhisattvas, buddhas in essence, in seed. If you can find out the center of your being you have found the very center of existence.

Just finding it, and immediately something starts growing in you – a huge buddha suddenly surfaces. You disappear. You are completely gone into the ocean, just like a dewdrop. You are no more, only life is – dancing, celebrating.

> Maneesha's question:
> Our Beloved Master,
> Nietzsche suggests that man only searches for truth because he presupposes that truth is a consolation, a cure. But, he says, perhaps truth "exists only for souls which are at once powerful and harmless, and full of joy and peace… just as it will no doubt be only such souls as these that will be capable of seeking truth."
> Do You agree with him?

Maneesha, I absolutely agree, because what he is saying is absolutely true. But it does not suit the lips of Friedrich Nietzsche. It would be perfectly right if a Gautam Buddha said it.

You have to understand the difference. Friedrich Nietzsche is only an intellectual; he came to this conclusion as a logical conclusion. He has stumbled almost on the right thing, but it is stumbling in the dark. A buddha does not stumble in the dark, he is living in an immense luminosity.

So what he is saying is right, but the man who is saying it is not right. I agree with the statement, I don't agree with Friedrich Nietzsche.

It will be a little difficult for you: the distinction is very delicate. His statement is correct, but it is not his experience. He himself was not a man of joy – very sad. He was not a man who could dance or sing; that was far below him. He was a serious philosopher. Philosophers don't dance. They look at the dancers as stupid – "What are you doing?"

But even without a clear-cut experience, Nietzsche is a rare phenomenon. Buddhas have always been saying that, but a man who is not enlightened has stumbled unconsciously on a truth that is not his experience but only a logical conclusion.

It is perfectly right that the majority of people are searching for truth, because they presuppose that truth is going to be a consolation, a cure. They are sick people. Their old consolation has gone away: God is dead. Now they are seeking for truth in place of God, so they can be again consoled.

Prayer is dead, so they are searching for meditation. Perhaps meditation can be the substitute. But these are the people who will not find it.

He says truth "exists only for souls which are at once powerful and harmless, and full of joy and peace." He was not full of joy or full of peace;

he was one of the most tense persons who has ever walked on the earth. And finally he had to be admitted into a madhouse. His anxiety became so serious that to keep him in the house was dangerous; he had to be handed over into a mad asylum.

But what he was saying is perfectly right. Only a man of peace, silence, joy, a man who is capable of singing and dancing, a man who is capable of celebrating, is the man who is capable of seeking and finding the truth.

I am trying in every possible way to make you nonserious, non-tense. Laugh, dance, sing, celebrate, because these are the people who will find immense power arising in themselves which is dormant. These are the people who will have power but will not harm anybody with their power. Their power will be a blessing to the world. It will not be the power that destroys, it will be the power that creates. These will be the creators.

And these will be the people who know. These will be the people who have disappeared in joy, in dance, and are no more. Only a consciousness, a pure consciousness remains. That pure consciousness we have called the awakened consciousness, the enlightened consciousness; we have called it samadhi or satori. Gautam Buddha is just a name, representative of this ultimate blossoming.

It is time to be nonserious, time for Sardar Gurudayal Singh....

Martha Grumble and Mildred Mousebreath, two middle-aged housewives, are sharing confidences over a cup of coffee.

"I don't know what to do about my husband anymore," sniffs Martha. "He never comes home until three in the morning."

"Oh dear!" sighs Mildred. "My husband used to be like that – but not anymore!"

"Really?" asks Martha. "What made him change?"

"What made him change, my dear," says Mildred, smiling, "is that every time he crept through the door at three o'clock in the morning, I would sweetly call out, 'Is that you, Raymond?'"

"Is that all there is to it?" asks Martha.

"That's right!" explains Mildred.

"But I don't understand," says Martha. "Why would that stop him?"

"Simple," explains Mildred. "Because his name is Sidney."

Jack Jerk stays out late one night and comes home at three o'clock in the morning. He walks into the bedroom and finds his wife, Jill Jerk, lying awake, naked, in the bed.

"Where the hell have you been until three in the morning?" screams Jill, furiously.

Ignoring her, Jack takes off his coat and opens the bedroom closet. To his amazement, he finds a naked man crouching on the floor.

"Who the hell is this guy?" shouts Jack.

Jill sits up in bed and cries, "Don't change the subject!"

It is a sunny morning on Cape Catastrophe beach, and Prunella Polygon, a very homely-looking girl, is rambling along daydreaming. She stumbles and trips over a bottle lying in the sand, and nearly faints when the top of the bottle flies off and, "Poof!" – a genie pops out.

The genie stretches and yawns and then looks at Prunella and announces, "Ah! I am forever in your debt, young lady. You have freed me from a prison of a thousand years. Ask anything, and I will fulfill your desire."

Prunella Polygon cannot believe her good luck and does not hesitate.

"I want a figure like Sophia Loren," she says, "and a smile like Raquel Welch, and hair like Bridgette Bardot and tits like Samantha Fox. And eyes like Elizabeth Taylor and an ass like Marilyn Monroe."

The genie takes a long look at Prunella and says, "Honey, please put me back in the bottle."

Nivedano...

Nivedano…

Be silent…
Close your eyes…
and feel your body to be completely frozen.
This is the right moment to turn in.
Gather all your energy…
and with a total consciousness,
rush towards your center of being.
The center of your being is just two inches below the navel,
inside your body.
All that you need is an urgency,
as if it is going to be the last moment of your life.
With great urgency and intensity, rush towards the center.
Faster and faster…
Deeper and deeper…
As you are coming close to your center,
a great silence descends over you just like soft rain.
You can feel it.
You can feel the coolness of it.
A little more deep, a little more close to the center…
and a tremendous peace arises in you, overwhelming you.
As you are coming closer,
suddenly there arises a luminosity:
your whole being becomes light.
Now step into the very center.
And you start feeling drunk with the divine.
This is what is called ecstasy.
Out of this ecstasy is all celebration.

Centered in your very being, you are no more.
You have come to the seed –
the bodhisattva has dissolved into the buddha.
The face of Gautam Buddha is the original face of every human being.

The only quality Gautam Buddha has is witnessing.
Witness that you are not the body.
Witness that you are not the mind.
And finally, witness that you are only a witness.
This pure witness – sakshin –
is your ultimate freedom.
It is your enlightenment, it is your liberation.
It is entering into the eternal dance of life.
It is because of this I say again and again, I celebrate.
To me, life is celebration.
Existence is celebration.
Witness the eternal dance that is happening inside you.
This dance has to become your very flavor,
your very fragrance.
And invisible flowers are showering over you.
You cannot celebrate alone,
existence participates from all dimensions.
Nature rejoices when anyone comes to the very center of being.
A part of nature has become awakened.

To make this witnessing deeper,
Nivedano…

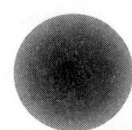

Relax…
Be in a let-go.
This is the peace, the joy, the silence,
the power that is harmless, that is creative.
This is what Nietzsche has stumbled on in his darkness and blindness.
But you are going with open eyes to the very heartbeat of the universe.
The whole universe except the so-called religions
is in immense celebration every moment –
in the birds, in the trees, in the rivers;
in the oceans, in the mountains, in the stars.
All around you there is nothing but celebration.

You have to participate in it.
Throw out all the barriers.
They are only fictitious,
and reality has immense power.
Witnessing will do the job.
Witnessing is another name for meditation.
At this moment,
Gautama the Buddha Auditorium is becoming an ocean of consciousness.
Ten thousand buddhas are melting like ice in the ocean –
no waves, no ripples, absolute silence.

Remember, enlightenment has three steps.
The first is that the buddha you are experiencing within you
follows behind you like a shadow.
It is your very nature, your dhamma. It is your tennen.
The second step, after experiencing the buddha behind you,
his warmth, his love, his truth, his compassion, his divine drunkenness…
you slowly become his shadow.
He comes in front of you –
that is the second step.
And your shadow starts disappearing, slowly slowly.
As you melt into the buddha –
that is the third and final step – you are no more.
Only the buddha is – you are no more.
Only an enlightened awareness is – you are no more.
Only life is celebrating.
A sheer dance of joy…
A song that has no words in it,
a music without any sound.
Eternity in your hands.
You become one with the cosmic whole.

I celebrate myself.
I hope soon you will be able to say the same:
"I celebrate myself."

Before Nivedano calls you, collect all these experiences.
You have to bring them to your day-to-day life.
The grace, the beauty, the truth, the honesty, the intensity of living –

and the witnessing has to be your very breath, your heartbeat.
And persuade the buddha – he is your nature;
you have never requested it, you have never welcomed it.
That's why it has been there hiding in the very center of your being.
Help it to come along with you.
It is bound to come.
It has come thousands of times,
to thousands of buddhas.
It is every living being's birthright.
Just ask him to come along with you
and he will transform your whole life –
in every gesture, in every word, in every silence
you will find his presence, his light.

Nivedano…

Come back…
but come as a buddha, full of joy.
A great serenity, a pure silence…
and sit down for a few moments just to recollect,
to remind yourself of the golden path that you have followed inwards,
and the silent, peaceful space that you have encountered.
You have seen your original face,
the face of the buddha.
Feel the presence of the buddha behind you –
the warmth, the coolness, together;
the power and humbleness together.
The silence – utter egolessness and yet a tremendous dignity.
This is what makes one celebrate life.
There cannot be anything more than existence is already.
Just participate in the dance.
Celebrate to your abandon,
and all the mysteries and all the secrets of existence and life
will be opened unto you.

It is my promise.
It is the promise of all the buddhas, past, present, future.

Okay, Maneesha?
Yes, Beloved Master.

BOOKS BY OSHO
ENGLISH LANGUAGE EDITIONS

Early Discourses and Writings
A Cup of Tea *Letters to Disciples*
From Sex to Superconsciousness
I Am the Gate
The Long and the Short and the All
The Silent Explosion

Meditation
And Now, and Here (Volumes 1&2)
The Book of the Secrets (Volumes 1–5)
  Vigyana Bhairava Tantra
Dimensions Beyond the Known
In Search of the Miraculous (Volume 1)
Meditation: The Art of Ecstasy
Meditation: The First and Last Freedom
The Orange Book *The Meditation Techniques of Bhagwan Shree Rajneesh*
The Perfect Way
The Psychology of the Esoteric

Buddha and Buddhist Masters
The Book of the Books (Volumes 1–4)
  The Dhammapada
The Diamond Sutra *The Vajrachchedika Prajnaparamita Sutra*
The Discipline of Transcendence (Volumes 1–4) *On the Sutra of 42 Chapters*
The Heart Sutra
  The Prajnaparamita Hridayam Sutra
The Book of Wisdom (Volumes 1&2)
  Atisha's Seven Points of Mind Training

Indian Mystics
The Bauls
The Beloved (Volumes 1&2)

Kabir
The Divine Melody
Ecstasy – The Forgotten Language

The Fish in the Sea is Not Thirsty
The Guest
The Path of Love
The Revolution

Krishna
Krishna: The Man and His Philosophy

Jesus and Christian Mystics
Come Follow Me (Volumes 1–4)
  The Sayings of Jesus
I Say Unto You (Volumes 1&2)
  The Sayings of Jesus
The Mustard Seed *The Gospel of Thomas*
Theologia Mystica
  The Treatise of St. Dionysius

Jewish Mystics
The Art of Dying
The True Sage

Sufism
Just Like That
The Perfect Master (Volumes 1&2)
The Secret
Sufis: The People of the Path (Volumes 1&2)
Unio Mystica (Volumes 1&2)
  The Hadiqa of Hakim Sanai
Until You Die
The Wisdom of the Sands (Volumes 1&2)

Tantra
Tantra, Spirituality and Sex
  Excerpts from The Book of the Secrets
Tantra: The Supreme Understanding
  Tilopa's Song of Mahamudra
The Tantra Vision (Volumes 1&2)
  The Royal Song of Saraha

Tao

The Empty Boat
The Stories of Chuang Tzu
The Secret of Secrets (Volumes 1&2)
The Secret of the Golden Flower
Tao: The Golden Gate (Volumes 1&2)
Tao: The Pathless Path (Volumes 1&2)
The Stories of Lieh Tzu
Tao: The Three Treasures (Volumes 1–4)
The Tao Te Ching of Lao Tzu
When the Shoe Fits
The Stories of Chuang Tzu

The Upanishads

I Am That *Isa Upanishad*
Philosophia Ultima *Mandukya Upanishad*
The Supreme Doctrine *Kenopanishad*
That Art Thou
  Sarvasar Upanishad,
  Kaivalya Upanishad,
  Adhyatma Upanishad
The Ultimate Alchemy
  (Volumes 1&2)
  Atma Pooja Upanishad
Vedanta: Seven Steps to Samadhi
  Akshya Upanishad

Western Mystics

Guida Spirituale *On the Desiderata*
The Hidden Harmony
  The Fragments of Heraclitus
The Messiah (Volumes 1&2)
  Commentaries on Kahlil Gibran's
  The Prophet
The New Alchemy: To Turn You On
  Mabel Collins' Light on the Path
Philosophia Perennis (Volumes 1&2)
  The Golden Verses of Pythagoras
Zarathustra: A God That Can Dance
  Commentaries on Friedrich Nietzsche's
  Thus Spoke Zarathustra
Zarathustra: The Laughing Prophet
  Commentaries on Friedrich Nietzsche's
  Thus Spoke Zarathustra

Yoga

Yoga: The Alpha and the Omega (Volumes 1–10) *The Yoga Sutras of Patanjali*
Yoga: The Science of the Soul (Volumes 1–3) *Original Title: Yoga:The Alpha and the Omega (Volumes 1–3)*

Zen and Zen Masters

Poona 1974-1981

Ah, This!
Ancient Music in the Pines
And the Flowers Showered
Dang Dang Doko Dang
The First Principle
The Grass Grows By Itself
Hsin Hsin Ming: The Book of Nothing
  Discourses on the Faith-Mind of Sosan
Nirvana: The Last Nightmare
No Water, No Moon
Returning to the Source
Roots and Wings
The Search *The Ten Bulls of Zen*
A Sudden Clash of Thunder
The Sun Rises in the Evening
Take it Easy (Volumes 1&2)
  Poems of Ikkyu
This Very Body the Buddha
  Hakuin's Song of Meditation
Walking in Zen, Sitting in Zen
The White Lotus
  The Sayings of Bodhidharma
Zen: The Path of Paradox (Volumes 1–3)
Zen: The Special Transmission

The Mystery School 1986-1989

Bodhidharma The Greatest Zen Master
  Commentaries on the Teachings of the
  Messenger of Zen from India to China
Christianity, the Deadliest Poison and
  Zen, the Antidote to All Poisons
Communism and Zen Fire, Zen Wind
God is Dead
  Now Zen is the Only Living Truth
The Great Zen Master Ta Hui
  Reflections on the Transformation of an
  Intellectual to Enlightenment

I Celebrate Myself
  God is No Where: Life is Now Here
Kyōzan: A True Man of Zen
No Mind: The Flowers of Eternity
One Seed Makes the Whole Earth Green
The Zen Manifesto
Zen: The Mystery and the Poetry
  of the Beyond
The World of Zen
  A boxed set of 5 volumes, containing: *
    Live Zen
    This. This. A Thousand Times This.
    Zen: The Quantum Leap from Mind
      to No-Mind
    Zen: The Solitary Bird, Cuckoo
      of the Forest
    Zen: The Diamond Thunderbolt
Zen: All the Colors of the Rainbow
  A boxed set of 5 volumes, containing: *
    The Miracle
    Turning In
    The Original Man
    The Language of Existence
    The Buddha: The Emptiness of the Heart
Osho Rajneesh: The Present Day
  Awakened One Speaks on
  the Ancient Masters of Zen
  A boxed set of 7 volumes, containing: *
    Dōgen, the Zen Master: A Search
      and a Fulfillment
    Ma Tzu: The Empty Mirror
    Hyakujō: The Everest of Zen,
      with Bashō's Haikus
    Nansen: The Point of Departure
    Jōshū: The Lion's Roar
    Rinzai: Master of the Irrational
    Isan: No Footprints in the Blue Sky
**Each volume is also available individually*

Responses to Questions
Poona 1974-1981
Be Still and Know
The Goose is Out!
My Way: The Way of the White Clouds
Walk Without Feet, Fly Without Wings
  and Think Without Mind
The Wild Geese and the Water
Zen: Zest, Zip, Zap and Zing

Rajneeshpuram
From Bondage to Freedom
  Answers to the Seekers of the Path
From Darkness to Light
  Answers to the Seekers of the Path
From Death to Deathlessness
  Answers to the Seekers of the Path
From the False to the Truth
  Answers to the Seekers of the Path
The Rajneesh Bible (Volumes 1–4)

The World Tour
Beyond Psychology *Talks in Uruguay*
Light on the Path *Talks in the Himalayas*
The Path of the Mystic *Talks in Uruguay*
Socrates Poisoned Again After
  25 Centuries *Talks in Greece*
The Sword and the Lotus
  Talks in the Himalayas
The Transmission of the Lamp
  Talks in Uruguay

The Mystery School 1986-1989
Beyond Enlightenment
The Golden Future
The Great Pilgrimage: From Here to Here
The Hidden Splendor
The Invitation
The New Dawn
The Rajneesh Upanishad
The Razor's Edge
The Rebel
The Rebellious Spirit
Sermons in Stones
YAA-HOO! The Mystic Rose

The Mantra Series:
  Satyam-Shivam-Sundram
    Truth-Godliness-Beauty
  Sat-Chit-Anand
    Truth-Consciousness-Bliss

Om Mani Padme Hum
   The Sound of Silence:
   The Diamond in the Lotus
Hari Om Tat Sat
   The Divine Sound: That is the Truth
Om Shantih Shantih Shantih
   The Soundless Sound:
   Peace, Peace, Peace

Personal Glimpses
Books I Have Loved
Glimpses of a Golden Childhood
Notes of a Madman

Interviews with the World Press
The Last Testament (Volume 1)

Intimate Talks between Master and Disciple – Darshan Diaries
Hammer on the Rock
   (December 10, 1975 – January 15, 1976)
Above All Don't Wobble
   (January 16 – February 12, 1976)
Nothing to Lose But Your Head
   (February 13 – March 12, 1976)
Be Realistic: Plan For a Miracle
   (March 13 – April 6, 1976)
Get Out of Your Own Way
   (April 7 – May 2, 1976)
Beloved of My Heart *(May 3 – 28, 1976)*
The Cypress in the Courtyard
   (May 29 – June 27, 1976)
A Rose is a Rose is a Rose
   (June 28 – July 27, 1976)
Dance Your Way to God
   (July 28 – August 20, 1976)
The Passion for the Impossible
   (August 21 – September 18, 1976)
The Great Nothing
   (September 19 – October 11, 1976)
God is Not for Sale
   (October 12 – November 7, 1976)
The Shadow of the Whip
   (November 8 – December 3, 1976)
Blessed are the Ignorant
   (December 4 – 31, 1976)
The Buddha Disease *(January 1977)*
What Is, Is, What Ain't, Ain't
   (February 1977)
The Zero Experience *(March 1977)*
For Madmen Only (Price of Admission:
   Your Mind) *(April 1977)*
This is It *(May 1977)*
The Further Shore *(June 1977)*
Far Beyond the Stars *(July 1977)*
The No Book (No Buddha, No Teaching,
   No Discipline) *(August 1977)*
Don't Just Do Something, Sit There
   (September 1977)
Only Losers Can Win in This Game
   (October 1977)
The Open Secret *(November 1977)*
The Open Door *(December 1977)*
The Sun Behind the Sun Behind the Sun
   (January 1978)
Believing the Impossible Before Breakfast
   (February 1978)
Don't Bite My Finger, Look Where I'm
   Pointing *(March 1978)*
Let Go! *(April 1978)*
The 99 Names of Nothingness *(May 1978)*
The Madman's Guide to Enlightenment
   (June 1978)
Don't Look Before You Leap *(July 1978)*
Hallelujah! *(August 1978)*
God's Got a Thing About You
   (September 1978)
The Tongue-Tip Taste of Tao
   (October 1978)
The Sacred Yes *(November 1978)*
Turn On, Tune In, and Drop the Lot
   (December 1978)
Zorba the Buddha *(January 1979)*
Won't You Join the Dance? *(February 1979)*
You Ain't Seen Nothin' Yet *(March 1979)*
The Shadow of the Bamboo *(April 1979)*
Just Around the Corner *(May 1979)*
Snap Your Fingers, Slap Your Face &
   Wake Up! *(June 1979)*
The Rainbow Bridge *(July 1979)*

Don't Let Yourself Be Upset by the Sutra,
 Rather Upset the Sutra Yourself
 (August/September 1979)
The Sound of One Hand Clapping
 (March 1981)

Compilations

Beyond the Frontiers of the Mind
Bhagwan Shree Rajneesh
 On Basic Human Rights
The Book *An Introduction to the
 Teachings of Bhagwan Shree Rajneesh*
 Series I from A – H
 Series II from I – Q
 Series III from R – Z
Death: The Greatest Fiction
Gold Nuggets
The Greatest Challenge: The Golden Future
I Teach Religiousness Not Religion
Jesus Crucified Again, This Time in
 Ronald Reagan's America
Life, Love, Laughter
More Gold Nuggets
More Words from a Man of No Words
The New Man: The Only Hope for the Future
A New Vision of Women's Liberation
Priests and Politicians: The Mafia of the Soul
The Rebel: The Very Salt of the Earth
Sex: Quotations from
 Bhagwan Shree Rajneesh
Words from a Man of No Words

Photobiographies

Shree Rajneesh: A Man of Many Climates,
 Seasons and Rainbows
 Through the Eye of the Camera
The Sound of Running Water *Bhagwan
 Shree Rajneesh and His Work 1974–1978*
This Very Place The Lotus Paradise
 *Bhagwan Shree Rajneesh and His Work
 1978–1984*

Books about Osho

Bhagwan Shree Rajneesh: The Most
 Dangerous Man Since Jesus Christ *(by
 Sue Appleton, LL.B.)*
Bhagwan: The Buddha For The Future
 *(by Juliet Forman,
 S.R.N., S.C.M., R.M.N.)*
Bhagwan: The Most Godless Yet The Most
 Godly Man *(by Dr. George Meredith,
 M.D. M.B.,B.S. M.R.C.P.)*
Bhagwan: Twelve Days That Shook The
 World *(by Juliet Forman,
 S.R.N., S.C.M., R.M.N.)*
Was Bhagwan Shree Rajneesh Poisoned
 By Ronald Reagan's America?
 (by Sue Appleton, LL.B.)

OTHER PUBLISHERS

NEW ZEALAND

After Middle Age: A Limitless Sky
 (Compilation, (Hazard Press)

UNITED KINGDOM

The Art of Dying *(Sheldon Press)*
The Book of the Secrets *(Volume 1,
 Thames & Hudson)*
Dimensions Beyond the Known
 (Sheldon Press)
The Hidden Harmony *(Sheldon Press)*
Meditation: The Art of Ecstasy
 (Sheldon Press)
The Mustard Seed *(Sheldon Press)*
Neither This Nor That *(Sheldon Press)*
No Water, No Moon *(Sheldon Press)*
Roots and Wings
 (Routledge & Kegan Paul)
Straight to Freedom *(Original title:
 Until You Die, Sheldon Press)*
The Supreme Understanding
 *(Original title: Tantra: The Supreme
 Understanding, Sheldon Press)*
The Supreme Doctrine
 (Routledge & Kegan Paul)
Tao: The Three Treasures *(Volume 1,
 Wildwood House)*

Books about Osho

The Way of the Heart: the Rajneesh Movement *by Judith Thompson and Paul Heelas, Department of Religious Studies, University of Lancaster (Aquarian Press)*

UNITED STATES OF AMERICA

And the Flowers Showered *(De Vorss)*
The Book of the Secrets *(Volumes 1–3, Harper & Row)*
Dimensions Beyond the Known *(Wisdom Garden Books)*
The Grass Grows By Itself *(De Vorss)*
The Great Challenge *(Grove Press)*
Hammer on the Rock *(Grove Press)*
I Am the Gate *(Harper & Row)*
Journey Toward the Heart *(Original title: Until You Die, Harper & Row)*
Meditation: The Art of Ecstasy *(Original title: Dynamics of Meditation, Harper & Row)*
Mojud, The Man with the Inexplicable Life *Excerpts from The Wisdom of the Sands (Ansu Publishing Co., Ltd.)*
The Mustard Seed *(Harper & Row)*
My Way: The Way of the White Clouds *(Grove Press)*
Nirvana: The Last Nightmare *(Wisdom Garden Books)*
Only One Sky *(Original title: Tantra: The Supreme Understanding, Dutton)*
The Psychology of the Esoteric *(Harper & Row)*
Roots and Wings *(Routledge & Kegan Paul)*
The Supreme Doctrine *(Routledge & Kegan Paul)*
When the Shoe Fits *(De Vorss)*
Words Like Fire *(Original title: Come Follow Me, Volume 1, Harper & Row)*

Books about Osho

The Awakened One: The Life and Work of Bhagwan Shree Rajneesh *by Vasant Joshi (Harper & Row)*
Dying for Enlightenment *by Bernard Gunther (Harper & Row)*
Rajneeshpuram and the Abuse of Power *by Ted Shay, Ph.D. (Scout Creek Press)*
Rajneeshpuram, the Unwelcome Society *by Kirk Braun (Scout Creek Press)*
The Rajneesh Story: The Bhagwan's Garden *by Dell Murphy (Linwood Press, Oregon)*

FOREIGN LANGUAGE EDITIONS

Books by Osho have been translated and published in the following languages:

Chinese	Greek	Marathi	Sindhi
Czech	Gujrati	Nepali	Spanish
Danish	Hebrew	Polish	Swedish
Dutch	Hindi	Portuguese	Tamil
Finnish	Italian	Punjabi	Telugu
French	Japanese	Russian	Urdu
German	Korean	Serbo-Croat	

WORLDWIDE DISTRIBUTION CENTERS FOR THE WORKS OF OSHO

EUROPE

Belgium
Osho Indu Distribution
Coebergerstraat 40
2018 Antwerpen
Tel.   03/237 2037
Fax   03/216 9871

Denmark
Anwar Distribution
Thorupgaard Allee 20, 2-3
2720 Vanlose, Copenhagen
Tel.   03179/2149
Comp. node 45-10

Finland
Unio Mystica Shop
for Meditative Books & Tapes
Albertinkatu 10
P.O. Box 186
00121 Helsinki
Tel.   03580/665 811
Fax   03580/665 811

Italy
News Services Corporation
Via XX Settembre 12
28041 Arona (NO)
Tel.   02/839 2194 (Milan office)
Fax   02/832 3683

Netherlands
Rajneesh Publikaties Nederland
Vianenstraat 48
1106 DD Amsterdam
Tel.   020/969 372
Fax   020/890 241

Norway
Osho Devananda Meditation Center
P.O. Box 177 Vinderen
0319 Oslo 3
Tel.   02/732 370

Spain
Distribuciones "El Rebelde"
Estellencs
07192 Mallorca - Baleares
Tel.   071/410 470
Fax   071/719 027

Sweden
Osho Madhur Meditation Center
Fridhemsgatan 41
5 -112 46 Stockholm
Tel.   08/514 270
Fax   08/184 972

Switzerland
Osho Mingus Meditation Center
Asylstrasse 11
8032 Zurich
Tel.   01/252 2012

United Kingdom
Osho Purnima
Centre for Meditation
Spring House, Spring Place
London NW5 3BH
Tel.   01/284 1415
Fax   01/267 1848

West Germany
The Rebel Publishing House GmbH*
Venloer Strasse 5-7
5000 Cologne 1
Tel.   0221/574 0742
Fax   0221/523 930

*All books available AT COST PRICE

Osho Verlag GmbH
Venloer Strasse 5-7
5000 Cologne 1
Tel.   0221/574 0743
Fax   0221/523 930

Tao Rajneesh Bookshop
Doerfchen Osho Meditation Center
Dahlmannstrasse 9
1000 Berlin 12
Tel.   030/320 0725

Tao Institut
Klenzestrasse 41
8000 Munich 5
Tel.   089/201 6657
Fax   089/201 3056

AUSTRALIA & NEW ZEALAND
Osho Meditation & Healing Centre
P.O. Box 1097
Fremantle, WA 6160
Tel.   09/430 4047
Fax   09/384 8557

Rebel Books Mail Order
P.O. Box 193
Papakura N.Z.
Tel.   09/292 2602

AMERICA

United States
Chidvilas
P.O. Box 17550
Boulder, CO 80308
Tel.   303/449 7811
Fax   303/449 7099
Order Dept. 800/777 7743

Osho Viha Meditation Center
P.O. Box 352
Mill Valley, CA 94942
Tel.   415/381 9861

Osho Nartano Distribution
P.O. Box 51171
Levittown,
Puerto Rico 00950-1171
Tel. 809/795 8829

Also available in bookstores nationwide at Walden Books

Canada
Publications Rajneesh
P.O. Box 331
Outremont, QUE. H2V 4N1
Tel.   514/276 2680

ASIA

India
Sadhana Foundation*
17 Koregaon Park
Poona 411 001, MS
Tel.   0212/660 963
Fax   0212/664 181

*All books available AT COST PRICE

Japan
Eer Osho Neo-Sannyas Commune
Mimura Building 6-21-34
Kikuna, Kohoku-ku
Yokohama 222
Tel.   045/434 1981
Fax   045/434 5565

OSHO MEDITATION CENTERS AND COMMUNES

There are many Osho Meditation Centers throughout the world which can be contacted for information about the teachings of Osho and which have His books available as well as audio and video tapes of His discourses. Centers exist in practically every country.

FOR FURTHER INFORMATION CONTACT

Osho Commune International
17 Koregaon Park, Poona 411 001, India